Praise for *Your New Money Story*

"This epic book will help you shatter your limiting beliefs and programming around money and will walk you step by step through a powerful, life-changing process that will help you achieve financial and life abundance. A must-read book for anyone who wants more money and the good life!" —**John Assaraf**, Chairman and CEO, NeuroGym; *New York Times* best-selling author of *Having It All*, *The Answer*, and *Innercise*

"In his earlier book, *The Secret Language of Money*, David Krueger powerfully and successfully explained the psychological, emotional, and personal impacts of money on us. Understanding these dimensions of money makes us more able to understand this powerful social trigger and, more importantly, how and why it affects us so much.

"Now David has taken this powerful and insightful analysis to a new level, with his new book *Your New Money Story: The Beliefs, Behaviors, and Brain Science to Rewire for Wealth*. Not only does he explain how the brain works but, more importantly, he discusses what you can do about it for your own personal benefit. This is an important contribution to understanding the trigger of money that drives most of Western society. Highly recommended for anyone attempting to create a wealth-based life journey." —**Jack Jacoby**, executive director, CEO Mentoring Pte Ltd, London/Singapore

"Learning what my own money story was and how to rewrite it with David as my guide and mentor has completely changed my life for the better. Instead of money controlling me and the decisions I was making, I am now in charge of my future, with money as the tool to help me achieve my goals.

"I am honored and proud to be a certified New Money Story® coach here in New Zealand, and I am now able to share my experiences and David's teachings in this new book with my own clients and help them transform their money stories as well." —**Lynda Moore**, cofounder, Money Mentalist Limited, B.Com, Grad Dip Arts (Psych)

"One of my most challenging roles as a Certified Financial Planner® Professional is helping and mentoring clients to change the money behaviors that don't serve them. For many clients, it is an elusive concept and a daunting journey to undertake. This book holds the key to unlocking those deep-rooted money stories and takes you on a step-by-step process of understanding and owning your money story, taking accountability, and ultimately changing that story. David inspires you to believe that it is possible to change the outcome of your life by changing your attitude and behavior toward money—that it is possible to change the money habits that no longer serve you into thoughts and actions where money is viewed as an enabler to living the life you really want to live." —**Kim Potgieter**, director and head of life planning, Chartered Wealth Solutions

"After a lifetime of sabotaging my finances, I swallowed my pride and worked through the ROADMAP process to effortlessly overcome my resistance to change. I doubled my income and halved my working hours, creating financial sustainability and working from home, by developing a world-class trader psychology program with the ROADMAP client workbook at its heart. I used my new understanding to empower traders of all financial markets to outsmart their own brains and behaviors, reduce stress, and develop confident trading skills for consistent trading results. Thank you, David, for sharing your life-transforming professional knowledge." —**Andrew Pertsoulis**, trader mentor from Sydney, Australia; licensed, specialty certified New Money Story® Mentor

Your New Money Story

The Beliefs, Behaviors, and Brain Science to Rewire for Wealth

David Krueger, MD

ROWMAN & LITTLEFIELD
Lanham • Boulder • New York • London

Published by Rowman & Littlefield
An imprint of The Rowman & Littlefield Publishing Group, Inc.
4501 Forbes Boulevard, Suite 200, Lanham, Maryland 20706
www.rowman.com

6 Tinworth Street, London SE11 5AL, United Kingdom

British Library Cataloguing in Publication Information Available

Library of Congress Cataloging-in-Publication Data

ISBN 978-1-5381-2399-7 (cloth: alk. paper)
ISBN 978-1-5381-2400-0 (electronic)

♾™ The paper used in this publication meets the minimum requirements of American National Standard for Information Sciences—Permanence of Paper for Printed Library Materials, ANSI/NISO Z39.48-1992.

Printed in the United States of America

To my beloved grandchildren:
Nicole, Jackson, Casey, Samantha, and Max Krueger
Caitlin, Norah, Julia, and Mairin Weeks

Those who do not have power over the story that dominates their lives, the power to retell it, rethink it, deconstruct it . . . and change it as times change, truly are powerless because they cannot think new thoughts.
—Salman Rushdie

CONTENTS

CONTENTS

PREFACE

A Quiz

Each of the following eight questions has a single-word answer:

1. What is the most popular legal substance to all peoples of the world?

2. What is the one true metaphor, the single commodity that can be translated into everything else?

3. What is the story you write each day, think about several times a day, and may not know how to tell yourself?

4. What is the legal tender of desires?

5. What is the one thing that can make any statement, carry any message, and represent any notion?

6. What is the universal, personal Rorschach inkblot?

7. What is the longest relationship you'll have in your life? The one that your parents discussed before you arrived, that will be deliberated after you're gone? A relationship that you'll never stop living each day of your life?

8. As a famous therapist once wrote, what kind of "questions will be treated by cultured people in the same manner as sexual matters, with the same inconsistency, prudishness, and hypocrisy"? (The year: 1913. The therapist: Sigmund Freud.)

See answers on next page.

Answers to Quiz

1. Money

2. Money

3. Money

4. Money

5. Money

6. Money

7. Money

8. Money

INTRODUCTION

Y*ou know, Dave, I don't know how to tell my money story to myself in order to know what to change.* This statement by an internationally known self-help guru and publisher struck me as both simple and profound. We each have personal narratives that shape our views of ourselves and of the world. The beliefs and assumptions of our inner voices can be expansive or limiting. Our brains are wired to process information in narrative form. We think in stories and tell stories throughout the day. Despite being natural storytellers, perhaps the greatest challenge is to examine our own stories in order to know what to change: to reflect on and develop mindfulness about our own experiences, to figure out who is really writing the script, to understand why we have chosen certain roles, to reflect on the challenges we face, to figure out how we can turn circumstances into possibilities, to convert challenges into strengths, to recognize money behaviors ghostwritten by hidden assumptions; to overcome the brain's patterned responses that lead to bad decisions, and to plan the next chapters.

Most people are secretly dissatisfied with their money stories. This dissatisfaction often stems from feeling either unfulfilled or ashamed of certain aspects of that story. We each have beliefs about money that we don't speak out loud, even to ourselves. This avoidance can create biases and can preclude taking in essential, important new information. Earlier downloads of expectations and experiences about money remain intact and unchallenged despite the passage of years, even decades.

A fact or a belief is an anatomical reality in the brain. Simply encountering a new fact or being presented with a better idea will not overwrite what we already know. Yet many of the methods we use to facilitate change are contrary to the way the mind and brain work. Most people are stuck because of the stories they tell themselves, the ones they use to operate their lives. Stuckness can result from an outdated story, such as the one that was tailor-made for a decade earlier but won't work today, or even an unconscious behavior pattern from childhood.

Neuroscientists now know that more than 90 percent of our operating system is unconscious and that the beliefs and patterns generated from those unconscious programs determine current decisions. How do we make our stories fully conscious to change what doesn't work and install successful new patterns? Many prescriptions for change ignite a discomfort with an old story, may even resolve old stories, but fail to offer an effective, systematic way to develop successful new stories.

In more than two decades of practicing and teaching psychotherapy and psychoanalysis and in the most recent dozen years as an executive mentor coach, I have helped people understand their relationship with money and how to successfully write new money stories.

In that time, I have come to see that the most fundamental understanding about our relationship with money is not an in-depth knowledge of money itself. It is about awareness of how our minds and brains work and how that affects our behaviors, including about money and finances. The beliefs, decisions, and seemingly inexplicable behavior involving money aren't fundamentally about money at all. Money becomes a portal to the immaterial and the intangible, a Rorschach onto which we project our needs and hopes. A money story is a large part of a life story. Some of the money issues are really about money, but many—most—are about other matters, private or even secret, hitchhiking on money.

Our relationship with money is complicated because some important aspects are emotional, unspoken, and even unconscious. Since our minds and brains determine financial decisions in unique ways, decision science can help us understand money mistakes and financial fallacies and how to program new, adaptive behaviors.

Your New Money Story will help you recognize, own, and assess each component of your money story. You can then decide what to change, map changes, author new story lines, and even program the changes to transform core identities according to that new story to make the transformation complete and lasting. This systematic stepwise process to inform and strategically catalyze behavior change will rewrite mind software and revise brain hardware related to money stories as they are interwoven with life, wellness, relationship, and career stories. This system of behavior, mind, and brain changes offers long-term successful strategies and can even crystallize a vision of your future self to significantly affect positive money decisions.

The ROADMAP System—an acronym for the seven steps to deconstruct the process of understanding a story and systematically construct a new one—will guide you to listen and to understand your present money story to develop the art and science of successful money strategies. The ROADMAP System is a proven method that integrates psychology, neuroscience, behavioral economics, and neuroeconomics with strategic coaching to make changes that last. The ROADMAP System is successfully used by licensed, specialty-certified mentor coaches whom I have trained as New Money Story® Mentors and New Life Story® Wellness Coaches.

We begin a journey to understand the choice architecture of your money story. You write your money story and live it and can revise it, or you can write an informed, powerful, new money story. You will then be better able to acquire, keep, use, and enjoy money.

Part I
UNDERSTANDING YOUR RELATIONSHIP WITH MONEY AND YOUR MONEY STORY

CHAPTER ONE

THE LONGEST RELATIONSHIP
OF YOUR LIFE

Y ou're writing a story that you may not know how to fully tell. It's
a very personal story with its own history and language. It's highly
visible to others but often not to you. In *The Unexpected Universe*,
Loren Eiseley observed, "Reality has a way of hiding from even its most
gifted observers."[1]

It's a story that you talk about every day, think about several times
a day. It is remarkably simple yet intricately complex. This story has an
internal and external dialogue, a secret language, and encrypted messages.

It's complicated because some important aspects are emotional, unspoken, even unconscious.

This story is about the longest relationship you'll have in your life.
Your parents discussed it before you arrived; people will deliberate it after
you die. Maybe you'll get 10 years out of a car, perhaps 50 with a spouse,
but this story you can never stop writing or living. You can't break up with
it, run away from it, or coax it into loving you more.

Even though it's unexamined and elusive, you orient life decisions
around it. You alone determine the genre: fiction or nonfiction, tragedy
or triumph. The story tells most about the teller.

This story ghostwrites every aspect of your life story: from what you eat
and drink to what you plan and play. Health, recreation, stresses—even the
water you drink—are all impacted by this story. At times, you've probably
used this story to regulate your moods, increase self-esteem, influence others, or soothe emotional pains.

And how you live this story will be what you teach your children.

The story's villain (or hero) is the most popular legal substance to all people of the world.

It speaks to you. You speak with it.

It's your *money story*.

Consider these questions:

- What's your money story?

- What would you ideally like your money story to be?

We give money meaning: we breathe life into it, give it emotional value, build a relationship with it, make it bigger than it is. Money can make any statement and carry any message.

Your money story is not your income, assets, expenses, or debt—it's your *relationship with money*. It's how you use money in story lines of what money means to you, what money says about you, and what you say with it.

It's a running dialogue about how much you feel you deserve and how much you believe you're worth—even how much you're capable of. It's about what if you had more—or less—and what your sense of *enough* is.

Your money story has little to do with math. If money were about math, no one would have debt—at least not personal debt. You can fulfill a desire you didn't know you had by spending money you don't have. You can define yourself by acquisitions not paid for. You can even borrow based on how much money you will be lent rather than how much you can pay back.

A secret language becomes most developed by emotionally powerful desires. A desire is not quieted by its satisfaction; desires can be created by filling them. Being the legal tender of desire, money becomes the inkblot of the Rorschach test: when our eyes look straight at it, there is only a design on paper. But when respondents are offered the chance to imbue the design with meaning, the interpretations will be as wishful and varied as those respondents' fantasies.

The messages will keep repeating themselves. People will keep writing the same money stories that imprison them until the stories are listened to.

Problems don't arise from wealth, position, possessions, or even chasing after happiness. Problems come when you lose yourself in the chase.

Your money story is a large part of your life story. Some of our money issues are really about money, while many are about other matters, private or even secret, hitchhiking on money. The more meaning we give to money, the less able we are to focus on what money means.

Money is the one true metaphor that can stand for anything.

Money is the portal to the immaterial and the intangible. We see it as both the path and the possession. Money always relies on the meaning we assign to it. We give it our power yet perceive the power to be its own.

You write your money story and live it. You can revise it or write an informed, powerful New Money Story®.

New Narratives in Old Brains: The Power of Story

We learn through stories. Stories are how we understand and how we remember—a way to hold information and to make sense of things. Defense lawyers know this. So do little kids standing next to broken vases. Muriel Rukeyser said, "The world is made up of stories, not atoms." Stories create both personal mastery and connection to others. A recent Princeton University study used brain scans to reveal that when one person tells a story and the other actively and empathically listens, the two brain patterns begin to synchronize. The neural activity of one mirrors the other and vice versa. If the listener fails, however, to comprehend what the speaker is trying to communicate, their brain patterns decouple.

A life story contains silent assumptions and emotional scripts. Our assumptions tell us what to look for and how to perceive and process experiences. Some of our beliefs and patterns may be invisible even to ourselves. We make a story out of events in order to infer relationship and assign causality. We personify the economy or the stock market as if each were a story of its own. "The market was cautious today, anticipating the impact of the upcoming Fed announcement." Marketers know this, which explains the profusion of stories in advertisements.

Each of us has a personal story with a plot and story lines. Our beliefs and assumptions ghostwrite that story. From an infinite sea of possibilities, our software determines what we perceive and process. The brain needs a story. It will always infer one, so we need to know the lexicon.

A story can define possibility. In centuries of recorded time, no one ran the mile in less than four minutes. People believed it couldn't be done. Then in 1954, Roger Bannister broke the four-minute mile. Within the next 18 months, more than a dozen other runners broke the four-minute mile. The obstacle of the impossible could no longer be constructed. Today, this is common. When the mind-set of what is possible changes, reality changes as well.

A story can define reality. A placebo generates the effect of the accompanying story. A patient is prescribed an inert pill plus some expectations (a story). In the majority of cases, the story becomes the reality. By anticipating an experience, we can create it. The story generates a truth so powerful that it can even reverse the pharmacological effect of a real medicine. The placebo is a white lie, a fiction that becomes a truth. A recent study at the Massachusetts Institute of Technology showed that a more expensive placebo worked significantly better than a much cheaper one—same placebo, different stories.

We believe and remember only that which fits our plot. What we expect to happen in the present reveals instantly our experience in the past. Our expectations help us see; in fact, they determine what we see. But they may blind us to other things that we are not looking for. Near the end of class, a professor who is fond of telling stories asked whether the students had time for him to tell them a story before leaving. They looked at their watches and said, "Yes." When he immediately asked them what time it was, they had to look at their watches again. The first time they had checked not to see what time it was but to see if enough time was left before class ended. If we look for one thing, we may miss another.

A story can take over the author. A feeling that someone creates is perceived to act on its creator—rather than seeing ourselves as the author of the stories we create, we may see ourselves as their victims: "My doubt paralyzed me." "My work eroded my free time." To our stories, our own creations, we ascribe minds of their own.

When you change the way you look at things, the things you look at change. Neuroscience shows that pure facts are a myth, a truth validated through quantum physics and the process of observing quarks.

An authentic belief in someone activates that person's brain to create a state of mind that transcends usual thinking and performance. Although proof of this comes from neuroscience, effective parents have known it for centuries.

We are hardwired to convert our lives into stories. Our narratives—the stories we tell about ourselves—both describe and determine what we do. We become the stories we tell about ourselves. Neuroimaging and cognitive neuropsychology have demonstrated how we create our "selves" through narrative. Our left brain specializes in personal self-narrating actions, emotions, and thoughts. This interpreter function is the glue that keeps our stories unified to create a cohesive sense of self. These language areas of the left hemisphere draw on memory from the midbrain hippocampal circuits and the planning regions in the orbital frontal cortex.

The transformative importance of the old story comes by learning from it. We become wiser for it, more adaptive. Rather than repeat the old story, we can recognize, own, and assess it in order to decide what to change. We extract the lesson from the past experience to write a new narrative in a current context. The past becomes memory, like our lap when we stand up to walk, rather than an active repetition intruding on the present. This places the memory on a library shelf in our mind, as a choice to revisit at will, rather than as an intrusive, unwelcome visitor. We remember in order to forget.

We Speak with Money

As a Tool

Money says *whatever you tell it to*. It can convey any message. The wonder of money is that it can represent anything. It's a stand-in for what we idealize and desire yet fear or lack, for what we covet, crave, spurn, chase, or follow. We use money to show how much we care—or how little. We use to it measure success and buy happiness—or try to. We use money to *communicate*.

We give money meaning: we breathe life into it, give it emotional value, build a relationship with it, and make it bigger than it is.

As a Self-Statement

Money can make *any statement.*

What we say and do are inevitable, unavoidable *statements* of our own beliefs and personal realities. All that we say is about ourselves. A life story or money story manifests through self-statements. The story tells most about the teller. A few examples:

- Proclamation of freedom

- Currency of caring

- Promissory note for happiness

- Embodiment of power

- Evidence of security

- Proof of worth

- License for opportunity

- Instrument of control

An example is the self-statement of spending money. We call it conspicuous *consumption* when you buy a bright-red BMW 550 and drive it in the middle of a busy street. *Contemptuous consumption* is when you buy a red BMW 550 in the middle of a midlife crisis and drive it by your ex-wife's house. (That's not a self-statement—I'd never buy a *bright-red* BMW.)

Without realizing it, we use money every day to tell a story about our lives and ourselves.

As Self-Talk

We tell ourselves various things about our personal meanings of money. These internal beliefs may include the following:

- People who have significant money are lucky.

- People with money are different from me.

- Truly spiritual people don't have money or wealth.

- Money will buy happiness.

External Dialogues

Part of what keeps the language of money a secret is the fact that it remains largely unspoken. Our social conventions create unusual pairings of spoken and unspoken agreements. A woman can speak of her dress size but not her weight, the cost of plastic surgery but not her age. We can debate financial markets and economics but not personal income or debt. Ask the host of your dinner party, "How much money do you make?," and you may not see the next dinner. Ask, "How much debt do you have?," and you may not see dessert.

An agent at a writers' conference discussed working with her authors over the years. She talked about the details of some of her contract negotiations. Someone in the audience asked, "Would you talk about how much money is involved in book deals, to give us an idea of what to expect?"

She looked shocked, responding immediately, "I've always felt that you don't talk about money." While she appeared to try to compose herself, an older man from the back row said, "I thought once you finished the book is when you finally do talk about money. You shut down your computer, change out of those sweat pants, and start selling your book."

Of course, he was right. His frankness and confrontation sparked a lively discussion about money and contracts. The presenter revealed the specific figures involved and went on to lead a discussion useful to an audience interested in writing books for a living.

A therapist once wrote, "Money questions will be treated by cultured people in the same manner as sexual matters, with the same inconsistency, prudishness, and hypocrisy." The year: 1913. The therapist: Sigmund Freud. Now, a century later, most of us have learned to talk more easily about sex yet remain secretive, embarrassed, or conflicted about certain aspects of our own money stories.

Guess who had this seasoned wisdom: "When we don't speak something, we make it more powerful."

The answer: Harry Potter.

Internal Dialogues

As long as we may not speak openly of something, our inner voice never takes up the conversation either. We have dialogues in our minds before making a decision to exchange our money—our time and energy—for something else.

Every exchange involves two asking prices: financial and emotional. The conversation, often silent and automatic, has many dialects:

- At an elaborate birthday party, the parent unconsciously whispers, "I'll give you what I never had as a child."

- The preamble to spending may be rationalization. "This seems like a lot of money to spend on a big-screen HD TV, but if I amortize it over the next 11 years, it only costs twenty-seven cents a day." (And my wife said, "Dave, if you want the TV . . ."). (Rationalized spending)

- We regard the same dollar differently depending on how it's obtained. "Found" money can be consumed frivolously. George Costanza said it simply: "This is found money. I've got to blow it on a horse." "Gifted" money we spend without debate. "Salary" money we use after serious comparative choice. "Savings" money we relinquish only with definite need or emergency. "It's the same dollar." (A framing bias)

- From a veteran of three bankruptcies on the verge of her fourth: "The high I get from shopping is more powerful than the low from bankruptcy." (Tilt)

- The parent: "I spend so much time at work, when I'm off I like to buy my child something to make up for it." (Justification bias)

Money Speaks to Us

A joint Stanford–Caltech study observed brain scans using functional magnetic resonance imaging while volunteers tasted five glasses of cabernet sauvignon.[2] (I follow research from around the world and collaborate with some behavioral economists and neuroeconomists, but I can *never* find studies like this to volunteer for.) Before tasting, the volunteers were told the price of each. As you might expect, they rated the wines according to the price they were told—the most expensive was the one they liked best and on down to the least expensive as the one they liked least. And their brains corresponded: the area of their brains that encodes the pleasantness of an experience (medial orbital frontal cortex) was more active with the more expensive wine and on down to the least activation with the cheapest wine.

Actually, the volunteers tasted *one wine* with *five different stories*. They experienced more pleasure—and their brains registered it—when they were in a more expensive story.

Money sometimes communicates to us just below the level of our conscious awareness. Money speaks to us as confidante, seducer, adversary, protector, or drug. Money can serve as a tangible container for hope, freedom, ambition, love, or disappointment.

Money Equations

Money can make any statement: worth, autonomy, security, freedom, love, opportunity, and power, to name only a few.

People may think money is a reflection of their personal self-worth or even their morals. One woman said, "I don't know why money is getting the best of me. I have good morals. I shouldn't have money problems." Of course, good money isn't related to good morals, or we'd have never heard of Madoff, Enron, Stanford, or Ponzi, to name only a few. Action gets you money; smart action gets you more; efficiency keeps your money.

Or their ethics. President Obama said, "If you work hard in America, you shouldn't be poor." But we know that's not true. You may work hard yet suffer a chronic illness, overspend, gamble, have a shopping addiction, live on Manhattan's Upper East Side, or have five children, three of them college age.

Who in America do you believe has the best work ethic?

As you consider this question, cast the broadest net possible to consider all cultures, jobs, and situations.

There is one group of people who get up every morning with a hustle—seven days a week, including holidays, 365 days a year. They can't let a single day go by without working. And it's not because their self-esteem suffers if they don't. One member of this group summarized it this way: "If I don't get up early tomorrow morning and hustle all day, the next day I'll die."

The answer? *Heroin addicts.*

The point is that work ethic must not be confused with performance ethic and especially not with success ethic.

Why Do We Make These Money Errors?

The moment we begin to make money more than the simple, tangible thing it is, we stop understanding it. The more meaning we give to money, the less we grasp what it really means.

We do strange things with money. Intelligent people spend money they don't have. Sophisticated people can scheme and get scammed. Rational people sometimes trade in leisure time for money to buy back some of what they just forfeited. Gifted people at times can't figure out how to exchange their talent for proportionate income. Otherwise balanced individuals spend extravagantly or hoard compulsively. Reliable people can ignore financial problems until they snowball into an avalanche. People with integrity sometimes write their own exceptions to rules about money.

Others operate on rules they were taught from the beginning. Burton Watson, chief executive officer of Cybernet, conned investors out of $120 million. When he was a boy, Burton's mother would tell him, "Exceptionally wealthy and exceptionally intelligent people don't have to follow the rules" (*American Greed* documentary).

The messages will keep repeating themselves—people will keep writing the same money stories that imprison them—until they are listened to and changed.

Money has become more abstract.

Here's an ultrabrief history of money. First, two goats were exchanged for five bags of rice. Then coins appeared as a unit of exchange. Paper bills were added, then paper checks, then plastic, then a pure abstraction of numbers stored and traded as configurations of electrons.

The vast majority of our money management occurs not through our hands or our brokers' hands but inside our minds in a complex interplay of thoughts, emotions, and neurological wiring.

Your Future Money Story

> To abstain from the enjoyment, which is in our power, or to seek distant rather than immediate results, are among the most painful exertions of the human will. —N. W. Senior (1790–1864)

Setting goals is easy. The challenge is sustaining the discipline to realize them. Resisting temptation is hard.

It's also difficult because there's an unequal battle between your present self and your future self. Your present self is real and in control. Your future self is an abstraction without its own power.

Your present self wants pleasure and to spend now. The pleasure center in your brain (the nucleus accumbens) opts for a little of something now rather than a lot in the future. Your future self needs planning and savings.

For every three baby boomers, the McKenzie Global Institute predicts that, in retirement, two will be unable to meet their preretirement financial needs.

Commitment devices level the playing field between our present and future selves. A commitment device needs to be structured so that you can't wiggle out of it or bargain with yourself. We helped our children learn about commitment devices when we gave them piggy banks.

Rather than use a commitment device to remind you of your lack of self-control, you can reframe it as a way to support making a good decision just once. As a simple example, you can decide to have the bank transfer money from your checking account to your retirement account once a month automatically.

We may also neglect our future selves because we don't—or can't—imagine what it would be like to be old.

Psychologist Dr. Daniel Goldstein, who studies decision making, uses computer simulation to help people imagine how they will look in the future.[3] When people are shown their projected image at an older age, most significantly increase their retirement savings.

A future money story depends on both imagining and planning.

The key element in writing a new money story is to begin with what is possible rather than what existed in the past.

Every choice we make is consistent with our money story. Whenever we buy a new car, purchase a trip, or buy a ski jacket, it fits with our identities and activates the part of the brain that orchestrates our sense of self.

Our identities are the stories we tell about ourselves, a composite set of beliefs of who we are, what we can and can't do, what we will and won't do. One of the strongest forces in our lives is consistency with this self-definition. Each of us has a model—a map or blueprint—of how we get our needs met and how we feel life should be. This personal blueprint governs how we perceive and process things, and it determines the meanings we attach to whatever happens to us.

When we encounter something that doesn't fit our story of how we feel life should be, we face a choice: either change the blueprint or change our story.

A fundamental quality of the human psyche is resistance to any change that is not part of our identity. We even tend to align with people who share our identities. And when we do change our behavior, we will ultimately return to our core identity *unless a new model is programmed in the mind.* That's what this book will show you how to do. The most common reason that people fail to change permanently, why they revert back to their original position after a temporary change, is that they have not changed their identity, of who and what they are, along with their behaviors. A habit is simply a series of choices, a collection of repetitions. It is not an identity.

Although we didn't learn it in high school, we now know that a fact or a belief is an anatomical reality in the brain. Simply encountering a new fact or being presented a better idea will not overwrite what we already know. Yet many of the methods we attempt to use to facilitate change are contrary to the way the mind and brain work. Most people are stuck because of the stories they tell themselves, the ones they use to operate their lives. Stuckness can result from an outdated story, such as one that was tailor-made for a decade earlier but won't work today, or even from an unconscious behavior pattern from childhood.

We are defined by the stories we tell ourselves. Is your story empowering you, or is it causing you to compromise? Is your story limiting any area of your life?

SURFACE AND SHADOW STORIES

The Cost of Money

I had my first official job—paid in real money—at age eight. On hot summer days I chopped cotton for my dad, earning a whopping 10 cents a row. (Back then, family farms were under the radar of child labor laws). The work was hot, hard, and dirty, but I was pleased to be earning money.

When school started and I saw my classmates enjoying the sodas and candies they bought, I joined them. But after my treats were quickly gone, questions lingered. "Was that candy worth one-half a row of cotton?" and "Is this soft drink worth one row of cotton chopping?" I soon answered "No" to both questions.

That experience was an early lesson about the *cost* of money. Not its *value*—I knew exactly how much candy a nickel would buy. The cost of money was the personal price I had to pay to get my hands on it. I learned that not only do you buy things with money, you also have to buy the *money*.

The next money lesson came in an unlikely way. At age ten, I entered into a joint venture with my dad. My first business! I fed all of his pigs in return for free food for my pig, Stubby. When the day came for me to sell my pig, my dad had to console me while I cried over giving up Stubby.

That was an early lesson about how every money exchange involves two prices—financial and emotional—and that internal dialogues have many dialects. "Gifted" money was no problem to spend; cotton-chopping money was for serious purchases; "Stubby" money survived all kinds of emergencies.

I developed a cost reference for bigger-ticket items. In the fifth grade, when I wanted a motor scooter, a used Cushman scooter would cost one Stubby. By age 13, I graduated to raising cattle, a small herd of registered Herefords—no pleading looks from them because I didn't have to sell them.

By the time I was 16, my dad let me grow my own cotton on 10 acres of land in return for doing work for him. I learned two lessons: the delayed gratification of doing work for myself without immediate payment, and, as I can officially tell you, there is no way to get emotionally involved with a cotton stalk.

I learned much later that everyone else also has internal and external conversations about money. We carry on dialogues in our minds before making a decision to exchange our money—our time and energy—for something else. When we really listen to those conversations, we can discern cost versus value and spending versus earning comparisons.

Operating Systems

Behavioral patterns and belief systems, especially those downloaded from parents in the first years of life, become automatic, operating without observation or awareness. Neuroscientists estimate that about 95 percent of our behaviors and core beliefs are preprogrammed in the unconscious mind, operating on autopilot. We only indirectly infer these behavior patterns and beliefs because they're unconscious. The conscious mind is a tiny processor that controls the mind and brain systems only 5 percent of the time.

That being so, we may create two stories simultaneously that go in opposite directions:

1. The *surface story*, the conscious intentions and aspirations that run our lives. This dialogue includes "This is what I want from life" and "These are my positive aspirations."

2. The *shadow story* that ghostwrites behaviors: "I can't really get what I want" or "The system keeps me from doing what I need" or "I don't have what it takes."

Another example:

1. The *surface story*: "I want to create wealth."

2. The *shadow story*: "Money is unspiritual" or "Some people were born to have money."

The step of rewriting your money story in order to change it calls for knowing yourself quite well, becoming self-observant. The keys are insight and reflection.

Whatever you experience in adulthood is something you either create or accept.

But positive thinking in *itself* doesn't reprogram beliefs. Positive thoughts are generated in the conscious mind. Using positive self-talk in order to change behavior will have the same impact as talking positively to a software program on your computer in order to change. You have to know how to *receive* the software. You must have a new story to be in before you can completely let go of the old one.

Each story line—including money—has an internal operating system with a set of beliefs and assumptions that inform behaviors. We are about to deconstruct that system in order to study it, understand it, and allow you to decide where it needs editing or updating.

Actual implementation of these ideas can be difficult because doing so often requires three changes about the way we think about money:

1. Breaking bad or outdated habits

2. Developing new ones

3. Remaining disciplined over the long haul, no matter what

Desire, Satisfaction, Greed, and Other Talismans

Several years ago, I was talking with a woman who had recently acquired a great deal of wealth. We were discussing restaurants, and she mentioned that she had dined the previous evening at the most fashionable and esteemed one in town, known for both "the poetry of French food" and its

17

sumptuous dessert cart with two dozen world-class choices. She said she had ordered one of everything on the dessert cart.

"Wow!" I said. "How was that experience?"

She said simply, "I was disappointed. I was surprised at how quickly I lost my desire."

Then I told her how, years ago, someone else had made the same discovery. The novelist Thomas Mann described how his father taught him about desire. Once in his life, his father assured him, he could eat as many cream puffs as the wanted. So, one day, he led Thomas to a pastry shop to make his dream come true. Mann got the lesson right away. As he put it, "I reached the limit of desire, which I had believed to be infinite."

If we want too much of something, it is sometimes because we are afraid of losing it and possibly never having it again. So we believe we have to consume—or hoard—to ensure that it will not go away or run out. We actually become greedy when what we get is not really what we want and it fails to satisfy. If one dessert doesn't do the trick, maybe the entire cart will. If $1 million isn't enough, then maybe $10 million will be. We become greedy out of the recognition that neither the dessert nor the dollar will truly satisfy, at least not well enough for long enough. We magically believe that more would be better and that more will satisfy the greed.

Yet our desires may be unrealistic for a reason: by excessive desires, our disappointment keeps us going. We experience a perpetual series of occasions for hope. We continue to desire goals just out of reach, or we configure them to ensure that we will never quite reach them. If someone feels that losing a final five pounds will bring happiness, then the five pounds will probably never be lost, as that person would then have to confront the illusion of happiness. We must be certain that we will never be fully satisfied; otherwise, we would then have to confront our fantasy. Wanting more means never giving up.

To the perfectionist, "good enough" is inadequate. Better to travel hopefully than to arrive, for arrival would reveal perfection as an illusion. The perfectionist clearly knows his desire yet avoids completion so as not to have to abandon hope.

Greed (defined as the rapacious desire for more) creates an insatiable desire for acquiring things, pleasures, and experiences. Greed ensures that we need not fear making the wrong choice or make choices at all. The fantasy of incredible wealth imagines unlimited choices. If you have everything, you don't need to choose. If you order everything on the dessert cart, you needn't make a choice. Then you can never be wrong or feel that you made an unwise choice. Had my friend chosen only one dessert, not only would she have had to mourn the unknown pleasures, but doing so would have persuaded her that she had made the wrong choice.

Greed, a state of mind of wanting to have everything, unlimited, at any time, defends against the fear of dissatisfaction and attempts a self-cure for helplessness. Links to an insatiable desire such as food, sex, or money become identifiable emblems of this process.

Although we usually want more then we have rather than notice that our desires may be unrealistic, we are more inclined to think that the world (or others) let us down.

When we achieve satisfaction in our lives, it is often by recognizing not only what we want and need but also what "good enough" is. When we are rich and can eat as much as we want, we quickly discover how much is enough. So, problems of food and money are really about energy and self-regulation. The most balanced individuals are those who self-regulate; they have a plan and stick to it.

The problem is not that our desire for love or money is insatiable. Perhaps it's the point, the purpose. How we handle the impossible and engage the ineffable ghostwrites our character.

Obstacles and Desires

Some time ago, I saw a cartoon of a dog straining at its leash, barking ferociously at a cat as if to say, "Just lemme at 'im!" The cat wasn't too shabby—he actually looked mean and was at least as big as the dog. All of a sudden in the middle of a ferocious bark, the leash snapped, so the dog was free to go after the cat. He looked astonished, scared to death. He quickly grabbed the leash, ran back, and tied a triple knot. Then he could once again safely strain at the leash and bark his fierce, "Just lemme at 'im!"

Every story of an obstacle has a shadow story of desire. The obstacle packs up and conceals the desire. What you seek is camouflaged in what you fear. Show me an obstacle, and I'll show you a desire.

There's a secret hiding in the open here. An obstacle is the unconscious mnemonic of desire. It reminds you of what you want but makes it safe to want if you're afraid.

When viewing a scene in a film you don't want to see, you cover your face with your hands as if to say, "No, I don't want to look." But then the desire creeps in, and you peek through your fingers at what you're drawn to see. The obstacle makes looking acceptable.

Sometimes we need an obstacle to free a desire. When the obstacle is unpacked, the forbidden desire also emerges. When Pandora's box was opened, all of the evils were released into the world. Remember the last thing to emerge? It was hope.

So rather than strategizing to overcome, avoid, or defeat an obstacle, a better approach is simply to consider not creating it. It's there only if you create it; instead, consider using your energy to generate something else, such as what you really want. It's your story to write, and every day is a blank page.

Pay attention to the obstacles that you construct, especially to your vocabulary of impediments. Worry simply holds onto things as a form of storage. When you find yourself focusing on an obstacle ("I can't find time to exercise" or "I can't put away any savings"), reflect on the underlying desire.

When you're ready to consider that you create the obstacle, you're also ready to consider the possibility of *not* creating it.

Imagine what it would be like to not create your obstacles.

The Enigmatic Promises of Money

In my earlier career of practicing psychiatry and psychoanalysis, I saw people who were quite wealthy by any standard yet were not happy. They knew something was missing yet had managed to keep hope alive by internal bargaining to up the ante. For example, when I'm worth $2 million, I'll really be happy. Then $5 million. Then a vacation home or ranch. As soon as each goal was met, those with insight consulted me to admit reluctantly that their plan wasn't working.

What do we really want when we want money? Is there a part of ourselves for which money is not (and never can be) the currency? In a culture that speaks of money, do we silence or distract this part of ourselves? We use money to wish with. Almost every adult wants more money than he or she needs, but acquiring more money inevitably creates more desire.

Money has become a way of describing the *more* that we apparently want and the *lack* that we apparently feel. Because it is instrumental in acquiring objects, money is something we're obliged to do something with. It is an action item, a transformational object that makes us feel better. Even if we hoard it and never use it, we cherish a fantasy of buying a future good.

Money, then, while promising to solve and satisfy, becomes our most successful tool for self-deception about our needs and desires. The experience of wanting may feel so helpless or so dangerous that we readily and gladly substitute another satisfaction. These fillers—possessions, food, drugs, alcohol—keep us from knowing our true needs and desires.

Although money can give us more of only certain things, we persuade ourselves that it can give us more of *everything*. Money is a way of thinking we know what we are getting. We think we know what money is by what it can do for us. Money promises to make accessible whatever we desire, to guarantee our expectations. If I pay this much for a car, I expect certain qualities.

Money always promises something other than itself. Even though it is worth only what it can buy, like all promises, it protects us from the fear that there is nothing that we really want or at least nothing worth having. Money helps us appreciate appetite.

The quintessential enigma is that we need money, yet money and what it buys can leave us feeling impoverished. At times, our appetites seem insatiable in that we want more than we need, and other times, we're not even sure what we want. This uncertainty can always focus on something specific and tangible, like money. Money can stand in for all that we desire as well as all that we abhor. As such, it tells us more about desiring than it does about money.

Consider how not desiring is more daunting than the unavailability of what you desire. In the same way, indifference is a less specific though far greater pain than death.

Perhaps one way to understand money is to think about what it cannot buy. One danger is that it becomes a negative ideal and creates the illusion of freeing those who abhor it. Opposition is only another form of engagement. Have you wondered what you would really want if you didn't want more money or what no amount of money could ever get?

In Charles Dickens's *Dombey and Son*,[1] a young Paul Dombey asked his father, "What's money . . . what can it do?" His father told him that it "can do anything." The boy then says, "I wonder why it didn't save my mama."

Spirituality and Money

One of my favorite descriptions of spirituality is from John Updike: "Pressed, I would define spirituality as the shadow of light humanity casts as it moves through the darkness of everything that can be explained."

This is one of the many unspoken, unexamined assumptions regarding money. For example, there does not have to be a split between spirituality and money. Spirituality and profitability can be quite compatible. There is nothing intrinsically unspiritual about money. It's analogous to the assumption of "starving artists": why should someone of exceptional talent have difficulty converting that ability into significant income?

Abundance, wealth, and spirituality are synonyms. Their antonyms are scarcity, poverty, and materialism.

You may not really know what it is truly like to be spiritual unless you are wealthy. How free are you to be spiritually resonant if you're worried about making the mortgage or rent payment by the first of the month? Remember that "wealthy" does not automatically equate with worldly riches. But it must incorporate aspects of freedom and choice in the context of the experience of abundance. If you spend some of your energy preoccupied with scarcity, with barely making it on your income each month, you may not have carved out the space to experience true spirituality. If you're running and a bear is chasing you, you don't have the freedom of a contemplative moment to think great thoughts or create new ideas.

When someone says, "I'm not in it for the money," I believe that person because I know the experience. But there's a caveat: it could be a rationalization for not making much money. Being truly immersed in what you're doing and passionate about it and delivering immense value is synonymous with abundant income—the result of alignment. Having an amazing experience of bringing value to people and making great money are seamlessly interwoven in a spiritual path. "Rich" and "spiritual" are synonyms.

You will improve your health by diminishing stress, for stress causes the body to be less healthy. You will create an attitude and an experience of abundance, which will also enhance wellness.

How Much Is Enough?

A passage in one of Schumann's piano sonatas is marked *so rasch wie möglich*, meaning "as fast as possible." A few bars later, he adds *schneller*—"faster"—and, a bit later, *noch schneller*—"still faster."

The Greek philosopher Epicurus said, "Nothing is good enough for the man for whom enough is too little."

So, how do you know how much is enough? Being able to answer this question means having a sense of "good enough" *inside*, an internal affirmation of worth. If you equate love and self-esteem with money and power, "more" will never be enough.

Much of our challenge with money stems from our difficulty in making one small distinction: what we *have* from who we *are*.

A Money Quiz

Answer the following two questions with a single, specific figure.

1. My current annual income is . . .

2. In order to ensure happiness and contentment financially, with no more money problems and worries, my annual income would need to be . . .

I have given this quiz to hundreds of people. In more than 9 of 10 cases, their answers indicate that their annual income would need to be about twice the current level for them to feel happy and free from money worries. Someone who makes $50,000 a year believes it would take roughly $100,000 a year in order to be financially content; someone who makes $500,000 believes that the figure would need to be about $1 million a year.

And, in follow-up discussions with people after they take this poll, there is a "trailing double" effect. People who have actually seen their income double over time have at the same time doubled their "happy and content" amount. In other words, once those who earned $50,000 achieve their hoped-for $100,000 goal, they raise the bar and believe that it would now take about $200,000 to be happy and content.

Even when you change the numbers, the story remains the same. The story in this case? "I need twice as much as I have to be happy." That's just one example of the common story threads; there are dozens of others, just as irrational and just as hypnotically compelling.

Making peace with our moving target isn't about learning how to aim better or how to create a fixed target that doesn't move even after we hit it. Creating financial targets (goals) is an important part of writing a new money story—but finding peace does not lie in the target. Your new money story begins with determining not what you want to *have* but who you want to *be*.

WHY DO WE RESIST CHANGE?

Why do we resist change, and even resist changing a story that doesn't work?

What keeps us from doing what we know we need to do for ourselves? Why will we repeat behavior that doesn't work, often do it harder, and expect a different result, even when it may lead to lower energy, debt, plateaued careers, or disappointing relationships?

Nassim Taleb asks in *The Black Swan*, "What are our minds made for? It looks like we have the wrong user's manual."[1]

We struggle to embrace change. Many of the methods for facilitating change fail to consider how the mind and brain work. Psychology, neuroscience, quantum physics, and strategic coaching have a lot to teach us about change and about resistance to change.

Our money stories tell us less about money and more about the human mind and its operations. At times, both our minds and our brains can work against us. When we think with one part of the brain and feel with another, we need a map.

The Psychology of Change

Part of the answer to why we resist change is in our minds.

Most lottery winners manage to spend or give away their newfound winnings to return to their previous situation. In fact, in the United States 80 percent of lottery winners of a million dollars or more file bankruptcy within the first five years.

Their money changed, but their mind-sets didn't. So much money moved them from their comfort zone, and they ended up returning to it.

A comfort zone is a familiar pattern of behavior. Getting to it is a gradual process, but once it's established, it makes us resist change. Think of a comfort zone like your home thermostat. If the temperature increases or decreases, it signals an adjustment to return to the set point—the comfort zone. Both our minds and our brains play their parts. We even have a comfort zone with our weight. We return to the familiar even when we don't like it or when it's uncomfortable.

A simple Scottish woman lived an ordinary life in a small village for more than 45 years. Then, suddenly, *Britain's Got Talent* catapulted Susan Boyle onto the world stage. Initially overwhelmed, she had to be hospitalized the day after the final competition. She, like the lottery winners, wasn't motivated to sabotage herself, but she got on overload way beyond her comfort zone.

In the beginning, departure from a comfort zone feels uncomfortable by definition—experienced as a rupture of continuity. A routine is broken. Sometimes letting go of a comfort zone occurs only when the pain is too great to remain in it.

The choices we make tend to come from our comfort zone. But a comfort zone trades passion for predictability, creativity for continuity, and the new for the familiar. A child reads *Goodnight Moon*, gets it the first time or two, and then reads it 98 more times or sees the same movie until he or she can say the lines.

An adult will repeat behavior that doesn't work, often doing it harder, and expect a different result. Why is repetition so compelling to intelligent people even though it's so illogical? Why can't we see that trying to leave an old story by simply writing a "better ending" only re-creates the same story and ensures that we remain in it? Why don't we see that a thousand better endings to an old story don't create a new story? Or why, too often, do we see ourselves as the victims of the stories that we author and the feelings we create?

We repeat the same story because it's our comfort zone: secure and predictable. A comfort zone may be limiting or uncomfortable, but it's familiar—a default model. *We repeat because we know how it will turn out, which creates the illusion of effectiveness.* The invisible decisions that we make every day become camouflaged as habits, our repertoire of repetitions. We remain loyal to the central theme, the plot, of our lives, forever returning to it. Any departure, even temporary, causes uncertainty and trepidation. Being in new territory as we seek to develop a new story creates anxiety. The easiest and fastest way to end this anxiety is to go back to the familiar, to the old story.

Coming to the end of an old story—or interrupting it—does not in itself generate a new story. You must concurrently create a new story.

People fail to change because they don't feel safe changing. Changing means leaving their home base of reality—the internal map that is synonymous with identity. We tend to return to our default mode.

Why can't someone just simply break out of a scarcity cycle—or chronic underachievement—and make a better life? Or launch a new business that they've dreamed often and planned well? A simple question. But there is no simple answer, for it's not a matter of intellect, willpower, or just moving into a better ZIP code. The question assumes an intact alternative, a substitute story waiting to be chosen, or another frame of mind to switch into from the one that has so permeated every cell of brain and mind. Assuming that this is possible would be like saying, "I know a better way to lead your life—just trust and go along with me to get there." No sensible person would or could do so, for it assumes that a new story awaits discovery and claim.

We know now that this is not the case. A new story is gradually and sometimes painfully constructed by a person who must, in the process, give up what is known, secure, and predictable. There is always the pull of the old and the fear of the new.

We are always loyal to the internal model that we create—not as a model but as the way things are. Repetition and resistance to change are initially perceived not as what they are but as reality:

- What are the repetitions in your life that are dead-end and dissatisfying?

- What are the things you'd like to change in your life in the next 90 days?

- If you could add three things of vital importance to your life beginning this month, what would these be?

CHAPTER THREE

The Neuroscience of Change

And part of the answer to why change is difficult is in our brains.
In a story from his childhood, the hypnotherapist Milton Erickson recalled that whenever it snowed, he would be the first to get up and go to school so that he could create a fresh path in the snow.[2] He intentionally created a circuitous path, with zigzags and indirect turns. He noticed that each person who followed him traced the same path until at the end of the day the path was well worn despite its circuitous route. *No one* started a new, more direct route. No matter how many turns and twists, each person in turn followed the path of least resistance.

This is how neural pathways are laid down in the brain: by early experiences, etched more deeply with each repetition, even if they don't work as well, even if they're circuitous and require far more work. Part of the answer to why change is difficult lies in the brain's preference and capacity for creating habits.

Experience converts to neuronal energy in the brain that runs along pathways that collectively form networks. These networks are templates representing particular ways of relating or habitual responses to certain stimuli in the environment. Consistent repetition of experience grooves these networks, strengthening them until they convert to automatic responses. The comfort or familiarity we feel from habitual behavior partly comes from the fact that habits require so little mental "processing" energy compared with that of fresh stimuli. The brain always strives for energetic economy, choosing first to transform experience as quickly as possible to habit by creating new networks and pathways for repeated behaviors.

An example of this would be learning a new dance step. Going through new movement patterns may be awkward and uncomfortable, triggering feelings of doubt and anxiety. These are predictable reactions in the mind and brain to new stimuli, requiring a shift from the automatic mode into an active level of processing. Change creates discontinuity and disrupts the "normal" state of cohesion. Enough practice, however, firmly establishes new neural pathways and networks and leads to a moment when the learner does the dance without much thought or physical effort. This is called "long-term potentiation."

This learning mechanism works consistently from the first years of life to form beliefs and attitudes that we come to regard as identities and character traits. Because it runs seamlessly and automatically, we can remain indefinitely unaware of how much we are a collection of habits. Our preference for security and comfort means we are not necessarily motivated to discover, question, or challenge it. Instead, we may attribute our stuckness to fate or to "just who we are."

But we are not hardwired for life. With new experiences, new neuronal pathways are created. This reprogramming can lead to more adaptive and successful modes. Stimulation for new insight is a circumstance in which the brain can't predict what will happen next. The catalyst for insight is a novel stimulus: new information or new context. New research shows that throughout our lives, we can rearrange and repurpose brain-cell connections (neuroplasticity) as well as produce new brain cells (neurogenesis). Neurons are both flexible and regenerative.

We now have the methods and tools to catalyze and accelerate the process of change. An infinite sea of new patterns and possibilities can be relearned or created to further new goals. But there's a caveat: you have to take action to diminish preprogrammed responses and write new script for new experiences. A new story has to replace the old one.

And there are no shortcuts because long-term change requires consistent practice to groove new neural pathways and establish new neuronal networks.

In the beginning, change is not only a disruption in the usual order of things but also an uncertain and precarious venture into new territory of mind and brain not yet etched like the old story. While you develop familiarity with the new story, there is always the likelihood, especially in times of stress or stimulation, whether good or bad, that you may move back to an old neural network. (Someone trips unexpectedly, and you immediately know his or her native language.) In extreme stress, the present context disappears: past, present, and future collapse into a repetition of the familiar. With a crisis, slippage to old neuronal pathways with accustomed story lines occurs; the repetition may not even be obvious until its pattern becomes complete. This stress activation of old and well-established networks and state of mind temporarily eclipses new growth and recent change, even making it seem to disappear.

Departure from the path of the familiar in behavior and brain involves the unknown, a sense of risk. Tolerance of the unknown, the new, requires holding a belief of successfully filling that space. At times, change is something one can get ready for only after it occurs. (And if you want to make an enemy, try to change someone.)

Both our minds and our brains react to leaving the familiar to engage new behavior. The uncertainty of this newness can be read as a warning not to proceed, as intuition of a wrong choice. Or it can be seen as a signpost of change and progress.

Discomfort and uncertainty begin any significant journey. Our brains even have an error-detection mechanism—located very close to the emotional center—that says, "This isn't normal" when we try something new. We'll investigate later how to use this mechanism as part of a powerful internal navigation system.

Why Are Bad Choices So Easy and Good Ones So Hard?

One trainee in my New Money Story® Mentor Training commented, "Everything you discussed about our resistance to change resonated with me. I understand how we naturally resist moving away from our comfort zone of familiarity not only because we know the outcome but also because it's the default mode grooved in both the mind and the brain. I'm wondering about something I've witnessed in others and myself: why is it relatively easy to make changes that undermine our best interests? Is the ease of making the 'bad change' the path of least resistance and just a reflection of our hedonistic tendencies?"

"Bad" choices (cheesecake, drugs, risk) usually involve *immediate* reward. Dopamine mediates the excitement of even anticipating a pleasure. "Good" choices (broccoli, exercise, saving money) involve *later* payoff. The good news is that with repeated new experiences, we can rewire our brains and revise mind software—create new pathways to new communities in the brain. The key success strategy for writing the next chapter of a life, wellness, or money story is having a structured *plan* and *sticking to it*. An aspect of that plan is to learn specifically from the past what you *don't* want to include.

Commitment devices can make good choices *consistent*. We can prioritize "shoulds" and then reward with "wants" to reframe the "wants" as part of a performance ethic. This contingency removes guilt from what you know you're going to do anyhow. As an example, a continuity program makes a good decision *automatic*, such as automatic withdrawals to fund a retirement account.

Why Are Our Money Stories So Elusive?

Neuroscientists study the responses and functioning of the brain by functional magnetic resonance imaging—a video of the brain in action—as it responds to different situations. These studies have disproven the long-standing assumption that people have a consistent and predictable set of preferences and responses that they choose based on logic. Different parts of the brain operate in radically different ways.

Money behavior and financial decisions are linked to both mind dynamics and brain activity:

- The prefrontal cortex says, "Let's think about the 12-month game plan and retirement savings." The limbic system says, "Ah, let's have that second cognac and order that 27-inch iMac." (My amygdala even specifies the brand of cognac—and can even pair it with the best cigar—it's kind of talented in that way.)

- Each part of the brain struggles over the same dollar, hopefully without tearing it.

- Emotions do not simply and only corrupt decision making. Emotions narrow attention and compress focus on the immediate. However, those individuals who feel no emotion are not good at making decisions.

- Making people happy is not simply a matter of giving them more of what they prefer. The brain's pleasure center quickly accommodates to new stimuli and expects them to continue.

- Gamblers interpret good fortune as skill. My wife and I play heads-up poker, and she finally confessed that one of my "tells" is that when I happen to draw a lucky hand, my slightly smug look suggests that I think I'm brilliant.

The important thing about your money story is to discern what works and what does not. The components that work don't need fixing. The ones that don't work need to be revised in order to enhance both your money and your life stories and help you discern what is really about money and what hitchhikes on money. Your life can be changed significantly by changing your money story.

Money is a magnifier. Like adversity, it *reveals* character. Whoever a person is, excess money will exaggerate. If someone is a problem drinker, money will make that person an even more problematic drunk. If someone is insecure, money will enhance paranoia. If someone is caring and generous, money can enhance philanthropy.

Our money stories are a large part of our life stories. Stories awaken emotion. And money resonates with the most basic emotions.

We live our money stories each day. With each monetary transaction, the themes may be unstated, but they are evident in each transaction.

When we understand the architecture of choice, we can revise our money stories or write new ones. We can strategically rewire our brains and reprogram our minds to create wealth and success.

The most fundamental understanding about a relationship with money is not an in-depth understanding of finances. It is recognizing how our minds and brains work, how that affects our behavior, including about money. The beliefs and decisions and seemingly inexplicable behavior involving money aren't really about money at all.

Money is a portal to the immaterial and the intangible.

Inverse Wisdom

I came home from college after my freshman year of college and announced to my mom that I'd decided to major in psychology. We talked; she was excited for me. Then she mentioned that she made an A in her college psychology course.

I said, "You must have really enjoyed it and studied a lot." Her reply was, "No, I just answered everything on the tests the opposite of what I thought was right."

So, in honor of my mom, who thought it was all opposite anyway, here's a list of nine inversions of conventional wisdom in writing a new money story.

1. *Burn your bridges.* One dramatic way to mark a story's ending is told of Spanish explorer Hernando Cortés. When he came ashore with his men at Veracruz, he knew that his men were extremely uneasy about both the exploration ahead and the danger. Some had called it hopeless. Facing a continent of unknown perils and adversaries, every member of his party was torn between a desire for adventure and the urge to flee. Cortes burned their ships. Make it impossible to go back to an old habit or way of being. If you decide to quit smoking, make it impossible in some way to restart. Create an uncomfortable scenario if you do start again. Focus on the present without the bad habit. Reward yourself for not going back.

2. *Do the opposite of what you'd normally do when you're afraid, worried, anxious, or uncomfortable.* If you're uncomfortable with public speaking, avoidance will increase the fear, so do more of it. Jump into the water; you can't learn to swim on paper. Prediction and expectation based on the past create *repetition*, but based in the present and anticipating the future, they create *possibilities.*

3. *Obstacles reveal desires.* Show me an obstacle, and I'll show you a desire. An obstacle conceals but simultaneously reveals the underlying desire. When you're ready to recognize that you create the obstacle, you're ready to consider the possibility of not creating it.

4. *Discomfort can be a sign of progress.* Repeated habits etch neuronal pathways and neural networks, the highways and villages in our brains, to create efficient operations and make routine behaviors easy. When these habits are confronted with a requirement to change, the midbrain's automatic pilot gets disrupted. We feel discomfort. Although change promises to develop a new, better default mode, the brain doesn't know that at first, so our minds have to lead the way with a plan.

5. *Lean into the unknown.* People fail to change because they don't feel safe changing. Changing means leaving their home

base of reality, the internal map synonymous with identity. A new story generates uncertainty, trepidation. The easiest and fastest way to end this discomfort is to go back to the familiar old story, but it won't give you the change you expect. You can tiptoe through life very carefully and arrive safely at—death.

6. *You do not attract what you want; you create what you focus on.* When you focus on what you want, what you don't want falls away—like your lap when you get up to walk.

7. *You see only what you believe.* Our beliefs are the software that writes our behavior. Our experiences are always consistent with our assumptions. And we're always right—because we write the story.

8. *Believe in someone, and then he or she will show you why you do.* Neuroscience has demonstrated that authentic belief in someone activates his or her brain to create a state of mind that transcends usual thinking and performance.

9. *Don't believe every thought you have.* Thoughts lie a lot. They're like my Uncle Ted (rest his soul, or I'd have to use a different example). You don't have to believe every thought that crosses your mind. You're not even stuck with the brain you have—you can make it better.

Eighteen Caveats on How to Avoid Money Story Ownership and Change

If you are adamantly opposed to change, these caveats will embellish your position. If you are considering change, they might illuminate beliefs or positions that need addressing.

1. *Focus on the system.* Devote special attention to the things that seem frustrating, out of your control, and impossible to address: politics, corporations, and economics. Systems must remain in focus as broad categories in order for you to feel distanced and disaffected.

2. *Maintain a focus on theory.* Avoid detail, singular aspects, *and application.* *Cling to your* theories and abstractions about how to transform various systems, about what needs to be done, maintaining the frustration of what continues to seem out of your control.

3. *Believe that the answer will appear when you step out of the box.* Simply opposing the system can be an end in itself.

4. *Keep the point of reference external.* Believe that the antithesis of conformity is opposition; know that one or the other of these external points of reference of conformity or opposition holds the real truth.

5. *Do not decide.* Allow the urgency of a situation to decide for you. The gravity of a last-minute emergency forces action and avoids planning. Waiting for the deadline excuses responsibility for thoroughness and excellence.

6. *Believe that the answer is more rules.* Further structure will provide greater compliance.

7. *Debate the obvious.* Give energy to the controversial.

8. *Believe in experts unequivocally.* Expertise is authoritative. Dismiss any notion that expertise is perceived, processed, and filtered through assumptions, belief systems, and prejudices of experts.

9. *Do not seek your own information or develop your own solutions.* You will always have experts to listen to. Find someone to provide a map for you and avoid anyone who wants to help you develop your own navigation system.

10. *Always find some cause-and-effect relationship to explain things you can't otherwise understand.* Some tangible explanation will inevitably offer a specific, concrete focus on what is wrong or who can be blamed. Warning: much work is required to maintain this position. You must be certain the obstacle can never be totally removed; otherwise, its causal effect would

have to be confronted as inaccurate. The perceived cause must always be just beyond reach and remedy in order to remain as effective blame.

11. *Keep doing the same thing and expect a different outcome.* If the outcome doesn't change for the better, do the same thing harder.

12. *Be suspicious of new ideas.* Feedback from others can confuse and derail.

13. *New ideas must be curbed or even silenced.* Any perturbation of the existing system threatens disruption.

14. *Meticulously guard against mistakes.* The best way to be sure to avoid mistakes is to keep doing the same thing again and again with perfection as the goal.

15. *Maintain a focus on avoiding failure.* Give failures the proper respect of fear so that they remain ever in focus with their guiding principles of avoidance.

16. *Be extremely wary of new strategies and solutions.* Invest instead in enforcement of the existing approach.

17. *When you make mistakes, focus on the mistakes.* Redouble efforts to get them right.

18. *Continue to hold prejudices.* They are excellent markers of emotional land mines.

Don't Believe Everything You Think

The illusionist and hypnotist Derren Brown did an experiment on London's Regent Street in which he placed his wallet, with money clearly sticking out, on the sidewalk.[3] He then drew a circle with yellow chalk around the wallet—much like the crime scenes on TV. Then he walked away, leaving the wallet lying there. Hundreds of people walked past this wallet. Most saw it, many stopped to look at it, but no one would pick it up. The yellow chalk circle created a barrier—an assumption that limited people from simply picking up the wallet.

Belief systems are both powerful and enduring. Beliefs come first, expectations follow. We form our beliefs from various personal experiences with family, friends, colleagues, and culture. Then, after forming those beliefs, we seek to validate, even to justify and rationalize them. We confirm the beliefs by cherry-picking data to support them and become blind to data that diverge from them.

Our perceptions of reality rely on the beliefs we hold. The brain is fundamentally a belief engine. Beliefs are the software that organizes both what we perceive, from an infinite sea of stimuli, and how we process them and the patterns we deem meaningful.

From behavioral economics, we have learned that the more heavily invested we are in a belief, the harder it is to let go of, especially if we have no new belief to replace it. The sunk costs of our beliefs seduce us. (Sunk-cost fallacy refers to the decision to justify spending more money when we can't recover what we've already spent.) When conditions clearly dictate to mountain climbers partway up Everest that they should turn around, they tend to continue because of how far they've come.

How do you form a new belief?

Changing your belief system changes the neurophysiology of your brain, making creating a new story both an art and a science. Whether the content of the belief system is about life possibilities, money, or other personal stories, change is challenging. Many of the ways that we try to facilitate change are contrary to the way the mind and brain work.

We change not because we seek transformation or enlightenment but because what we've been doing doesn't work—often dramatically so. Because it is lonely and unpleasant inside our own stuckness, we begin to look for other possibilities and options. The ability to admit that we are wrong depends on our willingness to tolerate the unpleasantness associated with being wrong.

For guys only: remember being hopelessly lost, yet stopping for directions was *not* an option? C. S. Lewis addressed this challenge: "If you are on the wrong road, progress means doing an about turn and walking back to the right road; and in that case the man who turns back soonest is the most progressive man." (Notice he even specified "man.")

Being wrong is, first and last, an emotional experience. Our mistakes become a moment of actual alienation from our sense of self:

"That wasn't me." What's our ultimate challenge? Not believing everything we think.

Our sense of self comprises a number of beliefs, any one of which can be mistaken. Every one of us has had ideas about ourselves—beliefs—that have evolved over time if not collapsed abruptly. Remember when you thought you didn't want children or knew you'd grow up to be a lawyer or reasoned that you would be happy only if you lived in New York City?

What is your yellow chalk circle? Hint: any assumption that limits you.

Adventures in Error

> For those who believe, no proof is necessary. For those who don't believe, no proof is possible. —Stuart Chase

You can't entirely let go of an old story until you have a new one to inhabit. This is, after all, the way scientific theory works. Science philosopher Thomas Kuhn summarized it like this: "A scientific theory is declared invalid only if an alternate candidate is available to take its place."

Some change is slow. Consider how, at an earlier age, you were adamant about a particular point of view. A dozen years later, looking back, you may even mock your former position. In between, a gradual process of transformation allowed you to let go of a belief and take on a new one. This is the stuff of time-lapse photography: slow and gradual, imperceptible in any moment or month.

Our sunk costs in a belief determine how loyal we are to it. The more emotional currency we invest in a belief, the harder we find extracting ourselves from it. We leave the security of our known stories, the certainty and predictability of how those stories—and we—will turn out. It feels like a lack of control, so it motivates us to avoid new information, especially if we expect bad news. The ultimate mistake? Avoiding the truth about ourselves.

Embracing change by recognizing the limitations of a belief or admitting the wrongfulness of a notion brings with it various emotions. Initially, we can feel lost, alone, perhaps scared. Neuroscience teaches us that a fundamental belief is an anatomical reality in our brains. Changing it can feel like an amputation, even an insult to our identity.

No matter how psychologically minded or resilient we are, facing up to mistaken beliefs challenges us. Since the past can't be changed, restitution involves admitting mistakes and using them to inform a different story.

Invincibility bias—that seemingly inextinguishable sense of immortality that crested in adolescence—still has whispers in adulthood. Here's some validation for this error:[4]

- 19 percent of people believe they're in the upper 1 percent income bracket.

- 75 percent of people believe they are healthier than average.

- 90 percent of people believe they are better-than-average drivers.

The challenge is to recognize, own, and assess certain aspects of our own stories:

- We tend to seek information that confirms rather than disproves our beliefs.

- New information may cause unpleasant feelings and a departure from our comfort zone.

- Different behavior disrupts our default mode; for example, people are afraid to go to the doctor not because they're afraid of doctors but because they're afraid of confronting their denial.

Fixed versus Growth Mind-Sets

Each of us has a running account of what's happening, what it means, and what we should do. Our minds constantly monitor and interpret. Mind-sets frame and fuel the stories we create about ourselves.

Jackson Pollack had little native talent for art, and it showed when experts looked at his early products. Experts also agreed later that he became one of the greatest American painters of the twentieth century and revolutionized modern art. How did he get from point A to point B?

Dedication. Pollack was wildly in love with the idea of being an artist, thought about art all the time, and created it all the time. He got others to take him seriously and mentor him until he developed his ability and began to produce startlingly original works.

Twyla Tharp, the famous choreographer and dancer, wrote a book called *The Creative Habit.*[5] She argues that creativity is not a magical act of inspiration but rather the result of hard work and dedication.

By consensus among the experts, the two hardest-working athletes in the history of sports, by no means naturals, were Larry Bird and Michael Jordan.

In business, sports, or the arts, those with a growth mind-set keep on learning. They are not worried about measuring or protecting their fixed abilities; instead, they look directly at their mistakes, use feedback, and alter their strategies to become better at what they do. Throughout the process, they maintain a healthy sense of confidence.

The view you adopt—the software program of mind-set you use—can significantly affect the way you live your life. Let's examine two simple versions of mind-sets.

Fixed Mind-Set

Those with a fixed mind-set try to make sure they succeed. A consuming goal is to prove oneself: in the classroom, in a career, or in a relationship. Each situation calls for a confirmation of intelligence, personality, or character. The repeated internal questions are these: Will I succeed or fail? Will I look smart or dumb? Will I be rejected or accepted? Will I be a loser or a winner?

Yet with a fixed mind-set and preoccupied with how you'll be judged, no amount of confirmation can dislodge the hypothesis of mediocrity or the need for proof.

A fixed mind-set shares some of these characteristics:

- People learn things, but intelligence is basic and essentially unchangeable.

- Since traits are fixed, success is about proving that you are talented or smart.

- Problems indicate character flaws.

- Self-esteem repair occurs by assigning blame or making excuses.

- I won't attempt something new unless I know I'll be great at it.

Growth Mind-Set

A growth mind-set is based on the belief that we can enhance and develop our skills. We are open to accurate information about talents and abilities and use that information to improve and grow.

A growth mind-set of learning is based on a belief that we can develop and improve on our basic qualities. The fundamental assumption of a growth mind-set is that everyone can change and grow through experience and application—that people can even improve their intelligence.

Dr. Howard Gardner, in his book *Extraordinary Minds*, concludes that exceptional individuals with growth mind-sets have a "special talent for identifying their own strengths and weaknesses."[6]

Whatever remains unconscious will be attributed to fate. Beliefs are often unconscious, yet we can pay attention to the best indicators of beliefs: our behavior. We can nudge ourselves toward a growth mind-set:

- Am I taking ownership of my mistakes?

- What can I learn from this?

- How can I improve?

In adulthood, whatever we experience, we either create or accept.

Mental Models

A mental model is a representation of external reality inside our heads. A mental model incorporates knowledge and principles about the world. Each of us has several mental models—stories—in our head, metaphors that explain both the tangible and the intangible.

If we have too few mental models, we tend to overuse the ones we have. To a man with a hammer, every problem looks like a nail. We overreach and apply the same mental model to more problems than it can actually solve. For this reason, the models that we choose need to come from different disciplines. One discipline can't encompass all the wisdom of the world.

An example of a mind-set in action is how we make decisions to purchase a particular product. Neuroscience studies have shown that if a product attracts us, it is often because we identify with it. The product fits into the picture we have of ourselves or of who we want to become, as increased brain activity in scanning experiments has shown. Mental models are stored in the hippocampus, the brain's memory focal point.

The magazine *Science* recently reported discovery of a new cell type, known as border cells.[7] Border cells are active in discerning the limits of one ending and a new beginning. This means that the brain functions like a Google map: it creates multiple independent maps while finding its way in the world. When a new situation arises, the map changes. When one context or environment ends and another begins, the brain boots up another map. This mechanism explains how we have different contexts or frames (mind-sets) for different situations. These maps are stored in the unconscious.

We began to download these mental models, including beliefs and behaviors, in our first years of life. For example, our money scripts began to be written by what our early caregivers consciously taught and unconsciously modeled.

These scripts are often so deeply ingrained that they are not conscious, yet we can rewrite these programs in our minds. Using the seven-step ROADMAP process (chapters 7–13), we can systematically examine existing stories and provide a method to write new ones.

A Young Business Partner

Many years ago, one of my psychoanalytic patients said, "You know, Doc, it's a lot easier for me to talk about dead people and bad dreams than it is for me to hand this check to you each month."

A poll of 20,000 people reported in *Money* magazine revealed that half of parents had never discussed finances with their children and that two-thirds had never revealed their income.[8] Youngsters who have had no comfortable discussion with parents or real information about money fill the vacuum by fantasy and personal myth. Children often conclude that things treated secretly and uncomfortably are bad and taboo. Their logic, based on the behavior they observe, can therefore create a lifelong legacy of discomfort around money.

The strictest rules in any family are the ones never spoken.

Several years ago, on a cruise ship headed for a family adventure vacation, my son first encountered casino gambling. It fascinated us both, so we decided to form a business partnership to play blackjack. Being a minor, he couldn't actively participate, so he sat behind me as my "consultant" where he could see our cards and the action on the blackjack table, whispering strategy and directions in my ear.

To my surprise, at age 14, he turned out to be a considerably more accomplished gambler than I. Although we had been investing in stocks together since he was 12, this gave us a wonderful opportunity to talk about some principles of business. Aware that the most common reason small businesses fail is inadequate capitalization, we decided to capitalize our venture at $25 each. This $50 seemed sufficient for losses that might otherwise disillusion or stop us, when we might need some "bounceback money." We also decided that we would never risk more than $25, half our initial investment, on a single evening session. Beyond that, we evolved principles, agreeing on when we would hold, when we would ask for another card, the amount of our standard bet, and under what circumstances we would deviate from our standard. We recognized the value of having established this business plan once we were in the stimulating atmosphere of the blackjack table. On the two or three occasions that we abandoned our rules, we learned important and expensive lessons that served to reestablish our principles even more firmly.

We gambled for approximately an hour and a half on each night of the cruise. At the end of six evenings, we were, happily, ahead about 300 percent. In that time, we had seen roughly 40 to 50 people at our table come and go. We made observations about the similarities among those who lost, especially those who lost spectacularly. We saw initially two groups of people who lost. One group had no consistent "business plan" or discernible principles on which to operate. Those who appeared to have some standards abandoned them when emotion was high: big wins, big losses, or sustained streaks of wins or losses. The emotionally motivated behaviors included anger at losing, overstimulation by winning big, or greed. No one seemed to have an established end point for loss or gain.

I was thankful for this opportunity for my son to see firsthand these basic business principles at work. And I loved our time together.

One evening, an older woman approached me indignantly when she saw what my son and I were doing. "I suppose you're proud to be teaching your son how to gamble?"

"No ma'am," I said. "I'm proud that he's teaching me." (Ryan now owns a very successful capital-management firm, overseeing significant wealth in his own mutual funds and hedge fund, advising many clients, including me, about investing [but not about how to play blackjack].)

Possibility Thinking and Your Money Story

What we believe is what we'll see. This means that we are not only data determined but also hypothesis determined. The brain as computer and as biological evolutionary system determines whatever story we construct and call reality.

What is the practical value in this? About decision making? About how to change some mental models? Consider some lessons from neuroscience, psychology, and strategic coaching:

1. For any situation, look at the data but also at the hypothesis—the default assumption that appears as "given."

2. Since we shape and filter the world by our hypotheses, they need to be continuously tested.

3. Examine which of your hypotheses work and which don't.

4. Challenge your thinking and assumptions.

5. We become comfortable with and dependent on our old habits; uncertainty and discomfort are the result of moving away from existing internal models.

6. Use data to test a hypothesis rather than to automatically confirm it.

7. Distinguish between transforming your thinking and being caught up in a new fad.

8. The best way to excise something from your life is not to ignore it. The best way to avoid something is to be informed by it.

9. You are always free to change your mind.

By avoiding something, you engage it and keep it central in your life. Ignoring it takes energy and moves you from a centered, balanced position. Decide what you want to keep, what you want to avoid, and what you want to let go.

Focus on the foreground without losing sight of the background's big picture. Repeat zooming in and out to keep perspective. Both microscopic and macroscopic views offer benefits.

Interact with diverse people and keep an open "beginner's mind" rather than quickly closing off some new idea. Life as a series of experiments keeps a system open to the new. Premature closure comes about in two ways: by too-rapid judgment and by trying to fit a new idea into an existing model, thereby losing the new model's context. This style of dismissal occurs frequently among very bright people with significant life experiences who immediately relate new information to something that they already know, absorbing it into an old context or meaning without sufficient examination.

RORSCHACH TESTS

R on consulted me for executive coaching with an unusual presentation: he had run out of wall space. After receiving a coveted national award in architectural design as one of its outstanding practitioners, he placed this award on his only remaining wall space. His office walls, as well as his trophy case, were now completely filled with awards and medals. He had already met his goal of yearly net earnings of $500,000. With each accomplishment, he bargained with himself that the next success would make him feel complete and happy. His pursuit of happiness seemed elusive though attainable; each higher monetary goal offered the hope of contentment.

Years before, he had believed he would feel comfortable when he had the security of fully funding his retirement plan. After that, he upped the ante to pay off his house mortgage and then his vacation property and then to achieve a net worth of $5 million.

He recognized that he was trying to make money speak the language of fulfillment, yet it was not saying back to him what he wanted. There were no admired colleagues more senior to applaud him. There were no higher awards to achieve. He did not need more money. He was not happy, and now his hope of contentment seemed illusory.

Money kept score for Ron, but score of what? He recognized his orientation to money and how he used it to garner the responses and admiration of others. Each round of applause had worked for a little while, just never well enough or long enough. He felt a relentless desire for more, yet more never made him happy. He was finally forced to confront his illusion that more would be enough when he had no remaining wall space for more awards. The lostness he felt crystallized a baffled review of what was missing.

Yet Ron admonished me not to take his earlier symbolism too lightly. He commented, "I've never seen a problem that money made worse. I know that money can't buy happiness. Then again, happiness can't buy government-insured bonds."

We examined his ideals—his internal values that serve as guiding principles. His ideals centered on achievement and mastery, yet his goals of further awards and more money by definition could not be met. "More" has no end point.

Ron quickly recognized that achieving his goals had only partially met his fundamental needs to be acknowledged and to feel significant. His ideals were not in alignment with his goals—or his passion. After some reflection, he decided to devote his professional time to architectural projects selected for reasons other than those on which he had based his earlier choices. Rather than take on all available business, he chose projects that he could do uniquely well and those he felt passionate about. He also shifted from his work habit of putting in 12- to 14-hour days to a *productivity* habit, focusing on success and satisfaction with each day's accomplishments.

This transition led Ron to work more happily, make even more money, and have more discretionary time. He devoted some of that extra time to funding and organizing Big Brother events.

Symbolic and Emotional Meanings of Money

Money is a Rorschach blot onto which we project various self-statements of personal meaning. As a mirror of the unspoken self, money can reveal hidden ideas and rarely divulged desires.

The hope that more money will bring happiness brings into focus what "enough" is. Only with an end point of "good enough" can you know when you reach a goal. This presupposes having a goal and a game plan about how to reach that goal.

The more unfulfilled needs or wants that money represents, the more promise of happiness it holds. The perpetual hope that more money will provide happiness sharply focuses on what is "enough." Someone who assumes that more money will bring more security or freedom may find that more money paradoxically brings a lessened sense of security and freedom.

Or, if we can have just the right amount of money, *then* we can do exactly what we *really* want to do and have what we want. The "right amount" may be a specific figure, but if it is a floating figure defined by "more," it is perpetually elusive. This illusion may not even have to be confronted as long as the amount extends beyond what's been realized, and about double is a safe lead.

An individual may recognize that what he or she thought would bring happiness does not. In the end, a symbol is only a symbol. Confronting the illusion of the symbol can precipitate a serious, often disappointing review of what money is and is not.

Money is an idea as well as a fact. Money is a medium of exchange of goods and services, and its value can theoretically be distinguished from emotional and symbolic assignments. Money is also one of the most emotionally charged objects in contemporary life as an emblem of feelings, significance, and striving. Perhaps the other two vehicles on which so much hitchhikes emotionally are food and sex. The symbolic and realistic meanings of money are important, probably inseparable for each of us, but particularly fused in emotionally charged situations, for example, in a marriage.

Money was always intended to be a symbol, so it is a ready stand-in for personal meanings of what we idealize, want, fear we have too little of, feel we don't deserve, or can never have. Particular emotions predominate in the money arena, for example, fear and greed. Strategies and game plans may be abandoned at times of excess stimulation—when things are going particularly bad or especially good—so that bad investment decisions prevail. Money carries unique personal meanings for each of us from past experiences, social ideas, and our own unique emotional development. Even in coming to know our personal myths and ourselves quite well, we may have omitted consideration of the personal complex meanings of money, how it affects our beliefs, behaviors, feelings, and relationships.

The Psychology of Money

If we move beyond the simplistic view that money is money, we can see how much emotional complexity we attach to it. Every one of us accords both conscious and unconscious significance to money: to represent power, security, self-worth, love, happiness, control, dirtiness, freedom, status, sexiness, worldliness, acceptance, in fact, any of a host of personal meanings. It may be an icon of achievement, of immortality concretized and passed to succeeding generations. Our symbolic representations and perceptions of money are influenced by cultural background, family values, developmental experiences, and emotional needs.

Although society adds some metaphors of its own, our money symbolism is uniquely subjective. Money and meanings are woven into our personality from our life history, sensitivities, experiences, internal conflicts, emotional needs, and basic sense of self. Some of these symbolic meanings are outside the realm of intellect, reason, and logic. Money symbolism may reside entirely in our right forebrain, the emotional part, at times disconnected from the left forebrain, home of reason and logic. Money issues may quickly spark ambition, insecurity, envy, fear, jealousy, competition, guilt, or any of a number of emotional reactions. For a person who's competitive, insecure, or prone to fantasize and worry, money is always a tangible yardstick. Hope can be rolled into a "someday" fantasy, very often given a numeric value. The pursuit of "more" may not be combined with the clarity of what constitutes "enough."

Many emotional and relationship issues manifest vividly in the financial arena, focusing on money as the answer, the problem, the cause, or the result. Money may be the common language of success phobia, impulsivity, or even fear of autonomy, such as creating financial crises from which to be rescued. Money symptoms include compulsions of gambling, shopping, or hoarding. Money may become the currency of addictions in work, financial risk taking, money acquisition, or impulsive spending.

While we often make decisions on an emotional basis, the particular meanings and significance we attach to money constitute a readily available emotional trip wire for repetitive and limiting choices.

The Money Psychology of Shame

Ideals and needs are at the core of identity, part of the foundation of self. Ideals are internal standards of excellence. Ideals serve as a personal model of value—an internal guide to purpose. Living up to a personal, attainable ideal generates a sense of worth and esteem. On the other hand, failure to live up to an internal ideal produces a feeling of shame. Shame can be pervasive over a lifetime, even as it remains masked to its creator.

Two major detours from self-esteem lead to shame:

1. Unempathic parents, by failing to praise the child's efforts and achievements, set up a "good enough" ideal that the child can never attain. They may even make belittling remarks ("Who do you think you are?") that foster shame.

2. Other parents present their daughter with the ideal that she must always be loving, kind, and giving and have no needs of her own, or at least not act on them. If she lives up to this ideal, she fails at her own growth, but if she grows successfully, she fails to meet that ideal.

By the time the girl becomes an adult, this internal model is a shadow she can't escape, one that will darken the joy of any success. For a boy grown into a man, he must not be afraid or uncertain, always acting as if he feels no doubt.

Shame is one of our most primitive human emotions—the most painful and difficult to deal with, the sense of "I'm never good enough." Shame is tied to one's fear of disconnection. In childhood, failure to live up to the ideals of parents threatens disruption of that bond. In adulthood, failure to live up to one's own internal ideal threatens self-alienation. Since shame is the perpetual shadow story, behavior to counter this shame must persist.

The message of shame and shame-based dynamics is partly gender related, especially in their expression. Perfectionism is a common adaptation to shame. "If I can do it perfectly, I can avoid shame, judgment, and blame." An unspoken causal explanation is, "If I had just been more perfect, I could have avoided this."

Perfectionism looks different for males and females. Some expressions of attempts to counter shame are definitely gender specific:

- For females: be perfect, pretty, thin, quiet, helpful, loving, and giving to others—or the desire to spend and shop to counter the unconscious whispers of "You need to look better."

- For males: be stoic, strong, and unemotional and do more and make more—or the desire to compete physically or rely on expensive acquisitions to counter the unconscious whispers of "You lack evidence of worth."

I work with many individuals in developing their money stories who have continued to operate in the old shame-based story. With their new story that defines attainable ideals—including growth and success—self-esteem is generated internally. The result? New story lines of worth, belonging, and being "good enough."

Consider these questions:

- Are you writing your money story from a totally current model that allows abundance, gratitude, and fulfillment through attaining all that you are capable of doing and being?

- Do you have an end point of "good enough"?

The Neuroscience of Money

Many Brains in One

We tend to regard the human brain as one big mass of gray matter when it actually comprises various structures specialized for particular activities, ranging from such complex roles as speech and memory to such basic autonomic body functions as regulating temperature and keeping our hearts beating.

Scientists have cataloged hundreds, even thousands, of different areas within the brain, but one structural distinction is particularly important in terms of wealth and your money story. Our three stages of evolution are reflected in the brain's three distinct layers: reptilian (inner), mammalian (middle), and neocortical (outer).

Its innermost area, the *reptilian* brain, is the brain's oldest and most primitive structure, one we share with all animals possessing a backbone. Remaining virtually unchanged by evolution, the reptilian brain controls our most basic functions, such as breathing and temperature regulation. As that part of the brain most concerned with survival, the reptilian brain's function is also decidedly instinctive. Its actions are automatic—and *fast*.

In the evolution of human beings from reptiles to mammals, the *mammalian* brain developed around the reptilian core. In addition to taking over some of the temperature-regulation functions, the mammalian brain assumed an enhanced memory function, enabling its possessor to react on the basis of experience of past events rather than on the basis of pure instinct alone. The mammalian brain also brought with it conscious connections between feelings and events. For the first time, human beings could both feel fear and act on it. Two particular entities in this layer, the amygdala and the hippocampus, are central to the processing of emotional stimuli and attaching meaning to events.

The largest leap in brain evolution came with the development of the *neocortex*, the outermost layer we generally consider the truly *human* brain. This is the true "gray matter," made up of frontal, parietal, occipital, and temporal lobes. The neocortex comprises about 85 percent of the mass of the brain—and for good reason. It is the locus of abstract logic, imagination, complex emotion, and the high-level functions of speaking, reading, and writing—activities that require a lot of brain hardware.

The distinction between these different brain layers is not the human brain's only significant structural division. It is also divided into left and right hemispheres, connected by a thick bundle of nerve fibers called the corpus callosum. Over the past few decades, we've learned that as the cortical brain developed, extensive specialization also occurred in the different functions of right and left hemispheres. The left hemisphere is highly verbal, systematic, logical, and process driven. The right hemisphere is image driven, spatial, intuitive, and concerned with feelings and emotions. Either side of the brain may be more or less active, depending on the activity of the moment.

Rational Money and Emotional Money

Not surprisingly, all this brain complexity significantly affects our financial dealings. On the surface, dealing with money should be an entirely logical matter. After all, it's just *math*—simple operations like the sum of our next two paychecks, the rate of return on our investments, or the discount on a new pair of shoes. Analysis by the left brain, it seems, should yield the right decision almost every time. Economists call such a logical approach to money *rational*. It assumes that human beings are logical creatures who always strive to maximize their gain in any situation. This assumption of rationality has dominated the field of economics from day one.

But the reality is not that simple. Advances in neuroeconomics show clearly that we're *not* logical creatures—at least not all the time. We're often driven by emotions, and emotional processing and logical reasoning reside at different neural addresses.

Suppose you're driving along calmly and peacefully when suddenly you see an oncoming car swerve into your lane, headed directly for you. Your life could be over in a matter of seconds. In an instant, you react. Reflexively, without thinking, you hit the brake pedal and horn while sharply banking the steering wheel to the right.

In a flash, your physiology has changed radically, triggering the release of chemicals that course through your system, instantly shifting your state of mind from reflection and thought to survival and drastic action. The transformation will last for less than a minute, but its repercussions will echo through your nerves and blood vessels for hours.

You pull over to the side of the road to recoup for a moment, and as you do, you realize you're short of breath and your pulse is racing. Later that day, you wonder why you are so exhausted.

This is a dramatic example, but the truth is that *every* thought or feeling has a chemical consequence, and the changing flow of chemicals alters both body and brain.

The brain's *limbic system*, a neural network that drives the instantaneous functions of instinct and basic emotions, is in charge of such fight-or-flight reactions. Strong emotions—such as the desire evoked by the prospect of food or sex, the fear on seeing an approaching pedestrian who just might be a mugger, or the panic sparked by the swerving car heading toward us—light up the limbic system, activating the more primitive areas of reptilian and mammalian brain and overriding the more rational neocortex.

When this happens, we temporarily lose access to exactly that brain software we need to perform the kinds of long-term analysis and reasoned decision making that smart money actions require.

The chemicals of our emotional state hijack the rational brain, causing us to process information as though we were in a mortal crisis. This automatic alarm system, essential for survival in the wild, instead leads to mistaken perception and judgment. A hot stock tip, a business deal gone sour, a family tragedy—any one of these or a thousand other situations may touch off an emotional state of mind and alarm response geared for survival at any cost rather than the more measured responses that are probably more appropriate to the situation. As other experiments have shown, such primitive, survival-focused brain activity can even influence ethical decisions.

The stock market does not function like a store or a catalog: *it's an auction*. But instead of a simple auction where bidders drive the price up and the highest bidder wins, in the stock market auction, bidders drive the price up, down, up, and down repeatedly. Intelligent, financially informed people sometimes act as if they're not using their heads—because they're not using their *whole* heads. More accurately, they're using only a specific *part* of their heads: the reptilian part.

No wonder we can get so readily caught up in the prevailing market mood of exuberance or depression. Extreme emotions, such as fear or greed, may easily derail us from our normal neocortical brain tracks and shift our state of mind. Decisions made in a fearful state of mind follow the survival mode—quite different principles from logical ones suited to long-term investing. Present fear renders the past and the future as inaccessible as logical and reason.

The film *Fear and Loathing in Las Vegas*, based on the real-life experiences of "gonzo" journalist Hunter Thompson, includes a scene in a Vegas lounge where Thompson (played by Johnny Depp), under the influence of massive amounts of hallucinogens, sees all the bar's "lounge lizard" patrons transformed into actual, human-sized lizards. As surreal as Thompson's drug-induced vision seems, the neurophysiological insights gleaned from studies using functional magnetic resonance imaging (fMRI) tell us that during a bad day on Wall Street, this is essentially what happens: thousands of reptilian brains are reacting to the day's financial news, their lizard responses draped in a disguise of human language.

As the stock market came crashing down in the fall of 2008, the U.S. government rushed to pump $700 billion into the nation's credit system. Why? As frightening as the looming economic crisis was, the majority of Americans still had their jobs, their homes, and food on the table. The toppling of such Wall Street icons as Lehman Brothers, Merrill Lynch, and AIG and the specter of others possibly following in their wake did not represent a genuine fiscal hardship for most of the public as much as it indicated a crisis of confidence. When President Franklin Roosevelt famously said in his 1933 inauguration, "The only thing we have to fear is fear itself," he was illustrating the same point: the crisis was in our *state of mind*.

The $700 billion bailout's principal goal was *to restore public confidence*. A quarter of a trillion dollars is quite a price tag for a public relations campaign aimed at changing an emotion, but that only underscores the truth about money and the human brain: it is a fragile combination. Physiologically speaking, the $700 billion package was really a massive public works program designed to shift the population's focus a mere two inches from midbrain to forebrain.

Neuroscientists use fMRI to study how the brain responds to and functions when presented with various emotional stimuli. Findings from these studies can be used to help people make decisions that are in their long-term best interest.

Here are some additional examples of how, at times, logic takes a backseat in financial decision making:

- As fMRI studies show, when people feel they are being treated unfairly, a portion of the midbrain called the interior insula lights up and overwhelms the logical considerations of the prefrontal cortex. The same response occurs when someone bites into a rotten apple.

- Making an example of people such as Ken Lay and the prosecution of other executives for their crimes does not work and will not work. If it did, Ponzi would have been the last to teach us this lesson. Making an example is an abstraction, something the emotional brain can't deal with.

Example, prior knowledge, and logic are *not* how the brain creates and succumbs to bubbles.

Mastery with money and investing requires having principles, consistency, and a game plan that includes an understanding of how your mind works. When investors lose money, it's most likely the result of emotional decisions that trumped otherwise good information, advice, and strategy. At times of stress, relying on emotional stamina to resist impulsive reaction is as difficult as it is important. When you are in a highly charged emotional state, the hardest thing to do is nothing.

In contrast, a calm and focused state of mind will permit rational thinking and intuitive knowledge to come together to allow you to access and synthesize different realms of knowledge. This reflective thinking mode also contrasts with working hard at performing a task.

We can get caught up in a prevailing market mood of exuberance or depression. Dramatic events, such as the 1987 and 2008 stock market crashes, provoke anxiety; the surging tech stocks of the late 1990s induced greed. Such extreme emotions as fear or greed may derail one's mental process from the usual brain tracks and consequently shift one's state of mind.

Emotions can override logic and game plan in money management and investing. Certain situations and characteristics of the emotional components of investing and money have the potential to derail reason and logic so that the emotional brain comes to dominate decision making.

Fear of losing money is a dominant motivation for those investors more influenced by past loss than by prospects for future gain.

Abandoning a game plan at a time of excess emotional stimulation (fear, greed, and euphoria) may overrule an objective view and knowledgeable input, such as a methodical investment plan. When emotion dominates, past lessons and future plans can collapse into an impulsive reaction. In a radical market, emotion prevails. One solution is to focus on what you can determine (loyalty to your game plan) and accept what you can't control (the market) so that you stay grounded rather than being swept into emotionally reactive decisions and changes. Many studies confirm that losses after investment decisions made in fearful attitudes and the grip of emotion far exceed losses from decisions based on fact, stock selection, or system.

The relationship to risk is a highly subjective and emotional matter. Risk here refers to the subjective emotional perception rather than to various business models, investing measures, and techniques of lowering the likelihood of loss (such as asset allocation, diversification, or buy and sell disciplines). Past experiences of loss in any emotional arena and even of trauma color the perception of risk, as risk is often associated with loss. If loss is highly charged emotionally, then even a usual degree of risk may feel exaggerated so that the investor will avoid or react to situations based on feeling rather than fact.

Nostalgic Cookies

Revisionist History

Proust smelled a cookie and launched tens of thousands of words of nostalgic remembrances.

Nostalgia remembers things not as they were but as we wished them to be. Nostalgia recalls the ideal rather than the real. Has anyone become less popular in memory replays or gotten worse in high school and college sports as the years go on? (For example, I was very close to being all-state in basketball twice in one season. And that was the season—as best I recall—that we were undefeated.)

We remember our past as it was and also as it would have been, for nostalgia is a historical revisionist. Nostalgia, generally thought to refer to positive reflections about the past, to memories infused with pleasure and warmth, occurs universally. Often accompanied by an expansive mood and infatuated state, it adds something to the memory that was absent in actuality.

Nostalgia is an instrument of forgetting dressed in the attire of memory, framed by the idealization and hope of a former period. It is still a memory but a memory of what never was, even at the time. We remember gratifying times in adolescence, former loves, and school or sporting experiences and nostalgically resonate with the expansive, hopeful, idealized aspects of the era. The enigma is that changing one's past may have significant consequences on the future.

Nostalgia bridges the present to a better past, airbrushed memories informed by yearning, backlit by retrospective idealization. Memory is about what happened, the register of perception at that moment in time; nostalgia seems more about what did not quite happen, though it came so close as to record a near miss, circumscribing fantasy while igniting hope. Memory's longing and past incidents speak the same voice in the moment of nostalgia. The ideal becomes the real of remembered experience, defending against too-painful actual reality.

Nostalgics collect memories, but only ones that have been edited, reshaped, possibly even recast, and set on a different stage. Often cued by particular music, a certain smell, or the resemblance of a person or object to past experiences, real memories and real fantasies blur. A nostalgic portrait as reality, such as an idealized picture of a parent during childhood, may substitute for the disappointment of repeated empathic failures.

Nostalgia is aesthetically, often expensively, crystallized and enshrined in art, antiques, and memorabilia. The bittersweet elation of nostalgia reminds us of what was missed and, at the same time, engages the absent experience, to be remodeled by wishing's archetype.

More extreme nostalgia longs for the past without accepting that it is over: the past is not irrevocable, for it is re-created as ideal. Blind to the paradox that hope exists presently within a past context, an obsessional attachment to the past may impoverish current experiences. The particular missed experiences, woven into the plot of nostalgia as dreamy remembrances, become part of one's identity, often paralleling and defending against emptiness and hurt. This investment in idealized memory filters all that is inconsistent with the plot of the pleasant past, defensively camouflaging painful aspects.

Nostalgic Resilience and Adaptation

What cued your mood to watch an old movie or an old episode of *Cheers* or *Friends*? Are there triggers that will prompt you to crave a piece of the same brand of candy you ate in childhood?

Neuromarketing strategies tap into nostalgic experiences. It's easier and faster to associate a product with idealized memories than to create a new product identity. A nostalgic trigger is coupled with new information. Arnold Palmer and that old tractor—two classics—preserved by one particular motor oil.

A consortium of neuroscientists examined situations that led people to prefer nostalgic products—those that remind them of the past—over contemporary products. In a series of experiments, they found that the key to preferring nostalgic products is the need to belong. The studies revealed that a situation in which people feel a heightened need to belong to a group or to feel socially connected will prompt a preference for nostalgic products.

In one study, excluding participants from a ball-tossing computer game prompted their choice of vintage products that had specific emotional ties for each person, including movies, TV shows, food brands, and cars. The scientists discovered that when participants were excluded, not only did they feel a greater need to belong, but this need was "cured" by eating a "nostalgic cookie"—a brand that had been popular in the past.

Mindfulness: Psychoanalysis Meets Quantum Physics on the Buddhist Trail to Neuroscience

Activation of the self-conscious mind occurs most vividly at the beginning of a new, exciting endeavor. This "honeymoon period" generates the most energetic attention and passionate engagement. The conscious awareness focuses on present attitudes and beliefs. When our conscious minds are more in charge, we generate the behaviors and qualities we most aspire to. Buddhist spiritual practice—its impact now affirmed by biology and physics—terms this "mindfulness."

This neurochemistry of the excited, honeymoon phase with dopamine and epinephrine then transforms to the maintenance system of norepinephrine, when habitual traits programmed into the unconscious mind take over.

Mindfulness is an awareness of what's happening while it's happening. Mindful attention—a full awareness of self—is an inherent human capacity. The Buddhist tradition offers one effective way to access and refine this mindful attention (in some Asian languages the words for "mind" and "heart" are the same). Mindfulness includes self-regulation, with mastery of states of mind.

Psychoanalysis addresses coming to the end of an old story but not strategic creation of a new one. Quantum physics recognizes the observer's participation in the creation of reality, but it omits motivation. Neuroscience illuminates workings of the conscious and unconscious mind while disregarding the spirit. Psychology helps us understand the developmental role of effectiveness and mastery yet remains silent on brain contributions. Early interpersonal development shapes both brain and psyche capacity for insight and empathy.

Approaches to revising limited and outdated beliefs to rewire brain pathways require that we keep our self-conscious mind focused in the present, attuned to specific purpose and intent. Unless we can do that, it automatically reverts to the default mode.

We can systematically rewrite even long-standing behavioral programs. For example, strategic coaching guides a client along the pathway of desired intentions, a journey to move from passive to active, responder to initiator, victim to creator.

Our brains and the unconscious programs are not fixed or unchangeable. We can rewrite mind software and rewire brain hardware to create new life and money stories.

As Good as Gold and Other Arbitrary Notions

A newspaper columnist said to me recently, "In your book *The Secret Language of Money*, you use the phrase 'as good as gold.' But isn't the value we place on gold and so-called precious stones arbitrary?"

Of course it is. Same with tulip bulbs, Beanie Babies, and dot-com initial public offerings. For any stock, the value is arbitrary—based on what another bidder is willing to pay at that moment.

The stock market isn't really a market; rather, it's an auction that activates the variables of mind and brain. The stock doesn't know who owns it any more than war bonds knew about the war.

Gold coins are tangible, real—you can hold them, bite them, wear them, even hide them, and they're still there. And gold glitters. (Call me a mind reader, but not one of my readers wants an iron Rolex.)

Ponzi, Madoff, and Stanford didn't do their sleight of hand with gold coins. They used symbols of symbols—derivatives of little-understood equities.

As money becomes more abstracted, transactions are easier, but our understanding of money fades. And our relationship with it changes.

MASTER MONEY STATES OF MIND

I magine that you are at an auction and the room is filled with 75 sophisticated-looking people in business attire. The auctioneer holds a $100 bill before your group. He explains the auction scenario: "Bids move in five-dollar increments. The highest bidder wins the bill. The second-highest bidder pays the bid but gets nothing in return. And this is real money." Within seconds, the bids pass $100. Some of the 75 people push the bidding up to $300.

Two of the people get into a bidding war. One of them ends up paying $465 for the $100 bill. The other owes $460 and gets nothing. You are dumbfounded. How could reasonable people pay more for something than it's worth?

Actually, this scenario has already happened—more than 600 times.[1] The auctioneer? Professor Max Bazerman. The setting? Harvard's John F. Kennedy School of Government. The participants? Investment specialists and economic gurus. Some of the brightest financial experts consistently pay three to four times the worth of the $100 bill just because of the way their minds work. (This isn't a stock—whose perceived value is determined *only* by the bid.)

Professor Bazerman commented, "I've never seen bidding stop below $100 in any of the more than 600 times that I've done it."

What happened?

What mind matters and brain business secrets are hiding in the open? Here's what we know.

Some contributions from the mind:

- Loss aversion: "I'm not going to be the second-highest bidder, still pay, and get nothing." Studies show that losing $100 makes you twice as unhappy as gaining $100 makes you happy.

- Sunk-cost fallacy: "I've already bid $260—I'll just go $10 higher."

We justify continuing because of what we've already put into it.
Some contributions from the brain:

- The prefrontal cortex says, "Stop at $95."

- The limbic system says, "I'm excited. I'm gonna win. I can't stop now."

Our states of mind are vulnerable to emotional contagion. Brains in that auction room were on a collective tilt—the herd mentality running wild.
But here's the conversation even without the contagion:

- The prefrontal cortex says, "Let's save for retirement."

- The limbic system says, "Let's go to Hawaii."

Money behavior and financial decisions are sometimes—rarely—actually about money.

Four hundred and thirty-three people voted on a proposal. It failed. If only 12 of those 433 people had voted "yes" instead of "no" the outcome would have been exactly the opposite. The result? In the next few hours, the stock market lost $1.2 trillion. Here's what one senior equity trader on Wall Street said: "You just felt like the world was unraveling. People started to sell, and they sold hard. It didn't matter what you had—you sold."

This collective tilt shows how states of mind are vulnerable to emotional contagion. This vote on the mortgage bailout in late 2008 crystallized an entire economic scenario of events.

Chuck Prince, the head of Citigroup, said, "As long as the music's playing, you've got to get up and dance."

Greed, emotional contagion, and peer pressure trump logic. When you see friends making significant profits trading stocks or flipping real estate, the natural inclination is to want in on the action. As more join the movement, prices rise, and for a while, it is a self-fulfilling prophecy. But then some event reverses the momentum, bursts the bubble, and turns optimism to panic. Herd mentality pushes people to join the momentum either to buy or to flee the market.

People aren't stupid—they're just not regulated. They make mistakes. They buy low and sell high because they either have no plan or, if they have one, don't stick to it when emotion vaults beyond the fence of that plan. Even when they're finance or economic experts, they pay $350 for a $100 bill.

Google, Inc., announced its financial results for the fourth quarter of 2005 on January 31, 2006: revenues were up 97 percent, net profit up 82 percent—phenomenal growth, yet Wall Street analysts had predicted even better. Their expectations fell just short of the actual outcome. As a result, Google stock lost $22.3 billion in value in a matter of minutes before trading was halted.

The great investment analyst Benjamin Graham was asked what it takes to be a successful investor. His response? "People don't need extraordinary insight or intelligence. What they need most is the character to adopt simple rules and stick to them."

How to Understand States of Mind

A state of mind is a psychophysiological state, an organized software program of feelings, expectations, and attitudes. Each "software package" determines access and expression of memory, emotion, thinking, and behavior. Mastering state changes and regulating emotions—such as remaining calm in the face of danger—determines effectiveness.

We enter and leave states of mind as fluidly and invisibly as the precision passage of the baton between relay-team members. Our familiar repertoire can range from creative energization and quiet happiness through anxiety or boredom to relaxation. For some people, more extreme, reluctantly inhabited states exist: depression, nothingness, deadness, emptiness, and confusion. Feelings, the subjective experience of distinct emotions, are a component of each state of mind.

Within a particular state of mind, we perceive, remember, feel, think, behave, and respond in a consistent mode.

The regulation of feelings and states of mind involves the understanding and mastery of access to a particular state of mind without altering consciousness to get there (i.e., while "staying present").

Each of us has a continuum of states, with some awareness of what state works best for what endeavor, even of how to enter into and exit from different states. We become more or less cognizant of which state to enter for a creative endeavor, which state to enter for conceptual planning, and which state of attention and concentration works best for each task, ranging from the alertness needed for business endeavors to relaxation for sleep.

What does it mean to get centered in your body and experience? Connection of mind and body comes about through specific focus on attunement to present experience and state of mind.

To overcome a feeling of being detached from or not grounded in your body or experience, focus your awareness on very specific details of your physical body, including breathing and relaxation. Grounding yourself in your body allows you to center inside your experience and attain a fully "present" state of mind. This grounding and centering creates a sense of being relaxed yet alert, focused but not tense. The "present" state of mind allows full access to all aspects of experience, especially self-awareness and attunement.

How to Regulate States of Mind

The most important thing we can do to achieve success is to manage our emotions and regulate our states of mind.

What do the following people have in common?

- John Belushi

- Marilyn Monroe

- Elvis Presley

- Janis Joplin

- F. Scott Fitzgerald

They never learned the critical success strategy of managing their states of mind. Using drugs, alcohol, or some other addictive substance or process to regulate a state of mind and manage emotions leads to significant compromise. Your state of mind—the particular software program you use—determines the meaning you attach to a stimulus. The meaning you attach then determines your behavior.

There are two primary ways to regulate your state of mind: through physiology—how you use your body—and through focus—what you attend to.

A state of mind can be physically controlled by an immediate deep-breathing exercise: inhale for three seconds and exhale for three seconds. Accompany this physical process with a *focus*: breathing in relaxation and breathing out tension.

The questions we ask ourselves determine what we focus on. We are always asking two questions:

1. What does this mean?

2. What should I do?

If you have a habitual feeling you don't like, it can come from a habitual focus and habitual questions:

1. Why does this always happen to me? The presupposition is that you are in a passive position and ineffective.

2. Why am I overweight? The focus is on overweight.

You are always asking questions from the moment you wake up, although you may not be aware of them. If you immediately begin asking, "What could go wrong today?," you have already begun a scenario that establishes a negative state of mind.

Ask a better question: "What will I create today—and have more fun doing—that will be more powerful than I ever dreamed of?" Your brain follows your focus, positive or negative. We can learn to ask ourselves habitual questions that empower us. Rather than asking, "Why am I overweight?," we can ask, "What can I start to do today for better nutrition and physical shape?"

The power of focus is in asking effective questions to determine your state of mind.

Try this exercise: Write down three empowering questions that put you in a peak state. Each morning, answer these three questions and feel the answer. Remember, you are already asking questions. This just changes the focus so you can consciously engineer those questions that empower you.

Sleep on It: The Neuroeconomics of Striking When the Iron Is Cold

A man with a large trailer load of special organic mulch was canvassing my neighborhood to sell it. He approached me at 11:45 a.m., saying he would be in the neighborhood only until noon and wasn't coming back. His price was good, and I jumped into the small window of time remaining.

The result of my decision was a front-yard mushroom farm within two weeks.

Life presents us with few true emergencies. Investing in a stock, deciding on a summer vacation special good only until 5:00 p.m., or buying mulch from the guy who'll be in the neighborhood selling it only until noon—these are not among them. In an excited state of mind, you'll see the compelling stories of a hot deal differently from the way you see them the next day when you're in a cooler state of mind. A hot stock tip, a business deal gone sour, a family tragedy—any of these may create an alarm response and an emotional state of mind geared for survival rather than logic. A compelling social interaction may even engage a powerful brain circuit that makes us give money to strangers.

Each thought and feeling has a chemical consequence. The chemicals of emotion alter mind and body. Personal experience determines what software program (state of mind) to use to process the data, and how to proceed.

The following considerations apply to decision making regarding emotions and choices, cataloged by the chemical mediator.

Adrenalin/Cortisol: The Emergency System

When incoming data resemble threat or danger, they trigger an emotional and biochemical response within a fraction of a second. While necessary for survival, adrenalin and cortisol hijack the logical, rational brain. Emotion-based judgments supersede rational ones. This automatic alarm system may cause mistaken perception and reaction.

Additionally, increased tension produces emotional regression. With increased tension and advanced conflict, the stress-response reaction can move someone into a more emotional pattern characteristic of an earlier age. Increased emotion also narrows perspective; when emotion prevails, focus becomes more restricted to the more recent event.

Dopamine: The Pleasure System

Dopamine mediates the excitement of anticipating a reward or pleasure. Someone can create a cult-like following by promising great possibility coupled with the vagueness of hazy dreams. The result? Followers are stimulated to see what they want to see. Just as they do with money, people project their own desires onto the story and see their wishes crystallized into an illusion of reality. The essentials are dopamine and a projection screen (a good story).

Norepinephrine: The Maintenance System

We believe that certain accomplishments and acquisitions will give us lasting satisfaction. However, a new possession, such as a car, will be quickly assimilated into our bank of possessions and no longer be the subject of intense focus and desire. Receiving a reward shuts down the anticipatory release of dopamine, diminishing the energy and pleasure. The central nervous system shifts to the maintenance mode (necessary from an economic and evolutionary perspective), mediated primarily by norepinephrine.

The fastest way to relinquish a desire or to stop noticing something may be to buy it.

Oxytocin: The Social Connection System

Social interactions stimulate the release of the neurochemical oxytocin, especially when we are trusted; this induces a desire to reciprocate the trust we've been shown, even with strangers.

Con artists know how to stimulate oxytocin. In David Mamet's film *House of Games*, the confidence man played by Joe Mantegna explained to a previous mark, "It's called a confidence game. Why? Because you give me your confidence? No. Because I give you mine."

Think about the trust that bankers gave, until recently, to large numbers of people in the form of credit and mortgages. That trust was reciprocated; both sides suffered, as did some innocent bystanders.

A remedy? "I'll think about it" is a decision.

"I'll get back to you" is an option.

"I'll sleep on it" is a choice.

These decisions allow you to pause between the pick and the purchase. "Sleeping on it" allows movement through different states of mind to fresh perspectives the next day. Most important, it allows movement of these neurochemically mediated responses from the foreground to the background for a balanced decision.

Money and Mood

As we have shown, mind-set can determine money behavior. We make particular associations to certain economic decisions. Dr. Jennifer Lerner's Harvard lab studies emotion and decision making.[2] Specifically, she investigates how social and emotional factors influence judgment and decision making:

- In an attempt to elevate their mood, depressed people are willing to spend more money than when they feel cheerful. One example of how social events affect money behavior manifested on the day that Lehman Brothers failed. New York's high-end Madison Avenue shops had one of their best days in history. When the going gets tough, the tough go shopping.

- People who are angry will take on more financial risk.

- People who are sad take on less financial risk.

Researchers led by Cynthia Cryder found that sad people become self-focused and spend as much as 300 percent more for the same type of commodity—the same item—as when they are not sad. The new purchases distract them from what is bothering them; a new possession reduces both anxiety and sad mood because the act of spending stimulates the pleasure center of the brain in the same way as cocaine.

Both pain and pleasure seek a monetary enactment. Spending will make pain go away, or it will enhance and extend the pleasure.

Neuroeconomists have demonstrated that people who are fearful cling to what they have. Our nervous system shuts down in an adaptive effort at survival—the result is a restriction in the ability of our minds and bodies to function. Uncertainty or anxiety will rigidify principles into rules. At a time of crisis, fear, or uncertainty, people reduce spending. When fear is dominant, money is not only constricted but also hoarded. At such times, consumers become risk averse and hunker down. This has been called the "negative wealth effect."

A negative or depressed mood causes your attention to scatter because of low dopamine. Dopamine is the brain chemical of stimulation and excitement, serving as a gateway to the regulation of working memory. Other catalysts for dopamine activation that spike mood include food, stimulation, risk, or a new relationship.

A spike in dopamine, with excitement and its resultant focus in attention, alerts us to new opportunity. When a task becomes too easy or too routine, dopamine wanes, and the low stimulation leads to distraction. When a task is hard, people may give up. A plan and strategy can sustain attention and effort to create a steady flow of dopamine, while a specific goal enhances motivation. This sustained state of mind and flow is an important component to long-term happiness.

Since spending is an attempted self-regulation of mood, here are some useful principles to keep in mind:

- Make no purchases when sad or upset.

- Spend only cash when sad or upset and have a limited amount.

- Use other means of self-regulation: connection with friends, listening to music, and other distractions, such as reading or exercise.

Neuroscience has demonstrated that human beings have two decision systems: analytical and intuitive. Different situations and patterns activate different parts of the brain. Andrew Lo, professor of finance at the Massachusetts Institute of Technology, has found these relationships:[3]

- Financial success triggers the same dopamine neurocircuits as cocaine, the same system triggered by food and sex.

- With increasing financial success, investors become increasingly inured to risk and take greater chances.

- Risk is both stimulating and addictive. Taking risks creates a rush of excitement triggered by dopamine and adrenalin.

- A strategy planned while you are calm at your office or home may be abandoned if you're in a different state of mind, such as stress.

Marooned in the Right Brain

It is not only our primitive brains that can hold us hostage in times of stress and high-stakes decisions. Even when our forebrains are functioning fully, we can become thrown off balance and lurch into one hemisphere at the expense of the other, often with disastrous effects.

The study of trauma's effect on neurophysiology provides revealing insights into how emotions can override logic and short-circuit all our "reasonable" game plans when it comes to making decisions about money.

Normally, when we process information in our forebrain, we use both the left and the right frontal hemisphere, the left representing the more rational, logical executive function and the right evoking more the emotional feeling function.

Dr. Bessel van der Kolk, founder and medical director of the Trauma Center at the Justice Resource Institute in Brookline, Massachusetts, has demonstrated that for most people, during a time of emotional stimulus, both the right and the left cortex light up on a PET scan, and EEG activity also increases on both sides of the brain.[4] However, people who have suffered significant trauma in their histories respond differently to that same emotional stimulus: on the PET scan, only the right cortex (emotional) activity increases, and EEG readings reveal that the left cortex (logical) does not respond *at all*.

For these trauma-sensitized individuals, emotional responses dominate without the mediating balance of reason or logic. In other words, these people are put in the unfortunate position of having to process difficult information with the side of their brains that has the least ability to sort and analyze it rationally. They become marooned on the emotional island of the right brain, their left brain powerless to anchor them in any sort of logical or sequential reasoning.

To complicate matters still further, the right hemisphere is also wired to the mammalian brain, which in turn is connected to the reptilian brain, making it all the more likely for such "unthinking" reactions to bypass altogether the process of rational analysis.

Now, we could simply chalk all this up as one more aspect of posttraumatic stress—except that van der Kolk's findings don't stop there. Here's where it all becomes especially significant: further study reveals that during moments of especially strong emotional stimulation, *even those of us who have absolutely no history of trauma* make this same shift to emotional right-brain processing, effectively shutting off access to the logic and reason of the left brain.

This is why, when we are faced with very good or very bad news, we may suddenly abandon our best strategies and most carefully thought-out game plans. In extreme situations, such as when the stock market is robustly rallying or precipitously falling, it is most difficult to stay with investment strategies and planned principles. Greed or fear shifts us to right-brain dominance. Thus, in times of very good news (a large and unexpected bonus check) or very bad news (a stock market crash), we may suddenly abandon our best-laid financial plans. Emotional override creates myopia with regard to future consequences. Hyperfocused on the present moment, as if our very survival demanded it, we become absorbed exclusively in the question, "What will make me feel better *right now*?" The surprisingly large bonus check is turned into a new car or television instead of paying off our credit card or going into our 401(k), and the stock market crash triggers a complete abandonment of our carefully crafted "buy and hold" strategy. What might happen *later* is out of sight, out of mind, along with the reflection, "What is actually in my best interest?"

Mantras and Self-Regulation

When Southern Utah's University's new basketball coach Robert Reid arrived, his team ranked 217th in free-throw percentage, lowest in their division nationwide.

During practice, Reid had his players develop a mantra before each free throw—a three- or four-word phrase coupled with a deep breath for relaxation. He gave the example of "relaxed and smooth" when stepping up to the free-throw line but emphasized that each player should determine his own mantra. Additionally, he simulated game conditions by abruptly stopping a player in practice and asking him to shoot two free throws. Reid simulated the mind-set of pressure in a game situation by suddenly stopping the action with a request to shoot a free throw. If the player made the shot, he got to take a breather. If he missed, he had to sprint around the court.

Within two years, the team was ranked number one in their division nationwide.

Mantras can be used in various situations to regulate states of mind, especially for emotional triggers that can instantly change a state of mind. Many of my clients who are professional athletes and actors have used it to get grounded and centered for their performances.

Mantras can both calm you and keep you from overthinking in a high-pressure situation. Here's a three-part sequence for developing a mantra:

1. *Cue*: A physical cue to begin the process. An example is at the free throw line, you bounce the ball twice. In your office, it may be to make a circle with the index finger and thumb of both hands.

2. *Focus*: A three- or four-word phrase to focus your attention and energy for the success of your task. An example is "Relaxed and powerful." If you are kinesthetic, what may work for you is envisioning being enveloped in a white, warm, protective cone of light. Focus on the target, not on your mechanics. Think about your successful completion of a presentation, not on the preparation or the mechanism of delivery.

3. *Physiology*: Coupled with the cue and focus, take a single deep breath to breathe in relaxation and breathe out completely to release any tension.

Some additional considerations can facilitate the effectiveness of a mantra:

- Focus on the target, not your mechanisms.

- Think about your successful completion.

- Don't slow down. Slowing down allows you time to think about it, which will derail procedural memory flow.

- Practice under pressure. When you practice under the same conditions that you will face when performing, you establish the mind-set that will prepare you for the actual experience.

What's Your Investing Mind-Set?

- Do you consistently lose money on investments?

- Do you feel paralyzed or afraid when it comes to investing money?

- Do you feel overwhelmed by the prospect of learning more about managing and investing your money?

- Do you expect or allow other people to make money decisions for you, even if they are not experts?

- Do you respond to financial gains with feelings of guilt or an expansiveness of wanting to spend more?

- Do you respond to financial losses with self-recrimination, anger, or futility?

- Is it painful for you to admit mistakes or to cut your losses?

- Do you have trouble putting aside thoughts of "what might have been" or "if only" you had purchased or sold investments earlier (or later)?

- Do you resist seeking suggestions and advice, even differing opinions, to judge a prospective investment or business decision?

- Do you feel you are fully able to make all your own financial decisions by yourself—despite consistent evidence to the contrary?

Ten Principles for Applying Neuroscience to Investing

Consider these findings from neuroscience to inform your investment story and to counter incorrect brain forecasts with misleading patterns:

1. Divest emotion from investing. An objective, structured game plan includes goals, strategy, target points of date or money, and a regular (time or money) contribution to a savings and retirement fund.

2. Structure successful choices. For example, an automatic contribution to a retirement plan is a strategic procedure that consistently results in greater savings than voluntary plans.

3. Insulate your investment decisions from immediate emotional reaction. Keep your amygdala away from your money and out of your investing plans. Anxiety or panic in a crisis has led otherwise smart money out of the market and prevented its return for longer than necessary. Avoid frequent market monitoring to reduce exposure to stimuli that produce reaction (positive or negative information).

4. Meet regularly—a minimum of once a year—with your portfolio manager to review performance, objectives, needs, and new information.

5. When things are going very well or very badly—such as a bull or bear market or a spectacular rise or fall of your stock—do more research. It is at times of excess stimulation that both your brain and your mind have difficulty *not* reacting. Have your plan clearly in view, and when you are most tempted to abandon it, stick to your plan. A way to avoid seasickness in a rocking boat with turbulent waves and a constant swirl of motion is to find a fixed point on the distant horizon and focus on it. This spot, contrasted to everything else, doesn't move; consistent focus on it can be grounding. Your financial plan is that focus, especially in times of storm.

6. Consider having at least three piles of money: one for long-term retirement, one for value and growth investing, and one for speculative, aggressive growth—your gambling pile. Because the brain is wired to pursue the euphoria of reward and to succumb to a good story about the next McDonald's or Microsoft, a gambling pile insulates serious money from the vagaries of your amygdala and the yearnings of your dopamine receptor.

7. Since the brain responds to only two repetitions of an event to automatically predict the third, keep the big picture and the longer term in perspective. While looking backward and understanding that history doesn't chart the future, a short-term trend doesn't predict a long-term pattern either.

8. Diversification into different investments can spread emotional responsiveness and wisely protect from emotional reaction by others, such as major trends or overreactions. Jason Zweig concludes from his research that diversification "is the single most powerful way to prevent your brain from working against you," and an automatic investing plan "minimizes the opportunities for your brain to perceive trends that aren't there, to overreact when apparent trends turn out to be illusions, or to panic when fear is in the air."

9. Beware of the appeals designed to bypass the prefrontal cortex and target the emotional centers of your midbrain. An appeal for instant action, for a short-fuse deadline, or to get in quickly with a "chosen few" should all be pondered and researched. Remember the five great emotional motivators in marketing: fear, greed, exclusivity, guilt, and need for approval.

10. Alternatively, doing still more research and waiting to decide at some future point becomes an avoidance of action and commitment, a means of procrastination in fear of anticipated negative consequences.

Six Guidelines for Making Grounded Money Decisions

A safety deposit box requires two keys to open the box: one held by the bank and one by the owner. Financial decisions need the same thing: the keys of the left and right brains operating simultaneously. Here are seven guidelines that will help you keep your limbic system and your money separate so that the lizard in you doesn't get to make your money decisions.

1. *Avoid making important money decisions when you are emotional*: Heightened emotion—good or bad—narrows your perspective, cuts you off from your sense of the big picture, and makes it more difficult to logically see the long-term consequences of your choices. Paradoxically, attempting to use reason and logic with someone who is in a heightened emotional state only deepens the automatic alarm pattern and will usually lead the person to dig in his heels and spiral into more extreme and less considered impulses. Empathic listening and communication of understanding are far more effective at de-escalating things.

2. *Avoid making important money decisions under tension or fatigue*: Increased tension produces emotional regression. With increased tension and advanced conflict, the stress-response reaction can move someone into a more emotional pattern characteristic of a much earlier age. The same holds true for fatigue. Make important decisions after tension has eased and you are rested. "Never go to bed angry" is an ages-old maxim for healthy relationships—and with good reason. It's easier to fly off the handle when fatigued and say things we might later regret or to *buy* things we might later regret.

3. *Be willing to sleep on it*: There are few true emergencies in life. Investing isn't one of them, and neither is buying that plasma television. If it is a good decision today, it will be a good decision tomorrow, after you have had the state change and perspective of sleeping on it. Be clear on the distinction between being passive and making an informed decision not to act right now. "I'll sleep on it" *is* a decision. Especially in times

of traumatic or crisis situations, sleeping on it can revert a "hot state" to one of cooler reason. Recognize if you are vulnerable to emotional news or gyrations in order to devise a strategy to not react in the financial arena. Limit exposure to emotional triggers, such as checking a stock ticker each day.

4. *Have a well-informed and fully structured plan*: Look at the big picture and your long-term objectives and create a strategy and game plan based on facts rather than on emotions or instinctive reactions. Seek out whatever assistance you need to become fully informed on the issues involved. Periodically review your plan to make sure it is in alignment with objective expert advice by a money or investment specialist.

5. *Stick to your plan*. Especially in times of doing extremely well and feeling euphoric, stick to the plan. Get your excitement and take risk in areas other than financial.

6. *Worry about the right things*. Decide what you can control (your plan, your actions, your decisions) and what you can't (market conditions, external events) and put all your effort, energy, and focus into those things you can determine. When things happen that are beyond your control and that you cannot determine, stick to the plan.

Shopping Momentum and Money Psychology

Three groups of marketing researchers have a common finding and conclusion: once someone purchases an item, he or she is far more likely to continue to purchase other items. Shopping leads to more shopping.

This shopping momentum is a two-stage process. Initially, a shopper decides whether to purchase the first item, takes time, and weighs pros and cons. After this initial deliberation phase, once the shopper has made the decision to buy, significantly less effort is put into evaluating subsequent purchases on the same trip. The initial purchase—actually the *anticipation* of the purchase—creates a change of the state of mind of the shopper. Both making and spending money trigger the pleasure center of the brain to produce dopamine. This has a singular impact of shifting the state of mind. Once the state of mind is in the "buy" mode, other purchases simply sustain this state of mind.

When I previously practiced psychiatry and psychoanalysis, I worked with some executives who had addictions to various substances. One very wealthy shipbuilder described his reliance on cocaine: "I have always chased that initial high. The first time I used cocaine, I experienced an incredible rush. Every subsequent use has been less than that experience, but I am always chasing it, hoping to recapture it. It was incredible. It has led me to some very bad decisions and compromises in my life and business." Same with shopping. So how to strategize?

Minimize shopper's momentum with a plan: Make a list. Hold the conviction not to get swept up by sales or impulsive purchases and to not stray in any way from the list.

Pause between the pick and the purchase: Since the anticipation of the purchase and acquiring a new bling object releases dopamine to change a state of mind, disrupt the flow of that state with a contemplative pause. Never mind if the "bling" doesn't have glitter, such as a backpack from REI. It still leads to a greater likelihood of additional purchases, such as a sleeping bag and hiking boots. (I know these things.)

Monitor your energy: When you become depleted from a task, you succumb more quickly to the urge to respond according to emotion and impulse. Various activities that impose high demands of self-controlling concentration become depleting and have an impact by withdrawing energy from an emotional bank account.

Here are some of the ways this effect is expressed:

- Overspending on impulse purchases

- Abandoning a healthy diet

- Lowered threshold for annoyance or impulsivity

- Performing less well on cognitive tasks and logical decision making

- Persisting for less time in challenging tasks

NONSENSE NEUROSCIENCE AND BAD BEHAVIORAL ECONOMICS

Are You Addicted to Less?

The story of addictive behavior is not always one of *more*: it can also manifest as the relentless pursuit of *less*. The flip side of money addiction is addiction to scarcity. The money psychology of scarcity ranges from an opposition to wealth, to maintaining a comfort zone of focusing on what can go wrong, and even to the idealization of poverty as spiritual. Examples include gifted people who can't convert their talent into sufficient income or otherwise dependable people who ignore financial matters until they become serious.

A comfort zone is a familiar pattern of behavior—one that's predictable and automatic—so you always know the outcome. It's a gradual process, but once established, it resists change. Both our minds and our brains contribute to this default mode. We even have a comfort zone with our weight, with what we order at our regular restaurant, or with the difficulty of starting a savings program.

A "Yes" answer to any of these suggests examination of a pursuit of less:

1. Do you believe it is more virtuous or admirable to be poor than to be rich?

2. Do you believe being poor is more spiritual than being wealthy?

3. When you have an influx of money, do you tend to spend it quickly and/or impulsively and return rapidly to a familiar state of poverty?

4. Do you often refrain from making needed repairs on your car or your home or from getting medical care for yourself (such as regular checkups or dental cleaning) because you don't feel you can afford to spend the money?

5. Is it more comfortable for you to spend money on others than on yourself?

6. Do you undercharge for your work or your skills?

7. Do you fail to collect money due to you?

8. Is it uncomfortable for you to collect on fees that people owe you for your work?

9. Does it seem like whenever you are about to get ahead financially, some crisis happens in your life that gets in the way and stops your progress cold?

10. Do you persistently focus on what can go wrong or on what you can't do?

A belief is the mind's command to the brain. With the same belief, you will continue to have the same results. If you change your belief, you can have different results. The beliefs within us—our own internal map of reality—determine our perception of what surrounds us, including what and how we select, register, and process. We construct our story lines from these premises.

We have to bring our beliefs about money, finances, and wealth into conscious focus to assess how well they work in the present.

Hope for a Dollar

Each year, Americans spend $7 billion on movie tickets, $16 billion on sporting events, $24 billion on books, and $62 billion on lottery tickets. The lottery is the most popular paid entertainment in the country.

What fuels our national pastime? Why do people continue to play the lottery?

An ancient part of our brain gets excited about the possibility of making money. This deep midbrain area, the nucleus accumbens (the pleasure center), can trump the rational forebrain and can even collectively influence entire economies. Mirror neurons and active amygdalas contribute to the social contagion of everything from tulip bulbs to housing prices. Most of the factors influencing these decisions are outside conscious awareness.

But there's one area where it's all in the open—everyman's game: the lottery.

The anticipatory excitement mounts when three of your six numbers are called—or when two of the three scratch-off symbols match and a third is *still possible*. The close miss, as when the first two cherries align on the slot machine, ignites brain kindling. "Walk away," says the rational forebrain. "No way," counters the midbrain. "I almost won—just one more time."

Why not spend $1 for a brief time of (irrational) hope? The purchase of a momentary anticipation of pleasure is sustained for a time by hopeful "what-if" fantasies. Where else can you dream so fancifully for $1? Escape to a better life for a buck? Lotteries activate a simple bias of the human brain called the availability bias: the tendency to judge probabilities on the basis of how easily examples come to mind. Lottery organizers heavily promote jackpot winners, so we consistently hear about the big win. We hear nothing about the millions of tickets purchased by people who win nothing. The availability bias creates the illusion that people are much more likely to win than they are.

Yet hope serves a significant psychological function. Our pleasure in living is based partly on our current situation but also on what could be, on what we imagine our situation could become. Perhaps some of those millions who check their TV and computer screens on Wednesday and Saturday nights praying for their six numbers to appear use this framework to imagine, to vault beyond what their imagination could otherwise not conjure. A limitation of imagination is that we have to imagine within our own system. The lottery does indeed provide another system, fantastical though it may be, to allow hope for a dollar.

Does hope come any cheaper?

It is, of course, when one becomes habituated to the process of creating this hope that very small amounts of money become very smaller amounts of money.

We know from studies of the brain that it is the *anticipation* of pleasure or a win, rather than the win itself, that creates excitement and the release of dopamine (a chemical very appropriately named). When some-one approaches a slot machine, he or she experiences a spike in dopamine *before* actually touching the machine.

In all situations of bias and inequality of the rich and poor, in *one arena* everyone has an equal chance: the lottery. Never mind that it is al-most impossible; it is impartial. The lottery, at least in fantasy, is the great equalizer. Never mind that it is fanciful and illogical; for a brief and shiny emotional moment, it lights up an entire neighborhood in the brain—just not the one where good business practices prevail.

The truly rich spend time concealing their wealth, while those with-out spend time aspiring. On average, in state lotteries, households that make less than $12,400 a year spend 5 percent of their income on lotteries. A behavioral economics team at Carnegie Mellon University explained why poor people are so much more likely to buy tickets: they *feel* poor.[1] Sad, since playing the lottery, a massively losing proposition, exacerbates the poverty of those with low income.

Our helplessness inspires us; it is a catalyst to create both effectiveness and autonomy. If it is an ersatz mastery—a temporary illusion based on the anticipation of pleasure—each of these temporary stand-ins—drugs, alcohol, food, and risk—is self-limited and carries the danger of being used again and again.

Authentic versus Counterfeit Self

Does feeling like a fraud make someone more likely to commit fraud? Do people who buy fake goods to look good to others look worse to themselves?

Psychologists studied two groups of young women.[2] One group wore sunglasses from a box labeled "authentic"; the other group wore sunglasses from a box labeled "counterfeit" (both boxes were authentic). The re-searchers put the participants into various situations in which it was easy and tempting to cheat.

Although math performance was the same for the two groups, 30 percent of those in the "authentic" condition inflated their scores, while a whopping 71 percent of the counterfeit-wearing participants inflated their scores.

The researchers concluded, "When one feels like a fake, he/she is likely to behave like a fake."

The volunteers who wore counterfeits were more likely not only to act dishonestly but also to believe that others did too. Wearing sunglasses they thought were fake made them interpret the actions of others through a lens of dishonesty.

And they were *completely unaware* of both cheating more and judging others as more unethical. While people buy fake goods to look good to other people, the irony is that they look worse to themselves.

In this study, it was not their self-image that led them to cheat but rather the act of wearing fake shades (knockoffs) that triggered their dishonesty.

Why is this?

The brain has an error-detection mechanism that registers when something appears wrong. This innate capacity detects what neuroscientists call "errors": the differences between expectation and perceived actuality. This portion of the brain plays a central role in detecting mistakes as well as responding to them.

You can deceive others—even your own mind—but your brain always knows.

A Random Walk through Chaos to Arrive at a Virus: The Neuroscience of Premature Closure

In our quest to understand, we believe that merely giving something a name accurately explains. The unknown in medicine can be ascribed to a "virus." Mathematics constructs "chaos theory" to explain what defies logic and cannot be understood. The "random walk theory" of Wall Street officially postulates that the market cannot be predicted. We create the illusion of understanding and even of mastery by assigning a diagnosis.

The brain operates efficiently, to expend the least amount of energy to do a task. This efficiency means that the brain takes shortcuts based on what it already knows—to make pathways and networks for repeated tasks automatic. The shortcuts save energy. The shortcuts also mean that past experience necessarily shapes current perception and processing. Psychoanalysts call this transference. Neuroscientists call it the efficiency principle. Behavioral economists call it diagnosis bias (physicians should as well but often do not). For all of us, the brain perceives things in ways it has been trained to do. How we categorize something determines *what* we see.

This works great for many things. But the challenge is that imagination, which comes from perception, can be limited to what we already know. We can only imagine from our current experience and our known paradigms. Neuroscientist Gregory Berns examines the science of thinking differently—iconoclasts in particular—to emphasize how we need to put ourselves in new situations to see things differently and boost creativity.

When the brain encounters the unaccustomed or unexpected, perturbation occurs. The brain has to reorganize perception, which influences how we see things. We are pushed to see things in a different way—to be creative. Prompts include a novel stimulus, new information, or an unaccustomed context.

Creative stimulation can be enhanced in these ways:

- Be aware of the categories that you use for a person or idea—in order to go beyond or outside them.

- Seek out environments in which you have no experience.

- Bring together ideas from different disciplines and different perspectives to the same subject.

- Engage a mentor coach to challenge new ways of looking at things.

- Follow intuition and gut feelings: write them down.

- Brainstorm and free-associate: allow a stream of consciousness not bound by usual categories.

The Art and Neuroscience of New Learning

Why does someone begin a new endeavor with such excitement and then seem to lose momentum after a few weeks into it or purchase a long-awaited item and then have the excitement turn into complacency? The dynamics of new learning involve both mind and brain.

Mind Matters

New learning falls into four phases:

1. *Initial confusion and excitement* combine to launch new learning. Awareness of the unfamiliar and uncertain registers as curiosity or even anxiety, mixed in with excitement, which propels momentum.

2. *Increasing confidence* follows, both with the experience of effectiveness and with positive feedback.

3. *Mastery* results from effectiveness with movement to its own self-sustaining "flow" and validation.

4. *Entropy* occurs when the invigoration of a learning curve's newness levels off and declines. This leveling off may register as disillusionment.

Brain Business

Dopamine is the brain chemical that induces excitement by anticipating pleasure or reward. The rush from the release of dopamine motivates and even encourages one to take risks. The newness is exciting, adding to the release. But neuroscientists have shown that anticipating a reward is even more exciting than actually receiving it. Why? Because receiving a reward actually shuts down the anticipatory release of dopamine, diminishing the energy and pleasure. The central nervous system shifts to the maintenance mode (necessary from an economic and evolutionary perspective), mediated primarily by norepinephrine.

This shift explains the paradox that the *expectation* of an event or a purchase is more exciting than the *actual* experience:

- An investor will feel more positive when expecting a stock to rise yet feel less excited than anticipated when it actually does.

- The purchase of a big-ticket item—such as a new car—isn't as exciting as expected.

- The "hedonic treadmill" described by Daniel Kahneman, Princeton Nobel Prize winner, occurs when the brain adapts to a new state of wealth and possessions and increasing pleasure is sought.[3]

- Clients hit plateaus in coaching or mentoring after one to two months.

From Paradox to Progression

Both the mind and the brain contribute to new learning and its paradoxes. Our minds seek closure and infer causality, accurate or not. Additionally, we then defend our position or decision rather than examining it, making it static. Our brains attempt to end any dissonance, even prematurely shutting down inquiry.

So what can you do to maintain some aspects of this excitement—or at least ladder it—to generate ongoing creative stimulation?

- Knowledge is inert until it is activated, so put it into behavior.

- Foster attitudes that promote curiosity and openness.

- Recognize and assess emotional couplings that can derail logical choices (such as money equals freedom, evil, or greed).

- Monitor choices and question ideas.

- Probe your reasoning.

- Ask, "What works?" "What doesn't work?"

- Facilitate new behaviors and guide the development of new mental maps.

- Program new identity: incorporate your new experiences into your evolving self-concept. You are no longer defined by your habits or your old story.

Continue to look at things in novel ways. Everyone thought Goliath was too big to hit; David thought he was too big to miss.

The Negative Wealth Effect

I was talking with the owner of one of our favorite antique stores in an area close to our weekend ranch. He said, "People are just not spending money." The downtown area of the little town was somewhat dead, and the nursery we frequently visit had few customers.

He continued, "They don't seem to be out of jobs, no one is making any less money, but people just aren't spending."

Since I believe homespun research can, at times, approximate results from the neuroeconomics lab, I asked why he felt this was the case.

"Everybody is watching the news too much."

The positive wealth effect occurs when rising values of homes, stock portfolios, and retirement accounts make people feel wealthy. Even though no one takes a single dollar from these assets, the heightened mood leads to more spending.

People feel the impact of the economic downturn in an inverse way: the negative wealth effect. Even though they make the same money at their same job, people spend less.

We spend not according to how much money we have or even what we need but according to how we feel.

Neuroeconomists have demonstrated that fearful people cling to what they have. Our nervous systems constrict in a primitive but adaptive effort for survival. In a state of withdrawal and fear, people reduce spending. The condition that people seek to avoid becomes what they bring about. When fear is dominant, money may be not only constricted but also hoarded. Finding some conscious, logical basis for their decisions so that they make sense, consumers become "risk averse" and hunker down. Spending gets a bad reputation.

A University of Toronto study demonstrated that when people are in a positive mood, their visual cortex takes in more information. In a positive mood, people both see and process a greater number of possibilities in their environment. A good mood enhances the size of the window of their perspective.

In terms of spending, the emotional contagion ("collective tilt" or herd mentality) of the economic downturn has the reverse effect from an expanding economy—even without a direct impact on the individual. Increased tension both produces emotional regression and narrows perspective. The stress hormones of epinephrine and cortisol block the processing of information.

To regulate states of mind in times of both good and bad stress, a modicum of balance is crucial. When one's natural inclination is to remain hyperfocused, look instead for opportunities to see the big picture. Being grounded and centered allows an optimal state of mind for synthesis of thinking with access to existing knowledge. When you're relaxed and centered, you have the greatest access to all your states of mind—all the information you possess.

A Buddhist teaching bears this out: "Return to the earth now if your mind is troubled and your heart is uncertain, for it is by returning to the beginning that we can clearly see the path."

This, Too, Shall Pass: The Improbable Lessons of Our Biases

The king summoned the wisest man of his court and commanded him to present one statement that would apply for everything, for all of mankind, for all of time. He commanded him further not to come back until he had such a statement.

After a substantial time, the wise man returned with this statement for the king: "This, too, shall pass."

Our brain's wiring and mind programs are constructed to not recognize this simple fact. Because these biases involve patterns that affect money decisions, it's important to recognize each one of them if we want to outsmart our brains and revise our software:

- *Durability bias*: This bias assumes that an intense emotional experience—either really good or really bad—will continue at the same level of intensity for the foreseeable future. The brain is not wired to imagine a gradual dissipation of emotion over time. The fact is that emotions, good or bad, gradually gravitate back toward a preset emotional baseline. "This, too, shall end."

- *Extrapolation bias*: This bias projects the past, as well as the present, onto the future. We are wired to project the past, the present, and the context of both into the future and not to project change going forward. This distortion is compounded by the cognitive tendency to view events within their context and to assume the same context in the future.

- *Cause-and-effect bias*: Seeing patterns in random data and assigning causality brings closure in our minds and ends dissonance in our brains. Harry Houdini, the magician, commented on this phenomenon. Just because something is unexplained does not mean it's supernatural. Once something unpredictable has occurred, going forward, we're more likely to see that outcome as inevitable (the mortgage crisis of 2008 or Japan's trio of tsunami, earthquake, and nuclear disaster).

- *The gambler's fallacy*: When there are five outcomes of "red" in roulette, the expectation is that "black" is now due. We expect reversion to the mean. Studies also show that gamblers, given more information about the horses and jockeys they bet on, become biased on the basis of this greater information and assume they should do better. Those with more information systematically gamble more, with the result that they lose more money.

- *The hot-hand fallacy*: When observing an unusual streak of events, people continue to predict that the streak will continue.

- *Status quo bias*: People continue doing the same thing, even when it is compromised or limiting, expecting somehow that the same thing will bring about a different outcome. People know exactly what they need to do to change in three areas, yet they usually don't change: money, weight, and relationships. In each of these areas, people have tried and failed. They repeat patterns that don't work, become frustrated, and often come to believe that the cause is due to issues beyond their control: the economy, genes, or a partner's stubbornness. They fail to recognize how strong and unconscious their stories are.

- *My perpetual, hopeful bias*: People can change; they can write new stories. Jung reminds us, "We cannot live the afternoon of life according to the program of life's morning, for what was great in the morning will be little at evening, and what in the morning was true, at evening will have become a lie."

Life, Like the Stock Market, Is an Auction

For the second Christmas in a row, I gave my wife Charles Krypell jewelry from an exclusive jewelry boutique. That second year, I negotiated for a ring and a bracelet, just as the year before I'd done for a necklace and earrings. Both times, my negotiation reduced the marked price. Although my wife was astonished that I dared attempt to negotiate the price of designer jewelry at such an exclusive store, her pleasure in the gifts trumped the shock (and rather quickly, I might add).

The stock market is really not a "market" but an auction; the price of any stock is what someone is willing to bid at any moment based on the perception of the bidders and influenced by many factors, including their herd mentality.

The same principle is at work in life. Its distractions with the money tool play out in the brain as cognitive bartering and mental accounting. An opening "bid" is perceived as a mental anchor, the starting point for the psychological jockeying that follows. Even if we perceive an opening bid as inaccurate or unfair, it still serves as an anchor to shape the way the brain thinks about value and to determine subsequent bidding behavior.

In one study, a group of people were given the opportunity to bid for a bottle of wine.[4] Rationally, they calculated the value—which they were actually told—and bid accordingly. Immediately before the auction, they were asked to write down the last two digits of their Social Security number on their bid sheet. The people whose bids for the wine were highest were those with the highest Social Security numbers (51–99). They consistently and significantly outbid those with the lowest last two Social Security numbers (0–50). Unwittingly, they were influenced by a completely unrelated fact. Anchoring—the influence of the reference price—comes into play even when two unrelated digits are written down.

So much of life is an auction—buying a house, a car, an antique, or health care. One senior health care executive, a former executive mentor coaching client who had moved on to become chief executive officer of a non–health care corporation, told me that hospitals expect to collect 40 to 50 percent of their billing and thus, though the fact is never publicized, are always willing to negotiate.

Even death is negotiable, as you'll see if you read *Younger Next Year* by Henry Lodge Jr.[5] and *The Singularity Is Near* by Ray Kurdzweil.[6]

Neuroeconomics illuminates our life and, like the stock market, operates on herd mentality in developing bubbles and many of the other mind matters and brain business that constitute a mutable logic and influence behavior.

Awareness is the best antidote. Whatever remains unconscious will be attributed to fate (or to the economy).

Can Happiness Buy Money?

This may be a better question. While happiness is a result and not a goal, consider these assorted findings:[7]

- Several thousand college freshmen were rated according to their cheerfulness. Two decades later, those who ranked at the top of the cheerfulness measures earned an average income 31 percent higher than those of lower scores.

- A study of employees at three large U.S. companies over 18 months found that those with increased happiness had higher salary increases during that period.

- The life span of pre-1960 Major League Baseball players was studied. Those with the broadest smile lived 79.9 years; those with a slight smile averaged 75 years; those with no smile averaged 72.9 years. Smiling has been shown to reduce stress hormones such as cortisol and induce endorphins to decrease blood pressure.

- People with great left prefrontal cortex activity—the area of the brain that generates happiness—produce more antibodies and have stronger immune systems. Greater activity in this part of the brain also relates to lower levels of stress hormone.

- Dutch men and women who laughed more often and had more positive use of the future had a 25 percent lower risk of mortality than those less optimistic.

- Employees with a more consistently good mood missed fewer days of work.

- Happiness can help keep money. Unhappy people—specifically those who are sad—become self-focused and spend as much as 300 percent more for the same item. The act of spending stimulates the pleasure center of the brain and temporarily counters both sadness and anxiety.

These findings suggest that happiness—a register of positive energy—can increase the most tangible and universal emblem of energy: money.

Money and Happiness: The Real Relationship

Money can solve many problems, or at least make them easier. Someone once told me, "I've never seen a problem that money has made *worse.*" With the exception of substance addiction, he probably has a point.

But then we overreach to make money address more than it should. It gets pressed into service because it's a commonly accepted social and personal resource—it makes people feel self-sufficient.

The idea that more money will bring more happiness is one of the most pervasive and persistent money themes in modern culture. Is there any truth to it?

Our relationship with money assumes that we know what money can do for us—that we know what we're giving and getting for money. Some things *do* work this way: the more you pay, the more you get, such as a car, hotel, or house. But not so with other things—abstractions such as happiness, love, and authenticity, which may at times even have an inverse relationship to money.

Research suggests that money, like Prozac, doesn't make you happy. Both, however, can prevent certain forms of unhappiness. Money, for example, allows us to afford better medical care, safety, neighborhoods, gadgets, and, at times, mood.

Harvard psychologist Dr. Daniel Gilbert has demonstrated that both greater wealth and actual purchases have little permanent impact on happiness.[8] His research shows that those events we expect to make us happy often prove less exciting than we anticipated. The increased happiness and pleasure we predict from, for example, a raise in salary or a new gadget typically fall short of our expectations. And even in cases where financial gain does bring about a better mood, the good news doesn't last long. University of Illinois psychologist Dr. David Myers found that after an initial excitement with a burst of good fortune, such as inheritance, lottery, or job advance, people revert to their initial set point of basic mood.[9]

Consistent evidence shows that some experiences, such as a vacation, an evening at the theater, or a good dinner, make people happier than do material possessions they spent money for. One reason is that the process is more social: when you spend money on dinner with a loved one or a vacation with family, you create an entire experience. When you spend for a possession, you quickly grow accustomed to it, and the pleasure fades simply because a different neurochemical system takes over once the purchase is made. This drop in dopamine *after* you buy accounts for buyer's remorse. (The same drop *before* you buy is called coming to your senses.)

Money is the legal tender of desires. We use to it measure success as well as to try to buy happiness. We use money to communicate, to carry messages. So, in regard to happiness, as well as many other promises of money, we project our desire onto it like the Rorschach inkblot. Money is the cover story, seemingly promising one thing but often delivering another.

When we compare our inside to someone else's outside, we think money can bridge the differences. Money is a ceaselessly renewable promissory note for possibility. But happiness is not a goal or reward. It's a consequence.

We need money in order to know what can't be purchased.

Debt Cycle Stealth: Debt Psychology and Self-Deception

You can fulfill a desire you didn't know you had by spending money you don't have. You can define yourself by acquisitions not paid for. You can borrow based on how much money you will be lent rather than by how much money you can pay back.

Spending money generates the perception, both by the spender and by the observer, of having money. Fulfilling a wish creates the desire. When desires define identity, they can become relentless. Many people who fall heavily into debt do not necessarily have psychological problems, but their spending takes on a life of its own.

Spending money is addictive; it changes a state of mind.

Elastic boundaries distance the obligation of debt. A credit card separates the pleasure of purchase from the pain of future payment. Our optimism bias then makes rainy days and repayment an abstraction.

Four stages of a debt cycle can occur, in this order: compulsion, shame, disavowal, and compulsion:

1. *Compulsion*: A debt cycle begins with an urge to buy something unaffordable. We feel compelled to buy because of how we believe it will make us feel. Spending is emotional, prompting

an output of dopamine, the same brain chemical that creates the "high" of drug use.

2. *Shame*: Shame, the recognition of not living up to one's internal ideal, sets in with the recognition of spending money that we do not have.

3. *Disavowal*: Lawrence Ausubel, an economist at the University of Maryland, found that cardholders admit to only $4 of every $10 they owe.[10] Intelligent people willfully disavow 60 percent of their debt for the same reason that alcoholics underreport the number of drinks they have. People mentally wipe off their fingerprints to wish they hadn't done what they did, pretending that they actually didn't do it. Disavowal tactics may include not opening bills when they come in, paying only the minimum on credit card statements, hiding bills or statements from a partner, or lying about bills owed or balances due.

4. *Compulsion*: Compulsion sets in to remedy the discomfort of shame as well as to counter the initial feelings and desires that set the cycle in motion. An addiction is anything—or any process—that you feel you can't do without.

A Debt Quiz

Answer each of the following questions with a "Yes" or a "No," circling the scoring number in the corresponding column. For the first 10 questions, each "No" scores 5 points, and each "Yes" scores *minus* 5. The next two questions are worth 10 points each, and the last is worth 20. When you've answered all the questions and circled all your points, add up your total score.

	Yes	No
1. Do you routinely make minimum payments on credit card balances?	–5	5
2. Are the balances on your credit card statements gradually increasing every month?	–5	5

3. Do you have a balance on one or more cards of more than 50 percent of the credit limit for that card?	−5	5
4. Do you often use cash advances on your credit cards to pay other bills?	−5	5
5. Do you routinely "play the float" on cards (juggle payments between cards) in order to pay bills?	−5	5
6. Do you regularly have past-due bills, rent, or mortgage payments?	−5	5
7. Do you have little or no savings?	−5	5
8. Have you been denied credit or had a credit card purchase declined during the past quarter?	−5	5
9. Have you had one or more checks bounce during the past quarter?	−5	5
10. Have you had one or more notices or phone calls from a collection agency in the past quarter?	−5	5
11. Do you ever hide, misrepresent, or neglect to mention a debt to your spouse or other family member?	−10	10
12. Do you ever hide a bill or credit card statement from your spouse or other family member?	−10	10
13. Are you unable to state, offhand and without sitting down to go through your records, the exact total amount of money you presently owe?	−20	20
Total Score	___	___

Possible scores range from 90, a perfect score, suggesting you have no significant problem with debt, to *minus* 90. Obviously, the lower your score, the more likely you are to some extent caught in the debt cycle. Truthfully, though, if you answer *any* of these questions with an immediate "Yes," then there is probably at least some material in this chapter that has special meaning for you.

What is the solution? How does one escape from this vicious cycle? Because the entire sequence depends on playing "let's play pretend," relief starts by saying "no more games" and coming clean with the truth.

French Fries, Credit Cards, and Debt Psychology

The Tyranny of Small Decisions

How do two French fries weigh 40 pounds? Putting on 40 pounds over 10 years means gaining an average of four pounds per year.

- 40 pounds divided by 10 years equals 4 pounds per year.

- 4 pounds divided by 12 months equals .33 (1/3) of a pound per month.

- This is approximately 1/100 of a pound per day (1/3 pound divided by 30 days).

- One pound of stored fat represents 3,500 calories.

- 3,500 times 1/100 equals 35.

- To achieve the feat of gaining 40 pounds in 10 years, all you have to do is consume an extra 35 calories every day.

- 35 calories = two regular French fries.

Little things count. Economist Alfred Kahn described how we become trapped by the series of seemingly insignificant choices that we make—the tyranny of small decisions.[11] If we were able to see the end results of those small decisions, we might chart an entirely different course.

If you are burdened by credit card debt, it probably wasn't one huge purchase that created the problem. More likely, it was hundreds of small decisions all along the way. Some were necessary, some justified, some rationalized. "It's just a couple of French fries" thinking. Internal bargaining took care of others: "Just this one time" or "I'll pay it off next month." Separation of the pleasure of the purchase from the pain of payment obviated any lingering questions.

The Nobility of Small Decisions

Consider the inverse: the nobility of small decisions.

We recognize in parenting, from the very beginning, that we really don't know which interactions or words will be really important or even remembered. Knowing that we don't know, we have to assume that everything we do is important. Everything matters.

Consider the very small decision of stopping for a $4 coffee each day. Calculate how much that is per year, then, with interest, how much it would be in 10 years and in 20.

Epictetus asked 20 centuries ago, "What is a good person?" It's the one, he reflected, who achieves tranquillity by having formed the habit of asking on every occasion, "What is the right thing to do now?"

You can be held hostage by small decisions. Or you can be effective and achieve mastery and freedom by small decisions.

All you have to do in life is the next right thing.

At times, it may not be clear what the next right thing is, but you can almost always know what it isn't.

Part 2

ROADMAP FOR A
NEW MONEY STORY

The ROADMAP—an acronym for the seven steps for change in chapters 7 to 13—will guide you to understand your relationship with money and its meaning. The tools and exercises will mentor a journey to navigate the changes of behavior, mind, and brain to write a New Money Story®.

*R*ecognize authorship. You are writing your money story: the assumptions as well as every choice about earning, spending, and saving.

*O*wn your story. Accountability is a prerequisite to change.

*A*ssess plot and story lines. Recognize the behaviors, hidden messages, and elusive language of mind and emotion.

*D*ecide what to change. Make informed choices about what story components to keep, let go, change, and enhance.

*M*ap changes. Establish goals and success strategies.

*A*uthor new experiences. Create the new money story you desire.

*P*rogram new identity. Incorporate and sustain the changes by a corresponding internal growth.

STEP I
Recognize Authorship
of Your Money Story

Two anthropologists were chosen to enter separate, essentially identical ape colonies to live and observe for a year. They had remarkable similarities of personality, philosophy, and education. When the two anthropologists emerged to compare notes, they expected essential similarities but instead found remarkable discrepancies. One anthropologist, after an initial period of transition, was accepted by the apes, integrated into the colony, and achieved a unity and comfort with the apes. The other anthropologist never got beyond the social periphery of his colony, remained careful and vigilant, always seemed right on the cusp of a conflict, and never achieved harmony.

The anthropologists could not understand the discrepant results or find any reasons for them. They puzzled for months until they finally found the one difference. The anthropologist who was the uncomfortable, careful outsider carried a gun. His gun never showed; he never used it; the apes never knew he had it. But he knew he had it; he knew that if things got tough, he had an "out." The anthropologist who had no gun had a commitment: he knew from the beginning that he would either make it—or not—on his own.

In retrospect and reconstruction, both assumptions created the reality they experienced.

We tell our story. Then our story tells us.

You are writing your money story: the assumptions as well as every choice about earning, spending, and saving.

The first step toward enhancing a money story is to *recognize authorship* of your story. Story recognition makes possible a review of the assumptions and choices about earning, spending, and saving money. This systematic introduction to your relationship with money begins with recognition of you as its author.

Plot: The core unfolding of the themes and story lines informs what you look for and how you attribute meaning to what you find. You then create narratives of self-statement according to those assumptions since both brain and emotions are programmed to ignore facts that contradict beliefs.

Story line: Money's language speaks self-statements. A self-statement is a unique, personal communication of your experience and point of view. What you do and say are ubiquitous, unavoidable self-statements of your beliefs and personal reality. Three people may stand shoulder to shoulder and observe the same event, yet each of their stories of the event will be different. The three stories make up self-statements of each individual's perspective from unique life experiences.

Money can make any statement, carry any message, and represent any notion. Money language conveys messages that sometimes are invisible to the speaker yet quite decipherable to observers.

One of the first steps in changing our money stories is to know ourselves quite well, know our own story, and have our own voice in its construction. We can know ourselves by first developing the capacity to be self-observers. This requires us to be insightful, reflective, and self-observant—to have *mindfulness* of ourselves in order to be empathically attuned to the mind and experience of a client.

In adulthood, everything you experience you either *create* or *accept*.

But positive thinking *in itself* doesn't reprogram beliefs. Positive thoughts are generated in the conscious mind. Using positive self-talk in order to change behavior will have the same impact as talking positively to a software program on your computer in order to change it. You have to know how to revise the software. You have to know what to do with the old program as well as how to write a new one. And you may need a guide.

Each of our story lines—including money—has an internal operating system with a set of beliefs and assumptions that inform our behaviors. We are about to deconstruct that system in order to study it, understand it, and help you decide where it needs editing or updating.

The actual implementation of the ideas can be difficult because it often requires us to change our relationship to money in three ways:

- Breaking bad or just outdated habits
- Developing new ones
- Remaining disciplined over the long haul, no matter what

Principles of Recognizing Authorship

1. *Our experiences are always consistent with our assumptions.* Each of us writes our own personal story and makes sense of things by fitting incidents and events into our unique plot. This story fills in the blanks and connects the dots to complete the picture of who and what we are. Events, images, and experiences form the patterns and story lines of that plot. We construct meanings to make sense of our life and determine what is remembered as narrative in a coherent story of our identity. Reality validates and affirms those assumptions as we live out our expectations.

A farmer and an anthropologist pass through the same terrain of undeveloped land. The farmer sees the soil and envisions growing crops. The anthropologist sees signs of an ancient civilization and reconstructs its history. Both are right. The data that are viewed validate each individual's story.

Using our beliefs and assumptions, each of us creates our own personal story and the themes of that story. The plot defines and orients us in the present and guides us toward the future. The stories we tell about our life *become* our life. The stories we tell about our past *become* our past. Until the story is uncovered, questioned, and reevaluated, "the past" continues as the default mode.

Rather than question whether we're always right about our assumptions, we only further etch those beliefs as reality. And because we are always creating our own story, reality validates itself.

We perceive and remember what fits into our plot, which is our internal model of the world and ourselves. The plot—the core beliefs and assumptions of life and money stories—informs what people look for and how they attribute meaning to what they find. People then create narratives of self-statement according to that plot, as both brain and emotions are programmed to ignore facts that contradict assumptions. We ignore, mistrust, disbelieve, or, more likely, don't notice anything that doesn't fit into our pattern. These notions, prejudices, and fears, plus expectations from others, construct a self-concept. Some are conscious, and some are not. Unless we know how to examine and change them, we have difficulty even challenging these assumptions. In fact, any departure or change from a well-traveled plotline, even a positive one, may initially create anxiety and uncertainty.

Beliefs must be in conscious focus before we can revise the ones that don't work and create new ones to enhance a life and money story.

When you recognize the plot of your money story, you can understand the hidden assumptions and emotional agendas that ghostwrite your story lines. You can then revise your story to live it fully and successfully.

When you stop telling yourself all the things you should say and cease listening for what you ought to hear, you can begin to recognize your own story more fully. Half of the struggle occurs when you become tired of your old story: the story in which you work too many hours, feel under pressure at work, and perpetually feel short of time. Or the story in which you are the caretaker of others. Or the scapegoat. Or continue to fall in love with an ideal you hope someone will become rather than who that person is.

Perhaps you don't fully know your own story; you just realize there are aspects of it you don't much like. This is a beginning. And you don't need to know the story you should have written five years ago.

Growth and change begin with personal story ownership: the recognition that you are the author of your own story.

Taking ownership of a money story begins the process of inquiry. Only by accepting ownership can you proceed to assess the story lines and decide what to change.

2. *We become what we think and feel. Our beliefs become our reality.* The beliefs within us determine our perception of what surrounds us, including what and how we select, register, and process. A story can create its own reality.

The placebo effect generates a truth so powerful that it can even reverse the pharmacological effect of a real medicine. The placebo is a white lie, a fiction that becomes a truth.

To a large extent, we view our beliefs and assumptions as the truth, as the reality of the way things are. We validate our beliefs by experiences that affirm them and surround ourselves with individuals who share our values and hold similar points of view. And we live those assumptions by communicating to others how to respond to us. If you firmly believe you will be rejected or abandoned, you will either choose someone who will enact it or act in a way to generate that response. Because your belief system contains what you see as inevitable, without insight, the only degree of mastery you can exert is to determine how and when the inevitable happens.

Our assumptions are often in evidence but not always in our awareness because they are so basic to who we are. If you want to find out what you believe about yourself and the world, look around at your life. Your life is the self-statement, the mirror, of what exists inside you. When you feel chaotic or disorganized internally, you likely will notice that your house or office reflects that experience. You have created, promoted, and allowed everything in your present experience. All that you say, in the syntax of thought, feeling, and behavior, is about yourself.

You may regard your past as a series of episodes at times seeming to lack a theme or continuity. What you remember and how you remember it, however, fits into the plot you earlier incorporated and now accept in yourself and others. Your unconscious filter omits from perception or forgets any incident that doesn't fit comfortably into your plot. Like the words of an unknown foreign language, the brain doesn't record them for later retrieval or reference. Because of that filter, the episodes you recall of your past are not at all random. In fact, the incidents of your past are variations of a recurring, consistent plot. Without insight and change, new editions of the same story place a thousand different faces on the same central characters to repeat the same themes.

The beliefs *within* us—our own internal map of reality—determine our perception of what surrounds us, including what and how we select, register, and process. We construct our story lines from these premises.

Money depends on the meaning we give it. It doesn't know who owns it any more than war bonds knew about the war. Consider these examples of people's beliefs about money:

- I wasn't supposed to have a lot of money.

- Even though I'm wealthy, I'm supposed to act like I don't have much.

- If I spend on myself, I'm selfish.

- I'll keep some of what I spend a secret from my spouse.

- I feel ashamed of my debt, so I'll not think about it—not even be aware of how much.

"There is nothing either good or bad, but thinking makes it so," said a certain prince of Denmark called Hamlet.

We have to bring our beliefs about money, finances, and wealth into conscious focus to assess how well they work in the present time.

The choices we make as parents are models our children emulate. They look, experience, and take unconscious notes. Those notes get passed on. We know that a great many beliefs and behavioral patterns are downloaded during the first years of life without even conscious recognition by the child.

I received the following correspondence from a reader of *The Secret Language of Money*. He recognized how much he attributed to money, as if it were an entity with a mind and power of its own. These are some of his insights:

- Money could make me feel sad—when I was a kid, I saw my mom crying when we had none.

- I felt scared when we had no money. Money could make me feel bitter because no matter how hard anyone worked, I still felt poor.

- Money could make me feel sick when I think of the ability it has to rule me.

- Feeling guilty was another emotion I had to deal with; now that I am a multimillionaire, I don't feel I deserve it.

- I love money, yet I hate money for making me feel I can't live without it. I don't want to be mastered by it, yet I am. I don't want to admit this, yet I know I am setting myself free by admitting it.

3. *A new story can occur only by living in the present moment.* Someone has said that there is nothing but the present: the past is a present memory, and the future is a present anticipation.

Observing and owning repetitions of themes and story lines initiates understanding the core assumptions that generate these repetitions. Moment by moment and frame by frame, we actively construct the present scenarios and our experiences of them. Some of the story lines are visible, such as how we relate to family or respond to stress. One's own radar may not detect other story lines, such as an assumption that one can make only a limited amount of money.

When you acknowledge yourself as the author rather than the subject of your story, you recognize the active construction of experience. By analyzing the story, you can discern underlying assumptions.

4. *Our minds seek closure and infer causality, accurate or not.* In another series of studies reported by Dr. Daniel Gilbert of Harvard University, volunteers were shown words on a computer screen for a few milliseconds. This was such a short time that they were unaware that the words had been shown and couldn't even pick them out or guess from a multiple choice. And yet the volunteers were influenced by the words. When the word "hostile" was flashed, volunteers judged others negatively. When the word "elderly" was flashed, volunteers walked more slowly. When the word "stupid" was flashed, volunteers performed less well on tests.

When these volunteers were later asked why they judged, walked, or scored the way they did, they didn't know, nor did they acknowledge not knowing. Instead, they quickly considered the facts they were aware of and came up with some explanation. For example, those who walked more slowly stated, "I was a little tired when I did the test" or "I've been traveling for the last few days and haven't slept well."

None were aware that they were falsely attributing cause and effect.

These findings demonstrate in two ways our innate desire for closure:

- Our brains want to end dissonance by imposing certainty.

- Our minds create a complete story by a causal explanation that infers both closure and a sense of effectiveness. "Complete" trumps "accurate."

The Four Rs: Repeat and Rationalize versus Recognize and Reorganize

Repeat: Are you repeating an old story, hoping for a better outcome? The brain operates efficiently, expending the least amount of energy to do a task. This efficiency means that the brain takes shortcuts based on what it already knows—the tracks already laid down and neurons tailored to certain tasks. The shortcuts save energy. The shortcuts also mean that past experience shapes current perception and processing. The brain perceives things in ways it has been trained to do; how we categorize something forever determines *what* we see.

This works great for many things. But the challenge is that imagination, which comes from perception, can be limited to what we already know. We can imagine only from our current experience and our known paradigms. We need to put ourselves in new situations to see things differently and boost creativity.

Rationalize: Do you dismiss or compromise any aspect of your money story?

A repeating story line may be as bold as always looking for the next big deal or as quiet as habitually comparing yourself and your money to others or as pernicious as not being able to convert your talent into corresponding income.

If you feel trapped in your own recurring money story, such as chronic debt, consider your basic assumptions that ghostwrite the story lines. A better strategy will neither get you to a vague goal nor solve emotional conflict. Recognizing the internal origin of a process is difficult because an external drama always accompanies it. Some warning signs of this struggle include personal compromise, conflict with other people, limited success, unhappiness, or not living up to your full potential.

Recognize: Are your needs, ideals, passion, and talents all going in the same direction?

Listen to your language in regard to your goals. If you say you will *try* to reach a goal, you may be protecting yourself from anticipated failure. *Trying* speaks of less than a full commitment, a potential diversion to other alternatives against failure. The words of someone lacking commitment include "I'll try," "I should," "I ought to," or "I know I need to."

These build in an "out." When someone says, "I'm going to try to quit drinking," you know that he or she will continue to drink.

If your money story is not satisfying or if you haven't attained your objectives, look more closely: *You are always reaching your goals*, whether they are conscious or unconscious. It is helpful to know consciously and specifically what those goals are. You might be undermining your success by being imprecise in your objectives. Do you fear specifically yet dream vaguely?

Reorganize: Do all the story lines fit and advance the plot of your money story?

Once you've become aware of actively making choices, you can decide what's in your best interest and what furthers your story and what doesn't.

Your money story is the manifestation of your beliefs. You are always free to change your mind and always free to change your beliefs, including core assumptions about who you are. But first you have to become aware. Then you can assess what works and what doesn't. Then you can strategize about how to change and craft a plan to guide and map the progress for external and internal change.

Your Money Equations

You begin learning your money language by becoming clearly and consciously aware of the assumptions and beliefs you hold about money. The following exercise can help illuminate the invisible motives and meanings behind the financial decisions you make:

1. What were your three most recent purchases of more than $100?

2. What does each purchase mean to you? That is, how does it make you feel?

3. If it didn't give you that feeling, would you still make that purchase, at that price?

4. If you answered "No" to any of question 3, then how much *would* you spend on each purchase if it gave you only what you actually bought and not the feeling that came with it?

After you answer all the questions, take a moment to go over your answers to see if they provide any new insights about your own money meanings. Were you aware when you made these purchases exactly why you were making them—both the practical reasons and the emotional reasons?

Now, consider once more the earlier exercise to see if, given everything we've explored, your answer is any different.

Again, fill in the blank with a single word: *To me, money means . . .*

Beliefs Ghostwriting Your Money Story

We earlier looked at the question, "How much money do I need to be happy and content?" Now let's look at a related question: "What is the greatest annual income you can reasonably *expect to earn?*"

This isn't meant to be theoretical, as in what *anyone* can expect to earn. The question is about *you*, personally and individually—and not if you suddenly won the lottery or quit your job and in a fit of inspiration created the next Google, but what you can *reasonably* expect.

To get the most out of this exercise, answer the question with a specific dollar amount *before* you continue.

What is the greatest annual income I can reasonably expect to earn?

Now, let's take a close look at that answer. Why did you choose that number?

Do you know of anyone who earns more than that? There are people who earn many times the number you wrote, and there are also hundreds of thousands of people in the world who are no more intelligent, gifted, or born to advantage than you who have created large fortunes.

The question, then, is this: Where did that "reasonable expectation" come from? It comes from your story. In fact, this might be a more accurate way to ask that question:

What is the greatest annual income my money story will allow me to have?

You will be right about your assumption, whatever it is, because you live your life according to the script. You will let yourself make and keep only the money you think you're worth. Your belief system contains what is inevitable. Without awareness and ownership of your money story, the only way you can exert any mastery over a limiting assumption is to determine how and when the inevitable will happen, then bring it about by your own hand.

The Anatomy of a Money Story

To understand why we typically don't know our money stories, it's helpful to understand how we put them together in the first place. There are four distinct layers to a money story, each quite different from the others:

1. *Feelings*: our gut reactions connected with the strivings, emotional attributions, beliefs about, and representations of money in our lives and the world around us

2. *Behaviors*: the things we do for and with money

3. *Thoughts*: how and what we think about money and its symbolism

4. *Experiences*: our overall reactions and responses to money and its significance and symptoms in our lives

Feelings

We make money decisions based on underlying feelings, which give money its emotional meaning to us; over time, those money meanings crystallize into our beliefs about money.

Money can stir deep feelings of anger, resentment, admiration, compassion, lust, hostility—the entire spectrum of human emotion is a magnet for the symbolic potency of money. Of the four layers of story, feelings are the deepest; they form the core of our money story.

A feeling usually cues a particular state of mind. The state of mind determines the meaning we attach, which in turn generates the accompanying behavior.

Behaviors

Our behaviors are the clearest windows to our true beliefs about money. Unlike the hidden, internal world of our feelings, our actions are clearly visible. Our behaviors represent the secret language of money at its most obvious and *least* secretive. What we *say* we believe is one thing; what we *think* we believe may be yet another. What we *actually do* is the clearest expression of what we really do believe.

Thoughts

We don't often think logically or even consciously about our true money beliefs, but we do think about our money behaviors—at least sometimes. However, our thoughts are not usually central to the process (even when we believe otherwise). We tend to buy emotionally and *then* justify rationally, not the other way around. In other words, thoughts follow after the fact.

Thoughts are what we tell ourselves the story means, not necessarily what it really means. Like any "official" history of events made up after the fact, the story we tell ourselves is often a whitewashed version of what really happened. And this logical explanation often drives the real story underground.

Experiences

The various elements of our encounters with money all combine together to create an overall experience, which becomes what, to us, money *means*.

The experience surrounding money in its entire dimension, including our money behaviors, the feelings and beliefs that drive them, and the thoughts, opinions, and rationalizations we have about them, all go into the composition of what in time becomes the substance of our money stories.

STEP 2
Own Your Present Money Story

O ne couple married a week before Black Friday of 1929, which began the Great Depression. The poverty and scarcity of their situation centered on the reality and the metaphor of the Depression-era finances.

Money was elusive for this family after they produced seven children, and they often struggled even to have enough food. They were proud that they had never gone on relief—accepted welfare payments. To find enough work, the father was often away in other states for several months at a time.

Finally, after years of being exhausted and tired, the mother agreed to accept relief. Around this same time, she had bartered canning vegetables for almost three years to have her home painted. Someone in the welfare agency who passed by and saw her freshly painted house called her.

"If you can afford to have your house painted, does your family really need to be on relief?"

"Take it back," the proud woman responded. "Just take it back. I don't want it."

For this family, unearned money came with strings attached. Their experience of the scarcity of money became a legacy amalgamating their life and money stories.

Two generations later, the same woman's granddaughter, going through a postdivorce move and adjustment, was having a difficult time supporting her two children, but she was adamant about not asking for anything. She was determined "not to become one of those people who take welfare." She carried the same torch of pride as her grandmother.

She noted, "One of my children refused to eat the free lunch she was offered at school because choices were limited. Her great-grandmother learned that with a free lunch, you give up certain freedoms." Three generations and counting.

Ownership of a money story allows an understanding of hidden emotional themes—of money story lines and the assumptions that create them. Story recognition and ownership makes possible a review and assessment of plot and story lines.

This step involves systematically identifying and examining money narratives. Informed listening focuses on fundamentals such as repeated behaviors, money equations, beliefs ghostwriting financial decisions, and the anatomy of a money story.

Story Lines That Define

Because most of our initial story is gelled or ghostwritten before we are capable of being aware, it runs subconsciously, framing both what we experience and our subsequent responses. Once beliefs are established, our minds select supported data so seamlessly that we don't notice other possibilities. This automatic process ensures that we will experience only what we expect, ensuring that we will be right about the truth of our assumptions, our internal story.

Consequently, we may not be aware that what we are experiencing is a direct reflection of our internal thoughts and beliefs.

The transition from reactive to proactive begins when you reenergize and own authorship of your money story.

By taking ownership of your story, accepting that you are an agent rather than recipient/victim, you acknowledge that in adulthood, you either *accept* or *create* whatever you experience.

Because of the tendency of the mind/brain to follow the stronger neural pathways, making changes can be a gradual process, one with fluctuations, sometimes with two steps forward and one step back. As you become more conscious of and responsible for the story, you realize the pervasive quality of your programming, that it affects all areas of your life.

Once you own your story lines, you can then scrutinize them to determine the underlying assumptions in the construction of their narrative. Each story line reflects the self-concept and assumptions of its author. The quest then becomes, rather than adapting to an emotion, understanding the assumptions in its creation. If you feel anxious, the first step is to take ownership of that feeling as an active creation. A feeling is an actively constructed verb, not an existing noun. Anxiety is the reaction to danger. What is the danger you perceive? If there is no obvious danger, then examine the assumption to which you are responding anxiously. Assumptions ghostwrite behaviors, feelings, and thoughts.

Recognize Active versus Passive Positions

Sometimes the story seems to write itself, to just happen to you:

- "My thoughts ran away from me."

- "It just seems to keep happening."

- "I wasn't myself."

- "Uncertainty crept in."

Statements like these illustrate a passive mind-set in play, one that denies or doesn't recognize responsibility for thoughts, feelings, or actions. When this mind-set exists, you perceive yourself as the unwitting recipient rather than the author of the experience, with little hope that something can be learned or different choices made.

Rather than managing, overcoming, countering, or medicating a feeling such as anxiety, the first step is to acknowledge that even though it seemed to "just happen," you generated the experience.

When you take responsibility, you activate your capacity for change. Once you understand the major internal themes, you can begin to resolve the conflicts. That may include releasing long-held anger or resentments. Once you complete some of this "housecleaning," you can then focus on creating new and different feelings, responses, and behaviors. The clearer you become about your old stories, the more freedom you have to reframe your life and reinterpret the events in ways that empower instead of cripple you.

Some disclaimed action, attributed to insignificance or "just happening," makes its author seem like the passive recipient: "The thought came to my mind." "My mind refused to think about it." "My mind played tricks on me." "I couldn't help being late." These locutions disclaim oneself as agent, as creator of thoughts, feelings, and experiences. Passively expressed thoughts ("My doubt stopped me," "My anxiety paralyzed me") make the author the victim of his or her own creation. Other disclaimers include a slip of the tongue (sometimes attributed to Freud), being late, or various accidents not viewed as motivated, meaningful, and/or intended.

Ninety percent of our lives will be characterized by how we handle the 10 percent of what happens to us, yet most people look at that 10 percent and think of it as the characteristic 90 percent.

Experience is not just encountered, observed, or predetermined; it is also created moment by moment. You are the author of your story—its agent, creator, and casting director. When you acknowledge yourself as author of your story rather than passive participant, you recognize the active construction of experience. Discernment of a narrative or story line will reveal the underlying assumptions of the author who creates that narrative.

Once you own a feeling, such as anxiety, you can convert it to an intention. For example, fear of not being successful in a new venture can be converted to the intention to do research, become knowledgeable, and generate a game plan to proceed.

Ownership of a story is a gradual process, sometimes undertaken grudgingly and painstakingly, with few "Aha!" moments. Invisible assumptions and emotional agendas ghostwrite your life story and often manifest interpersonally. Every day of your life is a blank page for a portion of the next chapter of your life and money stories.

Peeling Back the Layers

To see your own money story for what it is, lay it out in the open to examine. To change it for the better, you need to see it in *all* its layers.

Look beyond your logical thoughts to truthfully answer these questions:

- Yes, but what have I done?
- What am I doing?
- Never mind my words—what are my actual behaviors?

To genuinely see your money story for what it is, we need to go even deeper than the simple behaviors themselves and explore the root feelings that lie behind the things you do with money. You need to examine the default assumptions and beliefs your story carries. The only way to get to work on the parts of your money story in need of change is to draw it out into the open, take a good look at it, and understand the hidden reasons why you do the things you do.

As you review your own story, both past and present, three steps can be helpful in directing your inquiry:

1. *What are the beliefs that form the premise of my money story?* You've already explored your feelings *about* money and the meanings you ascribe *to* money and its role in your life. These feelings and meanings crystallize as the beliefs you hold.

You may have learned some common money story themes from earlier models:

- Money doesn't grow on trees, you know. Do you think we're made of money?

- If it was good enough for your father and me, it's good enough for you.

- We deserve to have enough for the basic necessities; anything beyond that is greedy.

- You have to work really, really hard to make big money—and even if you do, it could be taken away from you.

- Money is the measure of what really counts; people can talk all they want, but until there's real money on the table, it's all hot air.

- Money and genuine value are mutually exclusive: there are people who chase money and people who do well in the world, and never the twain shall meet.

- Money *does* grow on trees: it's called credit, and if you're clever enough to know how to work it, there's an unlimited supply.

Although they appear as facts, beliefs, like actions, are personal creations. Fed by feelings, each belief emerged from an original adaptive decision at some point in your life and exists today as a decision that you continue to make. Remember that you are always free to change your mind.

2. *Can you track the point in time when you made the original decisions that led to each view or belief?* For some beliefs, an emotional coupling can follow a disappointment or painful episode. A child knowing about his parents' worries about money or the sudden loss of a job can lead to a decision to be anxious or cautious about finances. This guardedness may have beneficial results; for example, it may create a healthy motivation to save and prepare for the future or to carefully examine financial risks. But it can also lead to irrational and unhealthy money behaviors, such as a vague sense of shame that inhibits any honest discussion of money, avoiding even the reasonable risks necessary to growth, or difficulty charging a fair fee for your services as a way of not valuing your full worth.

Your genes do not carry monetary problems; however, an assumption such as victimhood or being chronically underpaid can become a powerfully organizing story line, even an aspect of identity.

3. *Look for the connection between the original decision and the view or perspective you now hold.* Acknowledge the impact your assumption has on your current life, the emotional and financial costs, and the exchanges that you make in its services. Examine each belief in turn, asking, regardless of its origin, whether it is serving you now?

For example, if your parents were secretive about money and uneasy talking about it, for you it was adaptive to restrain discussion about it. In other words, the decision may have served you at the time, but you may have now outgrown its usefulness. Is it still worth the price that you pay? Are you exchanging energy for your current restraint as well as missing out on valuable information or feedback?

Realize that you decide what to perceive. You also decide what meaning to attach—and you decide what behavior you'll associate with that meaning.

Assumptions and Motivations That Construct Story Lines

Beliefs and assumptions generate the possibilities that you see. They then govern how you process what you perceive as well as how successfully you perform. Beliefs become self-fulfilling prophecies.

Empowering Beliefs

- I will make a plan and follow it.

- I will do what's necessary to make good decisions.

- I am competent to achieve my goals.

- I can make the money I need.

- I can find a way to love my work.

Limiting beliefs also influence reality and behavior as well as having emotional and physical effects.

Limiting Beliefs

- What I do won't be seen as important.

- My opinion doesn't matter.

- I will never make all the money I need.

- No matter what I do, I will never get out of debt.

- I feel stuck in repeating negative actions.

As you transform beliefs, you write a new money story. Fundamental to any belief system is its point of reference. To initiate change, move your point of reference from external to internal, beginning with the following basic questions. Filling the space of the present moment with current feeling and experience leaves no space for old beliefs. Your old assumptions will not disappear, but you make them a memory rather than a lived experience.

You Can Change Your Mind, and It Will Change Your Life

- Is any pattern evident from your plot assessment?

- Do any themes stand out to you as you reflect on your responses?

- What do these patterns and themes articulate about how you think about yourself and others?
- How do they affect your money behavior?
- Do you see patterns repeating in your financial decisions?

Identify Basic Aspects of Your True Self

- What are you uniquely good at—better than almost anyone else?
- What are you most passionate about?
- What do you have special experience doing?
- What is your greatest personal ambition?

Create Your Own Experiences and Your Own Reality

- What is the biggest obstacle that you currently face?
- What is the biggest challenge you face now?
- What is the one thing you most want to change about your money story now?
- What is the one thing you most want to change about your relationship with money now?

Review Your Belief Systems

To challenge a belief, consider the following:

- Does this belief still work; does it help me to function optimally?
- If not, have I outgrown it or discovered that it is no longer true?
- What else would be possible if I were to discard it?
- What new belief would support me now?

Become Your Own Authority

- Have you taken ownership as author of your own story to examine the basic assumptions and motivations constructing your story lines?

- Are you doing what you want, or are you doing what you believe or feel you are supposed to do in each of the areas of your life?

- Are you using money in a compromising way?

- Are you avoiding decisions?

- Are you making bad decisions?

- Are you responding to the wants of others before meeting your own needs?

- What are you saying "Yes" to in your life that you need to say "No" to?

- What are you saying "No" to in your life that you need to say "Yes" to?

- Each of the story lines you create has its own history, its own consistency over time, and its own attachment pattern in your mind and brain.

You Are Both the Protagonist and the Antagonist in Your Story

Illuminating your money story, the plot and subplots, involves the same questions as understanding any other story:

- Identify and learn about the protagonist (you), your motives and conflicts, wishes and fears, the manifestations of your wishes and fears in your money drama, your entire internal experience, and how each scene ends: whether resolved or not, happy or not, complete or not.

- Identify the antagonist (you, also).

- Identify how the identified antagonist (your proxy) was carefully selected and identified as an external representation of some part of you. What part of you does the identified antagonist represent? It is not an accident that you chose the external antagonist out of millions of possibilities to be a specific representation of some part of you that is unrealized, disavowed, or repudiated.

- Is this antagonist like others in the past, with each relationship being the same process, only with different faces? For example, are you engaged in current financial struggles that are similar to those you had at earlier times in your life?

- Is there a consistent theme or pattern? For example, is the pleasure of purchasing an item greater than the pleasure of saving the same money for retirement?

These questions assess whether the past lives on in the present and in fact ghostwrites some of the present. Observing and owning repetitions of themes and story lines allow you to understand your core assumptions that generate these repetitions. You see what you believe and become it.

Listen for the Assumptions and Motivations Constructing Your Story Lines

Core assumptions form the basic beliefs about yourself. Organizing, powerful, and influential, they fashion the story lines of your life. The harder you try to disregard, disavow, or counter them, the more intense their influence becomes. The more intently you run from something, the more you engage it. You keep coming back to what you attempt to flee.

What behaviors have you tried in vain to change? Those instances point the way toward a core belief. Someone who is constantly trying to please, even to the point of subjugating personal needs and wants, may assume that love comes only from continually pleasing others by spending money on them. The best indicator of your beliefs and values is your behavior:

- What patterns can you find?

- Do any themes stand out to you as you reflect on your responses?

- What do you care passionately about?

- What is your greatest personal ambition?

- What do these patterns and themes articulate about how you think about yourself and others?

- How do they affect your behavior?

- Do you see the patterns repeating in various areas of your life?

Deconstruct a Money Concern (to See What It Teaches You)

If you have an active internal critic, let's consider how to transform your inner *critic* into an inner *coach* by listening to the rest of the story.

Write down the biggest money concern your inner critic says. Some examples are the following:

- I spend impulsively on things I don't need.

- I need to save more for retirement.

- I don't have a planned budget.

Listen for these four story lines in your concern: *anger, fear, request,* and *love*. Consider each statement from your internal critic as a self-care concern rather than a "dragon" that you have to eliminate. Listen for each of these four in the concern.

This is how each of the four story lines can sound—heard as a self-caring voice—for "I need to save more for retirement":

Anger: "I'm mad at you for not taking care of yourself and denying your future needs."

Fear: "I'm afraid you're neglecting to consider your needs in future years."

Request: "I want you to plan for a lifetime of financial well-being so that you don't have money worries in older years."

Love: "I want you to be around a long time, feel alive and energetic, and free from money worries."

You don't confront your dragons to defeat them; you confront them to get to know them—to learn what they've done for you so they can get the respect they deserve. Then, with the pride of a mission accomplished, those dragons can rest peacefully and let you proceed, knowing they're safe—and appreciated.

> Be careful lest in casting out your devil, you cast out the best thing in you. —Nietzsche

Can You Make and Enjoy Money?

Mark the following items "True" or "False":

1. Talking about money, even with my family, feels embarrassing and seems taboo.

2. I go on spending sprees I can't afford.

3. I seem to consistently lose money on investments.

4. I feel afraid and paralyzed about investing my money.

5. I don't seem to be taking the initiative to learn more about managing money or investing, and I still rely on other people to make decisions for me, even though they're not experts.

6. You've got to step on other people to really make money.

7. I need to have money in the bank to feel real.

8. No matter how much money I have, I always want more.

9. I use money to gain love and admiration, to compete with others, to show off my prosperity, or to gain revenge.

10. I grew up poor, and although I'm doing all right now, I still feel poor and insecure.

11. I have difficulty admitting my mistakes and cutting my losses.

12. I'm pretending to be content with my financial status only because I'm afraid to make any changes.

If you answered "True" to any of these questions, you're probably having some difficulty gaining, managing, or enjoying money. No matter what you earn, old perceptions may persist because the questions are about your feelings and assumptions. Feelings are at least as real as dollars. Both rich and poor are states of mind.

Money Myths

The more you understand the underlying meanings money holds for you, the more objective and functional will be your money goals and strategies. Money myths can shape personal behavior and lifestyle. Examples include a belief that money can solve all problems, purchase anything, or bring happiness.

The following exercise may illuminate any money myths you have. The goal is to see money simply as money:

1. Are your financial goals consistent with your self-image?

2. Are your financial goals consistent with the way you want to be?

3. Are you pretending to be content with your financial status only because you are afraid to try to change it?

4. Can you set specific, attainable financial goals? Or do you constantly feel that you need to achieve more?

5. When you arrive at a goal, do you feel satisfaction and enjoyment, or the ever-spiraling sense of wanting or needing more?

6. Are you willing to seek suggestions and advice, even differing opinions, to judge a prospective investment or business decision?

7. Are you derailing your own success by consistently avoiding the final step? Do you consistently pick the wrong investment?

8. Do you expect or allow other people to make money decisions for you, even if they are not experts?

9. Do you respond to your financial gains with depression? With a feeling of guilt?

10. Can you admit your mistakes and cut your losses?

11. Do you have trouble putting aside thoughts of "what might have been" if you had purchased or sold investments earlier?

12. Do you recognize your limits? Or do you feel that your expertise in one field will automatically transfer to another?

13. Do you go on spending binges you can't afford? Does shopping give you a "high"? Do you feel let down as soon as you bring home and unwrap a new purchase?

14. Do you spend money to compete with others, get revenge on others, or show off to others? Do you spend money to try to win other people's love or admiration?

15. Do you treat money as a permissible topic of discussion in your family? Is it the same as any other aspect of living rather than a taboo subject? In discussing money with your children, do you keep the conversation appropriate for your child's age and level of understanding?

16. Does money control your social life? Do you avoid going out with friends or dating because it costs too much? Do you go only to places and to events that are ostentatiously expensive? Do you hate to spend money, even in small quantities or on necessities?

17. Do you feel that you will ultimately have to pay in some way for doing well financially?

18. Do you have a clear game plan for your finances, with definite goals and methods of obtaining them?

19. Are your financial goals separate from your emotional goals as well as from your concept of happiness?

20. Do you have trouble establishing priorities or a balance of work and love or keeping boundaries between work and private life?

Seventeen Common Money Story Lines

The following common story lines use money to make their statement. The journey to assess your story involves first learning the language of money statements in order to recognize and own the story line. Then you can take steps to decide what to change, keep, enhance, or let go of.

Freedom

Fantasies abound that limitless wealth would solve problems of daily boredom, a sense of emptiness, or feelings of deprivation left over from childhood or that money will purchase internal freedom.

Money, a tangible commodity, doesn't buy intangibles, such as emotional freedom. Yet at some point, no money brings limitation. While money doesn't buy internal freedom, it certainly can purchase external ones, especially from those tasks that others are hired to do.

Love

A parent may substitute money or gifts in lieu of physical presence, such as in divorce situations. Money can be dealt with directly and tangibly. Cold cash can be used temporarily to satisfy a craving for warmth. It may seem easier to obtain and manipulate money than to build a loving relationship. John Lennon and Paul McCartney summarized the attempt: "I don't care too much for money, money can't buy me love."

Although not inherently equated with love, the language and expression of self-care does at times involve money. To love yourself requires earning the money you are worth and taking care of your money. Nurturing yourself includes the wise use of your money without subjugating your own needs.

Power

The ubiquitous fantasy of immense wealth—and thus of unlimited power—is a feature of the childhood desire to establish mastery.

Almost everyone equates wealth with power and aims for both. As a yardstick of achievement, money indicates the degree to which power and respect have been attained. Worth then becomes tangible and countable. When money symbolizes power, the story lines read as order, control, and responsibility. By social consensus, money measures power and status.

Autonomy

Individuals who have provided a model of success for their children offer an invaluable asset. Yet requiring success of their children in a prescribed way disrespects their autonomy and compromises the child's experience of mastery.

Dependency

Money is a tremendous force, one that determines where we live, how we live, and even what kind of food we eat. Money speaks the language of its author—as a declaration of dependence or a manifesto of independence.

Happiness

A fundamental human desire exists for happiness. At one time or another, everyone believes that more money will bring more happiness.

Research conclusions suggest that money, like Prozac, doesn't make you happy, but both can prevent certain forms of unhappiness. For example, money affords better medical care, safety, neighborhood, and gadgets and sometimes a better mood.

While a certain amount of money is necessary in order not to be preoccupied with it, beyond this point, greater money does not equal greater happiness. The most basic human motivation to be effective and experience mastery propels individuals to continue to work even when they no longer need money. Assets or acquisitions become yardsticks of achievement but not of happiness. The *process* creates happiness: the excitement and adventure of accomplishment, the scenarios of mastery. Money is the *result*.

Security

Financial security can simply be about money. Financial security is attainable. It requires a game plan with specific goals, a map to gauge progress, and measurable results to monitor arrival.

Emotional security using money will be a promise never kept. As long as someone continues to up the ante, the illusion of money as emotional comfort will never be confronted.

Worth

Reliance on the applause of external affirmation introduces vulnerability to money and possessions. But icons of self-worth won't be fully satisfactory without an internal standard, an ideal of "good enough."

Having clear, specific ideals and living up to them generates self-esteem. In fact, it is the only source of true self-esteem in adulthood.

Envy

Envy is an uncomfortable desire, sometimes infused with resentment, for what someone else possesses. Envy made the top seven of Dante's list of deadly sins. Jealousy, on the other hand, is the reaction to perceiving that someone is trying to take what is yours, such as in a love relationship.

A desire is not quieted by its satisfaction, and desires can be created by filling them. It is human sport to compare what others have to what you have. However, to compare your inside to someone else's outside is not an apples-to-apples measure. The desire for more riches, success, or power equals the fervor for possessions as the icons of that success.

Envy can be used productively. If we closely examine the enviable, we can learn what is useful and what is only image. Disclosures of salaries, bonuses, and perks can provide useful data, fuel motivation, or prompt appropriate dissatisfaction.

Opportunity

Expanding your thinking about money requires a parallel expansion of your thinking about life. Money is a promissory note for possibility but not for happiness or even success.

Those who operate on a scarcity model will live out this assumption and will struggle to acquire money. Those with an abundance model will create that for themselves.

Time

Money can buy time. You buy money with your time. You acquire money's energy by spending your effort and energy to purchase it. Time and money may influence how you think about your life. "How long does it take?" determines what you do. "How far away from work and school?" determines where you live. Yet time is time, and money is money.

After you purchase money with your time and energy, you buy back some of what you've forfeited. Every purchase is a dual transaction: you spend time and energy for money, then you spend that money for service (someone else's time) or goods (such as time-saving devices).

Clarify for yourself what time and energy you are spending, what you are buying, and what is the real cost and the value of each.

Alliance versus Exclusion

Spending money is a way of giving to yourself. And, like money, the process can be authentic or counterfeit. It can provide what you want and be a reward for accomplishment, or it can serve as a tangible proxy for an emotional need. Filling a want can obscure the need to take care of yourself emotionally or spiritually.

Desire versus Obstacle

Although desires are necessary and instructive, the pursuit of a desire can become so persistent that it becomes an identity. When the desire cannot be satisfied, its search intensifies. Unmet needs or disavowed values exaggerate desires. In *The Divine Comedy*, Dante wrote, "Hell is the state in which we are barred from receiving what we truly need because of the value we give to what we merely want."

The difference between need and want registers as deprivation. Wealth is when you have enough of what you don't need.

Control

Aren't even the best of parents slightly to surely guilty of manipulations and control of their children with money?

I recognized how blatantly obvious this was when each of my children left for college. After working out a reasonable budget, I stipulated that two things not on the budget were unlimited: the amount they spent for long-distance calls home and the amount for travel home. Of course, any calls or travel *other* than to come home *were* part of the budget. After all, there had to be limits.

Guilt

A parent may spend money on children to compensate for emotional or physical absence. The stereotype is the divorced "Disneyland Dad" who mitigates guilt by money and presents. Churches, charities, and florists frequently benefit from guilt payments.

Regulation

Earning money feels good. Money is a socially accepted metric of accomplishment and success in society. Sociological studies have demonstrated that both men and women feel good about making money and suffer downturns of emotional and physical health when they're no longer able to make money.

Competition

Money is a widely accepted yardstick of achievement. Those fortunate enough to realize their goals and dreams also face confrontation with what the success will and won't do, what it answers and what it doesn't. Getting the answer sometimes forces a change of the question.

STEP 3
Assess Your Money Story
Plot and Story Lines

R obert consulted me because he wanted to expand his business but felt stuck and dissatisfied. An acknowledged expert in a niche area, he supervised the work of some consultants he employed. Although he worked successfully on behalf of clients, his income didn't match his recognized expertise, and his work did not satisfy his own needs.

Robert knew that money resonated with emotional issues throughout his life. Money had been the language of care and love in his family, seemingly the tangible evidence that his parents loved him. He recognized that he had continued a story line: making substantial money meant he would give up his wish of being taken care of by someone else. Now, success and money accumulation meant taking care of himself. The impossible had become accessible—though now by his own efforts.

He recognized a disparity between his desire for achievement and success and his underlying wish to be taken care of. His wants, needs, and ideals were not in synchrony, nor were they aligned toward his goals.

He could now use this awareness as information to construct a new story rather than have it ghostwrite a new edition of the old story.

Robert recognized conflicting wants and needs as he progressed successfully toward goals in his business. He began taking care of himself in a much better way.

The result of our work was that Robert worked happily at doing what he did uniquely well. He leveraged his time and income by training and licensing people in his method and franchised a component of his firm to a national group for significant residual income.

The assumptions and beliefs that determine your money story deserve full attention. You are the sole author of your money story. You are always free to change your mind, beliefs, and assumptions.

After awareness and ownership, you can assess the behaviors, hidden messages, and elusive language of mind and emotion in your money story.

The ultimate practical purpose of the assessments is discovering what works and what doesn't work.

Assessment involves four components:

- Monitor your choices.

- Question your ideas.

- Probe your reasoning.

- Ask clearly and honestly, "Does it work?"

Money Memories, Meanings, and Maturity

The assumptions and beliefs that determine your money story deserve full attention. These exercises will illuminate invisible decisions camouflaged as beliefs and assumptions.

Money Memories

As you were growing up, what notions were presented to you regarding money, its use, and its importance?

Were the principles presented to you consistent with what you saw your parents doing?

How did your parents behave with money?

How did they regard those who had less money than they did?

How did they regard those who had more money than they did?

Spend a few minutes writing anything and everything that comes to mind about your childhood experiences, fantasies, attitudes, and ideas regarding money.

Money Meanings

Spend a few minutes writing every word, phrase, image, feeling, and experience that the word "money" brings to mind. Write about what you use money to express or do:

For yourself?
For (or to) others?
As a reward for obedience or performance?
To enhance growth?
To create opportunity?
For control (such as buying for others what you really want yourself)?
For punishment by withholding?
To manipulate behaviors or attachments?
What are your current beliefs about money and your attachment
    to it?

Some examples of beliefs:

- People who have considerable money are lucky.

- People get money when and if they deserve it.

- Wealth and spirituality are mutually exclusive.

- People of wealth are different.

- It's difficult to make a living in this economy.

Money Maturity

Be empathic with yourself rather than judgmental or critical. The observations can become reference points for what to keep, enhance, avoid, or let go:

How open are you about money details with your children?
How fully and honestly do you speak with your spouse or partner
    about money, finances, spending, goals, savings, and debt?
Step outside yourself and become your own mentor. Write the
    most important things you currently observe about money
    and your money story.

Does your current financial picture allow you to use your ability to achieve your personal mission? Professional mission? Do you have a money mission statement?

Distinguish and Address Ideals

Your ideals are your internal standards of excellence. They are your core values, your personal model of what has genuine worth. When we live up to our ideals, we feel a sense of worth and esteem. When we don't, we feel shame and lack of fulfillment. Your ideals resonate with the core essence of who you *are*.

There are dozens of possible ideals. The key is to identify those few that are your guiding priorities, those core ideals that are most important to you, those you most passionately believe in. Your core ideals may shift or evolve as you progress through life, but they will not stray far from the "home base" of who you are.

From the list below, choose the *three* ideals that are most important to you. Choose those values that inspire you, not those you think you *should* value, that society tells you to value, or that you see others holding as valuable.

This list is not exhaustive; feel free to add others. You may find it easier to work through the list choosing more than three and then go back over it again to narrow your list down. Once you've finished, fill in the three blanks at the bottom with your chosen three top ideals:

Achievement
Adventure
Beauty
Catalyze
Charity
Connectedness
Contribute
Creativity
Dignity
Discovery
Family
Feel
Freedom

Generosity
Growth
Happiness
Health
Honesty
Independence
Individuality
Influence
Intimacy
Justice
Kindness
Knowledge
Leadership
Learning
Mastery
Peace
Pleasure
Power
Self-esteem
Sensitivity
Spirituality
Success
Teaching
Truth
Winning
Other:

List your top three ideals in order of most to least important.

Guidelines for Living Your Ideals

Once you've clarified your ideals, consider ways you might begin to incorporate them into your life.

1. *See how they apply.* Consider the different areas of your life—career story, relationships, money story, and wellness story—and explore how each of the top three ideals you've identified here applies to or reveals itself in each of these areas.

2. *Honor your order of priorities.* Recognize and honor the hierarchy of ideals when making decisions. For example, the immediate needs of your child might supersede a desire to learn and be creative.

3. *The price.* Each ideal carries with it an accompanying personal cost in commitment to uphold and honor that ideal. For example, there will inevitably be sleepless nights and boring moments involved in raising a child.

4. *Live your ideals.* Think of yourself as a tigress and your ideals as your cubs: they are your life, and you will do anything and everything to protect them. If you feel you have not been entirely true to your ideals or protected them with that kind of fierce integrity, then choose this moment as your time to reclaim them.

If you are unclear about any one of the ideals you've identified, spend additional time focusing on it, and if you feel it's necessary, rewrite that list until it rings unquestionably true for you.

Distinguish and Address Needs

Unlike ideals, which are standards of value to which we aspire, a need is an essential in our lives, a necessity for mind, body, or spirit. Early in life, our needs consist of physical nurturance, empathic attunement, attachment, effectiveness, exploration, assertion, feeling and tension regulation, and sensory satisfactions. In adulthood, our needs become adult versions of these same basics, all providing for physical requirements, comfort, identity, affirmation, love, communication, safety, and sexual/sensual satisfactions.

Consistently meeting your own needs produces a sense of effectiveness and optimum functioning, like the satisfaction of having completed a task or project, knowing you have given it everything you have. Frustrated or unmet needs create the opposite feeling, one of constant discomfort and ineffectiveness. For example, when the basic need for human connection is derailed or nonexistent, we feel an emotional disharmony. A need may be most obvious when it is unmet.

As with ideals, each of us is unique and has a particular set of needs that we value more highly than the others. From the following list of needs, choose the *three* that are most important to you. This list isn't exhaustive; feel free to add others:

Acceptance
Accomplishment
Acknowledgment
Actualization
Care
Certainty
Comfort
Communication
Control
Duty
Effectiveness
Emotional security
Empathy
Financial security
Focus attention
Harmony
Intimacy
Nurturance
Order
Physical activity
Recognition
Regulation
Relaxation
Safety
Self-control
Significance
Simplicity
Strength
Time alone
Variety
Other:

List your top three needs in order of most to least important.

When your needs and ideals are in synchrony with each other and combined with a clear vision and defined goals, all of your efforts go in the same direction. It will feel right and lead to mastery.

A discrepancy can exist for organizational systems as well as for individuals. For example, corporate *ideals* might include teamwork, leadership, caring for and promoting the creativity of employees, innovation, and realizing human potential. Corporate *needs* include productivity and the bottom line of profit and loss. When the core ideals of a corporation parallel the core values of an individual within that corporation, both grow.

Distinguish Wants from Needs

Wants or desires are not fundamental constructs like needs or values. A want can be replaced with another want, and fantasies are readily interchangeable—but one need cannot substitute for another need.

While both ideals and needs spring from the very essence of who we are, wants are far more circumstantial. A particular want, for example, may arise as the temporary manifestation of an unmet need from the past, such as the unmet need for affirmation as a child, which results, in adulthood, in the relentless pursuit of validation, accolades, and accomplishments. While needs are universal, wants are tied to uniquely personal experiences with their own particular histories.

Unsatisfied wants may derive from not having a defined goal (not having a definition of *enough*) or from trying to satisfy a past want in present time. While you can get sick if you don't get enough of a need, you can also get sick if you get *too much* of a want. And you can never get enough of what you don't need.

If the desires you have don't serve you, *you can choose new ones* that are in alignment with your needs—and your ideals. For example, you can spend based on who you are, not on who you want to be. People may buy something to pursue a hope or dream, expecting it will change who they are. Disappointment sets in when the books on cameras don't make someone a photographer or tapes on learning a foreign language don't produce proficiency. Consider spending on some reward or when you need something rather than with the expectation that it will change who you are.

Ideals and Needs Decision Tree

Ideals and needs can be used to inform decisions and evaluate goals. This decision tree is one way to systematically assess and plan:

Ideal + Need → Goal → Commitment → Fulfillment → Self-validation

Conflicting needs, wants, and values hinder our performance and drive us to invest time, money, and energy in things that don't fulfill us. Accordingly, it makes sense to weigh every significant decision you make against your ideals, needs, and wants *before* you make the decision:

- If the decision meets all three, it's a "Yes."

- If the decision is in alignment with your ideals and needs but seems to be in conflict with a particular want, it's a "Maybe." Examine this particular want to see if it is significant enough to veto the decision. Since wants are more transitory than ideals and needs, a sound decision may overrule a want.

- If the decision opposes or does not meet one of your needs or ideals, then the decision can be "No" or "On hold."

This alignment of ideals, needs, and wants can be applied to establishing direction and goals in all significant areas of life: home, career, relationships, way of being, business, personal success, financial plan, and spiritual development.

We live in a culture that is often very goal oriented. There is nothing wrong with being focused on a goal—as long as the goal aligns well with your ideals and needs. If it does not, then you are working at cross-purposes and cannot possibly win because if you win, you lose.

Before adopting a goal as your own, examine it closely to see whether it is in synch with your top ideals and needs. If it does align well with your ideals and needs, then move to *commitment*. When the goal is aligned with your ideals and needs, it is an expression of who you are.

Once you have committed to the goal, then be loyal to yourself by *fulfilling* that commitment, not simply because you said you would but because that goal is an integral expression of your ideals and needs, and thus a full-out pursuit of it—not only its final accomplishment but also the journey along the way—serves as an essential *validation* of your genuine worth.

Listen to Your Self-Statements

We perceive from within our experience and perspective. What we say and do are inevitable self-statements of our beliefs and personal realities. We believe according to our self-images. Everything that we say is about ourselves.

The value of owning self-generating statements lies in being able to discover unconscious themes as they are played out in front of us.

We always perceive and create outside to match inside, so pay attention to what you consistently like and dislike in another. Everything you say and do is a self-statement. Acknowledge and own everything about yourself. Take yourself very personally. Listen carefully and explicitly to all the messages from your interior, to your whole truth. Feelings never lie; the body cannot deceive.

Everyone else also makes self-statements. What someone says about you has everything to do with him or her even though it's focused on you. If someone is being critical and judgmental of you, you can decide whether to believe and accept that point of view. Listen but don't take it personally (only a theory is ever this simple and clear). All anyone else can do is share their experience of you; it's still *their* experience and perception, their own point of view. You can share your own experience of someone else but be aware that your perceptions are also filtered through your own lens.

Sometimes you can recognize something the first time only by denying it.

Your old story may have included displacing aspects of yourself onto others, a desired or a disavowed part of yourself. You can even fall in love with who you hope someone will become rather than who he or she is. Or you can fall in love with your own ideal projected onto someone else. This hope may be for your own unmet needs or for a piece of your life not yet lived. In this way, however, hope is maintained in an old context, and past needs cannot be met in the present. Past needs become present wants.

Other disclaimed action has to do with one's mind, as if thoughts and feelings existed apart from one's mind, and passively insert themselves:

"The thought came to my mind." "My mind played tricks on me." "My doubt stopped me." These locutions disclaim oneself as agent, as author of thoughts, feelings, and experiences, as if your mind were the subject rather than the creator of your thoughts and feelings. Other disclaimers include a slip of the tongue (sometimes attributed to Freud), being late, or various accidents not viewed as motivated, meaningful, and/or intended.

Internal dramas can convert into interpersonal ones, assigning roles to others, roles that originate from an aspect of self, externalized and ghostwritten for another to enact. The most dramatic roles can convert into disavowed ones, such as in blaming someone else so that you yourself become the victim. The idealized version of oneself, never quite attained, may be assigned to a caretaker hero. The shining armor of this hero inevitably becomes rusty over time with disappointment and disillusionment. In order to grow, you must assume responsibility for your own life to become your own hero.

Understand Conflicted and Contradictory Story Lines

Invisible story lines and emotional agendas can make intelligent, sophisticated, reasonable, talented, dependable, ethical people act goofy about certain things. The messages will keep repeating themselves—people will keep writing the same money stories that imprison them—until they are listened to.

Here's a question to consider: As you look at your life and money stories, your thoughts and beliefs, do you perceive a flow, or does there appear to be some pattern of disharmony?

As you begin to discover them, you will likely find a collection of conflicting ideas. The conflicts are a direct result of how you accumulate beliefs as you grow and mature. Much of the programming is wired in the first years of life. Additions from relationships, school, community, and jobs further establish the programming. It is a mixture of unexamined material, the remnants and scraps of the stories of others, patched together by emotion and judgment. It becomes an inner voice as well as the blueprint from which the outer experience is built. It also explains why we may experience an internal tug-of-war, wanting something and not wanting it. Conflicting thoughts and feelings are like having a foot on the gas pedal and the other on the brake.

For success in any area, you must be in a state of coherence. Resolving the crosscurrents of conflict and gaining clarity about what you do want maximizes the likelihood you can create outer experiences to match the internal ones.

Ultimately, however, you must determine which obstacles are generated from within and which are external.

- In your life story, is all of yourself going in the same direction, or do you seem to undermine yourself in certain areas of your life?

- In your money story, do all the story lines fit and advance the plot?

Compromises Inventory

Compromise: Something you tolerate that takes time, energy, peacefulness, or money from you in a recurring, unsatisfying way. Compromises seemingly avoid conflict and strive to create a certain appearance.

Compromises of money behavior can be a result of using money to regulate mood or of equating money with many of the things that inherently have nothing to do with money.

Compromises of financial decisions can include not having a money mission statement, lack of a specific plan and goals, or engaging in one of several emotional fallacies regarding finances.

Compromises can result from disregarding a personal need or being disloyal to a personal ideal.

In the exercise that follows, list your three most significant current compromises of money behavior or financial decision making.

- Design a time goal by which you will resolve, reframe, or accept each compromise to reclaim the engagement and energy given to it.

- Choose to resolve it by a certain date, for example, to make a budget within seven days.

- Reframe the toleration by moving resolution to a certain future date to avoid its being a daily energy drain.

- Distinguish reframing from procrastination.

- Or accept a concession that you have no control over and cannot determine, such as the economy or taxes; move it to the acceptance list to disengage from it.

After each of the three primary financial compromises, write the need or value you will honor as you resolve the compromise.

Compromises Resolution Schedule

Financial Compromise No. 1
I choose to: ____ Eliminate by (give date):
           ____ Move to: Year 20___ list___
           ____ Accept and assign it to my:
              ____ Gratitude List
              ____ Worry List
              ____ Forever List
Strategy:
The need or value I will honor to resolve the compromise:

Financial Compromise No. 2
I choose to: ____ Eliminate by (give date):
           ____ Move to: Year 20___ list___
           ____ Accept and assign it to my:
              ____ Gratitude List
              ____ Worry List
              ____ Forever List
Strategy:
The need or value I will honor to resolve the compromise:

Financial Compromise No. 3
I choose to: ____ Eliminate by (give date):
           ____ Move to: Year 20___ list___
           ____ Accept and assign it to my:
              ____ Gratitude List

_____ Worry List

_____ Forever List

Strategy:

The need or value I will honor to resolve the compromise:

A Five-Phase Plot Outline

Phase 1. Assess your present situation

- Where are you now?

- What money behaviors and financial goals that are consistent with your beliefs and ideals are you willing to commit to?

- What has worked? What has not worked?

- What has been missing that if you added now would enhance your life?

Phase 2. Visualize and generate possibilities

- Where are you going?

- What defines success? How will it look and feel?

Phase 3. Design a specific plan

- Create a mission that is stronger than your fear.

- Design a plan that honors your uniqueness, needs, and values.

- Establish a strategy and a series of specific, compelling, and short-term goals to arrive at a big-picture goal.

Phase 4. Work through each initiative and next best action for each goal.

Phase 5. Consider the impact of change on your identity. Your vision may involve changes in such fundamental notions as how and who you see yourself to be.

Remember: A habit is not a definition. It's a choice that gets repeated.

STEP 4
Decide What to Change
in Your Money Story

Jean-Paul Sartre tells a story about a young married couple who have breakfast together each morning. After breakfast, the wife kisses her husband good-bye and sits by the window all day to cry until he returns. When he does, she perks up. The psychologically minded might see this young woman as suffering from separation anxiety.

Consider that she actually suffers from a fear of freedom. As soon as her husband leaves, she is free to do whatever she wants, but this freedom terrifies her—paralyzes her.

People are often experts about what is missing in their lives, experiences they haven't had, and what their lives would be like if they were to have them. Yet they also have a very limited repertoire of possibilities of how their lives would be better if these missing things were to actually happen.

While everyone wants more money, "more" has no end point. And beyond the initial flurry of the fantasy purchases, how would more money make your life different? What problems would it actually solve?

Alfred Adler, one of Freud's earlier followers, did an initial interview with a patient. After a comprehensive evaluation, a detailed family history, and an elaborate account of what the man was suffering from, Adler asked the man, "What would you do if you were cured?" The man answered him.

Adler said, "Well, go and do it then."

That was the treatment. This man did not need psychoanalytic interpretation, to mourn missed opportunities, or to understand the dynamics of conflict or unconscious motivation. Since his problem was initiating action, when he did that, he had no more problems.

Jung said that some problems can't be solved—they have to be outlived. When people change their minds and create new experiences, new neural networks and brain connections occur. Success involves creating a new story inside and outside: an evolving internal model combined with new experiences.

Four Basic Inquiries for Money Story Evaluation

1. What do you want to *change*? Anything you consider a problem, barrier, or obstacle is created by you and cannot continue to exist without you. It is not a simple matter of getting over it, countering, or adapting to it: it will remain until you create something else through thought, feeling, and action. Consider creating something else instead.

An example is fear of public speaking. One approach: to convert the fear into an action plan that includes joining Toastmasters to practice in a safe environment. By confronting the fear and setting goals that will resolve it, you overwrite the old story of ineffectiveness and convert the worry or fear into an intention.

What are three behaviors or beliefs that you could change, reverse, or leverage to help you toward financial success?

2. What do you want to *let go*? In order to change, you also have to know what you want to let go. The bottom line, no matter how entrenched the process or how strong the hope, is "Does it work?"

As you evaluate, you may find things that you wished and hoped were different but remain unsatisfied. This is the time to decide whether changing your strategy would make a difference or whether it's best to let go and free your attention for creating other things. Emotionally, this may be difficult, but determine to learn what you can from it so that it becomes an opportunity for self-awareness and correction that will enhance your future stories. In this way, you are learning to convert what could have been perceived as failure into growth.

Review your money beliefs and behaviors. If you could eliminate three of them from your life, which ones would have the most impact?

3. What do you want to *avoid*? There is always the pull of the old and the fear of the new. Yet there is no future in repetition. For example,

avoiding engagement with someone who is draining protects your energy for a more productive choice.

What three things can you avoid that will positively rewrite your money story?

4. What do you want to *keep and enhance*? Your money story, like your life story, is the manifestation of your beliefs. Changing your mind changes your brain and your life: beliefs, goals, and visions drive action. Choose carefully what you engage.

Choose three areas of your existing money story that you'd like to keep or enhance.

Principles of Change

Some change occurs from the inside out, from examining and altering thoughts and feelings, with the resultant change in behavior. Some change occurs from the outside in, from adapting to new experiences or situations. Each individual usually has a favorite mode of how he or she works best, from the inside out or the outside in. And at times, a situation mandates change. A change in behavior, feelings, or thinking can lead the way to affect the other two.

In my work as an executive mentor, there are some things I have come to appreciate about change that differ from my former work as a psychoanalyst:

- The prerequisite to change is not necessarily insight and understanding. You have to be in a new story before you can give up an old story. Significant life change occurs not by interpretation of the unconscious but by doing and experiencing things differently in the present moment.

- Someone does not have to be motivated to begin doing something. An action can generate its own motivation. The professional athletes and actors I work with are not motivated to go to the gym each day. They just do it because they know that's what they need to do. What is needed, rather than motivation, is having a plan and sticking to it.

- Change requires ownership of a story—an authorship that is active, self-determined, and not ghostwritten by past experiences or fate.

Four principles of change have powerful application in initial revision of a money story:

1. *Change begins with the recognition that you are the author of your own life and money stories.* The dramas of your everyday life do not just affect you—they are created by you. Whatever you think, feel, and experience is what you create each minute. Your experiences are always consistent with your theories.

As improbable as it may seem at times, you internally author your life drama. Even your most painful current scenarios originate within yourself. In order to create freedom, you first have to be aware that you are not free. Awareness begins the process, but awareness alone does not create change.

On the surface, people may hear what you say, but they also sense and react to the deeper levels of what you feel and believe. These levels sometimes conflict. You may attempt to project an air of confidence while being in doubt at deeper levels. This incongruence is detectable by others, whether consciously or not, and affects the way they will respond to you. You are always teaching others how to respond to you.

Habitual modes for doing things are still decisions. Everything we do is an active decision, even automatic responses using the default mode. When you have to make a choice and don't make it, you've already made it. We omit, disregard, or exclude the intolerable, the dangerous, and the unacceptable. We do not perceive the unimaginable. And we inevitably revise history to make it a continuity with the perceived present.

By opting for repetition, people sabotage invention and imprison creativity. The same behavior repeated long enough begins to seem like fate, an outlook that can lead to despair. However pristine the theory or esteemed the therapist, mentor, or coach, the ultimate question is, "Does it work?" New theories alone will not drive old lived experiences into extinction. Insight, understanding, and theory do not create change. Change requires a new lived experience to replace old lived experiences, coupled with evolving your internal model to incorporate that change, including how you regard yourself.

Two vignettes illustrate subtle repetitions cloaked in the disguise of learning:

- Brian, a professional coach I was mentoring, noted with exasperation about his client, "There's no place to put new learning in his head." His client linked new information to an existing or past experience, a focus that kept him from learning from the new information. I helped him address the process of repetition and introduce ways of rearranging to the position of "beginner's mind" to embrace curiosity and openness to stay in touch with new experiences and information to learn from it.

- Many years ago, a colleague who sat next to me at a professional meeting commented about his motivation to attend the meeting: "I come here to have what I do every day validated." His search for validation obfuscated some possibilities of finding new and different information or perspectives to consider.

In order to change, you first have to know what you want to change—that is, know what you do not want in your life and what you want to create instead. Without this awareness, meaningful and systematic change cannot occur.

Doing something differently, being a contrarian, is not change because it uses another person or idea as a point of reference and simply opposes it.

Reinvention begins with taking ownership of what you do rather than living out what just seems to happen or feeling victimized by forces beyond your control. You have written the script of your life and remained loyal to it, even those parts that may not work for your best and highest good. Your life is the manifestation of your beliefs. The world occurs to you in the way you believe it to be.

2. *If you want to change your life, first change your mind.* How do you take an inventory of beliefs that are self-limiting, conflictual, and compromising if they are experienced as reality? Think of it in terms of impressionist painting, with each of your experiences a dab of paint on a pointillist canvas. Only when you step back and view the entire picture do you recognize that the points form a pattern of a particular segment of life and that the

segments have their own unity. You create each experience, the patterns, and the composite image—and all are at different levels of awareness.

Beliefs may be conflicting, as in a woman who indicated that she wanted to lose weight yet wanted to enjoy life, food, and her summer free of dieting.

Letting go of a belief is a change. Outdated convictions inhabit a museum of beliefs, on the shelf near Santa Claus, neighbor to the inadequacy fear, set on the floor above that crack you cannot step on to protect your mother's back.

Informed change requires you to determine where you are now, decide where you want to go, and figure out how to get there. With a goal and a plan, you can stay on track, recognize and avoid detours and tangents, and move more effectively toward your goals.

Without a plan, you can't know where you are and can't strategize how to get to where you want to go. If you don't know where you want to go, you can't figure out how to get there. And once you create a plan, you have to remain loyal to it through consistent attention.

If you encounter a barrier or obstacle to your success, the solution is not getting over it, countering it, solving it, or getting around it. It is not there until you create it. Consider the possibility of not creating the obstacle, of shifting your focus to create something else instead—no longer problems but possibilities.

A component of every internal obstacle is the associated desire. Regard the obstacle not as the problem but as a guide to the hidden desire. For example, someone fears initiating a job interview. Rather than maintaining the obstacle by dwelling on previous unsatisfactory encounters, the fear can be converted to an intention with a preparation plan and a commitment for the interview. A century ago, philosopher and psychologist William James wrote that the greatest discovery of his generation was that human beings could alter their lives by altering their attitudes of mind. Billions of words and millions of therapy sessions later, the idea often still eludes us.

3. *You are always free to change your mind, always free to change your beliefs and core assumptions about who and what you are.* Changing your mind not only alters your brain but also transforms your life. But first you have to become aware. Prediction and expectation based on the past create repetition but based on the present and future create possibilities. A belief

system constructs an obstacle or an opportunity. Any effort to change your past is futile, as your past is over and gone.

For example, succeeding at a goal of being a giving person, subjugating your needs to those of someone else, may lead to a failure of your own growth and self-actualization. What you believe will come true. What you say to yourself, *all of it*, will make a difference. Know what you do not want to create and what you want to create instead.

No one can believe in you more than you can believe in yourself. Because you live the vision of yourself and actualize your goals, be absolutely certain that you clearly and consciously know your goals.

4. *You have to have a new story to be in before you can give up an old story.* To change, you have to develop a life story that contains the story lines you want. To stop doing something is not complete change—a new story incorporates new behavior and beliefs. You have to embody—actually live—this story you want. Good theory is not enough. Abstaining from an old story, such as excessive spending, is a beginning:

What is the biggest obstacle that you face currently?
What is the biggest challenge you face now?
What is the one thing you most want to change about your life now?
What is the one thing you most want to change about your finances now?

Regard of the Use of Money

This exercise requires looking at your money story from different perspectives:

- The three things you have done with money that make you most proud

- The three things you have done with money that are most embarrassing or shameful

- The three best money investments you have made

- The three worst mistakes you have made about money

- The three worst money investments you have made

- The three smartest money choices you've ever made

Personal Feedback Questionnaire

First determine who knows you best and who will give straightforward feedback (family, colleagues, boss, minister, etc.). Ask them to jot down their impressions, opinions, and suggestions about you and what each sees in you regarding the following:

- Strengths

- Potential

- Special skills

- Personal and career possibilities

- Blind spots

- Unrealized potential

- Winning strategy (personality style that you most rely on, even when it doesn't work)

- Next step to take

- Distractions/derailers

- Work environment in which you would perform best

- Work environment you should avoid

What did you learn from the feedback you received? How will you use their feedback to create a strategy for proceeding in each area of your life?

Knowing what you want to achieve is crucial, with a game plan, specific steps, and measurable results.

Review your responses in these four areas:

- What do you want to achieve?

- What do you want to maintain without change?

- What do you want to change?

- What do you want to eliminate or avoid?

Prioritizing Goals

1. Which of the issues will resolve itself without your doing anything?

2. What is the one thing that bothers you the most?

3. Choose the issue to resolve that would make the biggest difference in reducing your stress level.

4. Is there anything blocking your ability to get this done?

5. What have you learned that would be useful to you in this focus?

6. Can you imagine what would happen if you viewed a fear of making a mistake as an indication that a problem needs to be solved rather than as a sign of danger?

Twenty-four Considerations to Construct a New Money Story®

1. *You always have the right to say yes or no.* Don't hesitate to say "No" or "Yes." So don't hesitate to ask, such as a simple request for a fee or service equal to its value.

2. *You have to be free to say "No" before you can be free to say "Yes."* Unless you are free to say "No," "Yes" has no meaning.

3. *Coming to the end of your past, even resolving emotional issues isn't enough; you have to have a purpose, a dream, in order to give hope a blueprint.* The plot and financial strategies of your money story provide the organization; the goals provide the direction.

4. *Have a "big picture" of your money story and bring it into focus whenever necessary.* The big picture consists of your own ideals and principles and objectively organizing your life and decisions according to what you believe to be in your best interest.

5. *Distinguish need from want.* A *need* is an essential requirement, a necessity for mind, body, or spirit. *Wants* (wishes or desires) are replaceable with other wants, but a need cannot substitute for another need. And you can never get enough of what you don't need.

6. *Establish priorities.* Prioritize plans and pursuits based on core values and needs. Money and finances must be balanced with family, work, health, friendships, leisure, and taking care of yourself. Neglect or imbalance in one area may generate overcompensation in other areas. Every day, you will redefine and refine priorities and make decisions based on a fundamental question: What is really important?

7. *Disengage from "what might have been."* If you attempt to re-enter an old story and acquire what you missed in the past, it won't work because it is no longer the past. You lose today and tomorrow when you look back for yesterday. "If only" fantasies erode the power of today. When you let go of the past, you reclaim your aliveness in the present. To keep a goal just out of reach maintains the "someday" fantasies associated with it. "I'll make one more big deal, and then I'll be happy." The goal must remain elusive in order for you to continue to hold the hope of happiness. Only the unattainable becomes addictive. It's difficult to sell a stock that has declined significantly. The sale makes a reality of money loss rather than a theory of paper loss. The sale also banishes the hope of future gains.

8. *Seek out suggestions, critique, and advice.* Consult with people knowledgeable in specific areas. At times, this may be difficult emotionally, when it would seem easier to consult (collude) with someone who would mirror and agree with your own opinions. Seek those who are expert in areas other than your own and those with different points of view. Listen from another's perspective while not abandoning your own. Use new information from a flexible and informed position.

9. *Recognize that there are few true emergencies in life.* Weighing different factors, gathering data, and perhaps consulting experts are the best approaches to most decisions. Rarely does any legitimate crisis demand that these steps be skipped. A classic example is the promoter who tries to push you into an overnight decision, to make money decisions in a fraction of the time it took to earn the money. Decisions based on impulse, frustration, or anger may need to be postponed until objectivity is regained. Calling a *time-out* is a useful maneuver for emotionally charged matters. "Let me think about that and I'll get back to you" *is* a decision.

10. *What you decide to accept undergoes a change.*

11. *The current moment has its own needs.* To get what you always wanted in the past may not feel as good as you thought it would because it is no longer the past.

12. *To establish a goal, ask yourself, "What is good enough?"* The goal of "more money" can never be reached because it has no end point. More money, like perfection, is a quest never satisfied.

13. *The past may not be the best or the more relevant context in which to understand the present.* Peter Bernstein, the man *Money* magazine says knows more about investing than anyone alive, calls extrapolation errors investors' most common mistake. When we predict the future based on the past, we forget that anything can happen. We do not and cannot know the future.

14. *The capacity to endure uncertainty is the essence of growth.* And, as a wise mentor once told me, "Never speak more clearly than you think."

15. *Not only can you change, you can also choose how you change.* You are always free to change your mind. Just be sure it's for the right reasons. One year from now, what will you be glad you've done?

16. *Growth and change involve their own mourning.* You have to relinquish a past position in order to move ahead. Mourning

that fantasy of what might have been is more difficult than mourning the disappointment of what actually was. The more you focus on how much you missed, the more you lose now.

17. *The only familiar territory is behind you.* Danish philosopher Søren Kierkegaard said, "Life can only be understood backwards, but it must be lived forwards."

18. *Our outcomes are always consistent with our theories.* To attempt change by changing your behavior often produces new editions of the old experience. To truly change, you must also transform your basic model of how you understand new experiences.

19. *Align internal and external goals.* The clarity and consistency of your principles and goals can be called on at times of emergency or confusion to help bring the big picture into focus. Be certain there is a fit between your internal and external goals, that what you want to accomplish is consistent with your ideals. This consistency can provide an organizing structure and direction to your ambition.

20. *Know what reaching a goal will do.* It is important to know what achieving a goal will do in order to distinguish clearly what it will not do. For example, reaching a goal will neither undo the past nor make other troubles go away. Monetary wealth may bring many things, but it may not make your marriage better.

21. *You'll never do anything important that will feel comfortable in the beginning.*

22. *Trying to change your past is not change, as it will always be the way it was.*

23. *Decisions always limit some choices while expanding others.*

24. *You suffer most from your anticipations and limit yourself most by your assumptions.*

STEP 5
Map Changes: Inscribe New Code

A man approached financier J. P. Morgan, held up an envelope, and said, "Sir, in my hand I hold a guaranteed formula for success, which I will gladly sell you for $25,000."

"Sir," Morgan replied, "I do not know what is in the envelope; however, if you show it to me, and I like it, I give you my word as a gentleman that I will pay you what you ask."

The man agreed to the terms and handed over the envelope. Morgan opened it and extracted a single sheet of paper. He gave it one look, a mere glance, then handed the piece of paper back to the man and wrote him a check for $25,000.

There were two sentences on the page:

- Every morning, write a list of things that need to be done that day.

- Do them.

Dr. Vernon Smith won a Nobel Prize in Economics in part by demonstrating how market bubbles are created.[1] In a series of trading experiments with economics graduate students, they were informed that the fair value of a security was $3.00. These student traders knew the *actual worth* of the security—a significant advantage over the normal Wall Street trader situation. What happened in price bidding? They still ran the price up significantly past the $3.00 mark. When other traders in the experiment stopped paying a premium, the laboratory market crashed.

In a second experiment, the same group formed another, smaller bubble. It was only on the *third time* around that the investors wised up enough to stay with the security's actual value—even though they had known this from the very start. When Dr. Smith repeated the experiment with finance professors and other economic specialists, they formed the same kind of bubbles, followed by the same crashes.

Bubbles are formed by optimism and collective tilt getting in a feedback loop: increasing prices stimulate optimism, causing more buying with price increases until the bubble (the state of mind) shifts. It's the equivalent of the child who said, "The Emperor doesn't have on any clothes."

This seemingly irrational force that overrides our logic and knowledge and causes us to believe that rising prices will continue to rise indefinitely—or at least as long as we're betting on them—is called human behavior.

Fourteen Principles to Organize the Plot of Your New Money Story®

Using the following principles as a guide, consider what you want to change, let go, and avoid and enhance in your New Money Story.

1. *Your beliefs form the premise of your money story.* Review and reflect on the answers you completed in the section "Money Memories, Meanings, and Maturity" in chapter 9. Your beliefs generate the story lines that impact ways of being, quality of life, career, business, personal success, financial success, and spiritual development. Beliefs exist as decisions you make. Although they appear to be facts, beliefs as well as actions are personal creations.

Each belief emerged from an original decision that was once adaptive.

2. *Track when in time you made the original decision that led to each view or belief.* For example, an original decision often follows disappointments or painful episodes. A child knowing parents' worries about money or being without a job can lead to a decision to be anxious or cautious about finances. This guardedness may have beneficial results to motivate savings or to carefully examine risk. It could also result in shame to restrain discussion of money, fear to avoid risk necessary to growth, or difficulty charging a full, fair fee for your services as a way of not valuing your full worth.

Your genes do not carry problems, including monetary ones. However, an assumption such as victimhood or being chronically underpaid can be a powerfully organizing story line, even an aspect of identity.

3. *Look for the link/connection between the original decision and the view or perspective you hold.* Acknowledge the impact your assumption has on your current life, the emotional and financial costs, and the exchanges that you make.

Does each belief serve you now?

For example, if your parents were secretive about money and uneasy talking about it, it was adaptive to restrain discussion about it. At one time, the decision served you, but you may have outgrown its usefulness. Is it still worth the cost that you pay? Are you exchanging energy for your current restraint as well as missing out on valuable information or feedback?

Realize that you decide what to perceive. You also decide what meaning to attach. And you decide the associated behavior.

4. *Explore what is possible.* From the place of what is possible, clarify what you want to create and what action would be paired with it.

If love was spoken in your family of origin in the language of money, consider how you want to currently develop your own separate meanings and expressions for love and money.

5. *Try out new perspectives and possibilities.* You have to try on and live an experience to see how it fits—to get informed data of how it may bring a change to your life. But recognize that "comfortable" is not a place you begin. If you have buried all your cash in your backyard, any investment will initially provoke anxiety.

6. *Recognize and honor your uniqueness.* Assess your unique capacities and abilities. What do you do uniquely well, better than almost anyone else? What are you most passionate about? Are you doing what you love each day? The plot of your money story must recognize your needs and ideals. Place your energy on leveraging strengths rather than creating obstacles.

7. *Recognize what you can determine and what you can't.* Engage what you can determine. Embrace what benefits you and the elements that serve you. Accept and let go of what you cannot determine.

8. *Clarify decisions about how you use, invest, and refurbish your energy based on your personal mission statement.* You spend life energy for money.

Reflect carefully on what you pay and purchase. Make yourself a promise about how you use, invest, and refurbish your life energy based on your money story.

9. *Change is a process, only rarely an event.* Design short-term, stepwise measurable goals to validate your progress. Hold yourself accountable to the timetable of your goals.

10. *Acknowledge your compromises.* These are the things that irritate you and that you work around, without satisfaction, in each of four areas: physical, emotional, relationship, and financial.

11. *Create a mission that is stronger than your fear.* Old story: Uncertainty and anxiety equate with danger. Response: Head for cover.

New story: Uncertainty means you are in new territory—a new experience. Anxiety validates progress. Response: Proceed.

12. *Focus your energy on where you are—the present—and where you are headed—the future.* You can't change the past, but you can free yourself from its grips.

13. *Issues and struggles about money can be about money or about something else hitchhiking on money.* Marital conflict focusing on money may be about divergent meanings of money (security and the need to save versus freedom to spend and enjoy) or of other issues using money language (such as control, dependency, anger, or guilt). True money issues need to be addressed simply and unemotionally.

14. *Know what enough is.* "More" is not a goal; it can never be reached. Establish goals that are specific, measurable, attainable, relevant, and time/amount specific.

Seven Techniques to Edit the Plot of Your New Money Story

1. *Focus on the plot of your money story and the basic assumptions creating the story lines.* Beliefs drive behaviors; behaviors drive performance. Assessment begins with recognizing that you are the author of your money story, just as you are the author of your life story. Take ownership of your experience. It does not just happen, even though it may seem that way.

Your experiences are always consistent with your theories. You loyally align with the central theme, the plot, of your life. You perceive and process according to that plot, and any departure, even temporary, creates uncertainty. Developing a new story generates anxiety of the unfamiliar. The easiest and fastest way to end this uncertainty is to go back to the comfortable—but limiting—old story.

Examine beliefs and assumptions creating the story lines for each recurring money problem as well as each financial success. Both problems and successes exist when you create them. And both are lessons.

For each obstacle, look for its core assumption. For example, if you feel you have been treated unfairly in a business deal, did you silently hope that someone in authority would take care of you? Use the situation as a lesson to take better care of yourself. Recognize that there is no ultimate arbiter of fairness.

Are you susceptible to a good investment story? Do you want to buy a promise of fulfilling your hope rather than assessing the purchase with the same research you would in purchasing a computer or refrigerator?

2. *Assess the money story lines that work and those that do not.* Regardless of intent or motivation, promise or possibility, the bottom line is always, "Does it work now?"

After awareness, acceptance. After acceptance, action.

Define performance and not behavior. Intentions are worthless—usually an excuse masquerading as an explanation.

Do your recurring obstacles share a common theme, such as goals not aligned with needs and values? Or hearing the story you want to believe?

Core assumptions form the basic beliefs about yourself. Organizing, powerful, and influential, they fashion the story lines of your life. The more you try to disregard, disavow, or counter them, the more intense their influence becomes. These beliefs are not "just there"—you create them. The best indicator of your beliefs and values is your behavior.

What patterns do you see in your handling of finances?

3. *Recognize passive versus active positions regarding money.* Words reveal an internal model. Listen for explicit language reflecting a passive or active position and for an internal or external point of reference.

Active language reflects an active position and ownership of initiative. Rather than "I'll try," latch on to "I will."

Passive language derives from beliefs about fate, luck, destiny, victimhood, entitlement, or hope. The language of this position makes the creator both subject and victim: "My fear took over." "The market beat me up this week."

Pressure words indicate an external point of reference rather than an internal authority: "should," "have to," "ought to," "need to," or "must."

Limitation words reveal the assumption of constraint: "impossible," "can't," or "shouldn't."

Nonspecific actions and nouns generalize and universalize experiences rather than create a specific focus and action potential. "I came to an impasse." "My mind played tricks on me."

Abstract goals impede precise strategy. Wanting to be happy, to change, or to be comfortable with money requires conversion into specific, measurable goals and strategies.

Your language will both reflect and facilitate ownership of your story to become your own authority.

4. *Assess what you want to change.* Change begins when you recognize that you author your own story. If a problem recurs, rather than simply getting over it, countering it, or adapting to it, recognize that it is not there until you create it.

5. *Determine what you want to let go.* In order to change, you first have to know what you want to let go. The bottom line, no matter how entrenched the process or strong the hope, is "Does it work?" Unfulfilled hope—what might have been—becomes the most difficult good-bye. You are never more aware of what you've missed in the past than when you give it to yourself now.

6. *Know what you want to avoid.* The pull of the old and the fear of the new exist side by side. Yet there is no future in repetition.

Recognize what you can and can't determine. Disengage the impossible, especially trying to change another person. Avoid involvement in nonproductive, energy-draining struggles, such as arguments: What is the sound of one hand clapping?

7. *Clarify what you want to enhance.* Your money story, like your life, manifests your beliefs.

Changing your mind changes your life, as beliefs, goals, and visions drive action. Choose carefully what you engage. Your money story and your life story should be mutually enhancing. Both must have the same text: What is *really* important?

Six-Step Action Plan for Achieving Goals

If nothing were keeping you from reaching your objectives, you would have already done so. Until you identify the obstacles that stand between you and reaching your objectives, you are in denial.

Consider following this action plan sequence:

1. Outline obstacles that must be recognized in order not to create them.

2. Identify benefits (happier, more prosperous, and more secure).

3. Move resolution to decision (a commitment).

4. Determine what other people, groups, and organizations you need to work with to reach your objectives.

5. Compile additional information to accomplish this objective.

6. Set the date to reach the goal as part of your game plan.

Possibility Thinking

What you believe is what you'll see. This means that you are not only data determined but also hypothesis determined. The brain as computer and as biological evolutionary system determines a story constructed to be called reality.

What is the practical value in this? About decision making? About how to change some mental models?

1. *For any situation, look at the data but also at the hypothesis—the default assumption that appears as "given."*

2. *Since we shape and filter the world by our hypotheses, they need to be continuously tested.*

3. *Examine the hypotheses that work and the ones that don't.*

4. *Challenge your thinking and assumptions.* Interact with diverse people and keep an open "beginner's mind" rather than a quick foreclosure to a new idea. Life as a series of experiments keeps

a system open to the new. Premature closure occurs by too-rapid judgment as well as by moving a new idea into an already existing model to lose the context of a new model. This style of dismissal occurs frequently among very bright people with significant life experiences who immediately relate something new to something that they already know, absorbing it into an old context or meaning without sufficient examination.

5. *We become comfortable and dependent on our old habits. When we move away from existing internal models, uncertainty and discomfort are the result.*

6. *Use data to test a hypothesis rather than automatically confirm it.*

7. *Distinguish between transforming your thinking and being caught up in a new fad.* Focus on the foreground without losing sight of the background's big picture. Repeat zooming in and out to keep perspective. Both microscopic and macroscopic views offer benefits.

8. *The best way to excise something from your life is not to ignore it. The best way to avoid something is to be informed by it.* By avoiding something, you engage it and keep it central in your life. Ignoring it—or attempting to—takes energy and moves you from a centered, healthy place. Decide what you want to keep, what you want to avoid, and what you want to let go.

9. *You are always free to change your mind.*

Change Only What Doesn't Work

Two core questions in examining your story are "What works?" and "What does not work?" A simple plan is to keep doing the things that work and change the things that do not work.

While your behavior may not be intended as self-sabotage, that may be the end result. The cause of your behavior is not in your childhood, past victimhood, bad mother, cold father, or conflictual adolescence. The cause is what you generate at this moment. You create the present cause, which means you can also not create it, creating something quite different instead. Blame, fault, victimhood, and passivity all ensure continuation of the present story.

If you don't change, the future will continue to be played out as in the past and the present. Is this your preference?

Seven Guidelines to Anchor Yourself in Financial Reality

1. *Create a clear picture, on a single sheet of paper, of your total current debts.* This is an important first step toward financial health. In the debt quiz, knowing exactly how much you owe earns the most points of any single question.

Take out every credit card statement, mortgage, loan statement, and any other statement of money owed and list the full balances owed on a sheet of paper, then add all the balances to arrive at a single number.

Some people are able to do this in half an hour; for others, it may take hours or an entire day. If you have documents missing or don't have all the totals readily at hand, make the phone calls and do the research. Even if it takes a few days, commit to following through on every single debt until you have your entire debt picture nailed down on a *single piece of paper* and the totals added up to a *single number.*

It's hard to slay a dragon if you can't see it.

2. *Start paying off your debts, beginning with those that carry the highest interest rates.* Take that sheet you created in step 1 and sort those debts in order of priority. Those with the highest interest rates are generally those to pay off first. Once you've sorted them, rewrite the list on a new sheet to reflect this order of repayment. Keep this debt summary where you can find it and rewrite it once a month with updated numbers.

This sheet contains your marching orders. The point is to pay off each debt, one by one, down to zero. Note that paying the "minimum due" does not count as an actual payment—that's barely covering interest.

3. *Identify your unique vulnerability.* Whether it's clothes, eating out, or electronic gadgets, identify your particular hot buttons, those areas where you're most commonly tempted to make impulse purchases. Recognize that for you, these goods or services are like alcohol to an alcoholic. Be on your guard when they present themselves.

4. *If you need to, cut up the cards and close the accounts.* Depression, anxiety, or other forms of emotional stress can trigger compulsive spending.

Compulsive spenders have to stop the addictive spending—just as alcoholics must stop drinking—before they can begin to understand the underlying reasons for their addiction.

It makes no sense to try to stop drinking or quit smoking as long as you have alcohol or cigarettes in the house. The same goes for credit cards. Be kind to yourself: remove the temptation. Cut up the cards and close the store accounts.

5. *Every time you face a spending decision, consult the big picture.* The big picture boils down to these two orienting and focusing questions:

- What is in my (or our) best interest?

- A year from now, what will I be glad I've done?

Keeping the big picture in view doesn't mean that every decision will necessarily be correct. Even the most seasoned and well-adjusted financial experts don't bat a thousand when it comes to their own financial choices. But it will help keep you grounded and greatly improve the chances of your making the best decisions you can in the circumstances.

6. *Commit to accurately tracking your cash flow every month.* The act of keeping track will automatically help you become more conscious about your spending.

Don't make this complicated. The point is to have a clear picture of how much money comes in each month, how much goes out, and where it goes. Whether you keep a handwritten checkbook register or keep track on your computer doesn't matter. Use whatever system seems easiest for you.

7. *Consult a professional to develop a plan for retiring your debt.* You may do just fine on your own, creating your debt summary and prioritizing your debt payment plan as described above. But if you feel you need to, don't hesitate to hire a pro. For a very reasonable fee, a certified debt counselor can help you create a simple, practical plan that will chart your best path out of the woods.

If you scored poorly on the debt quiz or believe you are seriously stuck in the compulsive spending and/or debt cycle, consider Debtors Anonymous or a quality service such as Financial Recovery (http://www.FinancialRecovery.com).

Seven Guidelines for Establishing a Healthy Money Story

1. *Remember that money is money.* Owing money does not "mean" anything about you or your value as a person, just as having a lot of money does not mean anything about who you are as a person. It's only money. Let go of whatever complexity and emotional drama you have attached to your money, your spending, your debts, your possessions, your net worth, and all the rest. As crucial as it is for you to deal with it responsibly and consciously, remember that it is only money.

The foundation of all sound financial decisions and behaviors is a firm grasp of this fundamental principle: "Money is simply money."

2. *Understand that internal satisfaction can transcend money.* Money means less when true inner peace exists; it becomes a simple medium of exchange, free from complex meanings or hopes of enhanced self-worth.

We live in a society that tends to equate "success" with financial prowess. But many forms of success have no relationship at all to financial success. The most genuinely successful people typically find work in an area they enjoy that is intrinsically motivating, and their financial success is in essence a by-product of that larger *life* success.

The German poet and philosopher Johann Wolfgang von Goethe, when asked for the secret of life, replied, "The secret of life is living."

3. *Know that there's also nothing wrong with money.* Be careful not to idealize poverty and rationalize the lack of success as somehow nobler than wealth. Money bestows on the possessor many choices not otherwise available. As Albert Camus put it, "It is a kind of spiritual snobbery that makes people think they can be happy without money."

4. *Learn how to balance money for today with money for tomorrow.* Money can be used constructively to enhance enjoyment and satisfaction in life. These joys should be balanced with the accumulation of money for future security.

5. *Create a financial plan that reflects your values and priorities.* If you don't know where you're going, any map will do. Money problems arise from falling prey to easy credit availability, but we fall prey to easy credit only when we lack a clear larger plan.

A financial plan doesn't have to be complicated; in fact, an uncomplicated plan is better. Identify your priorities in life, create the financial goals that support those priorities, and chart a path to get there.

6. *Seek out suggestions and advice from an expert.* The decision to seek consultation from people knowledgeable in specific areas is logically sound but emotionally difficult. Consulting someone who will mirror and agree with your own opinions is far easier than listening objectively to critical or contradictory information without responding defensively or remaining stubbornly attached to your original position.

The point of consulting experts is not simply to follow their advice and wholly abandon your own perspective but also to maintain your own viewpoint while staying open to what you can learn from theirs. Then use this new information to form a flexible and better-informed position.

7. *Go on a media diet.* The broadcast and print media are remarkably effective at fanning the flames of compulsive spending. The message the media give you generally goes something like this: *You are overweight, unfit, unattractive, your life is boring, you're in incredible danger, you may even smell bad—and the solutions to all these problems are just a purchase away.*

Start noticing the choices you make, including what you buy and consume, based on what television, magazines, and other media tell you. Seek out one specific media source each week that you disagree with or dislike. Experience the difference from your previous perception.

Start making your media choices conscious; exercise your prerogative to watch, read, and listen to only those specific media resources that you choose—and savor them well.

Fasting is good for the soul: consider giving yourself one fully media-free day per week.

STEP 6
Author New Experiences:
Write New Software

Ben Fletcher at the University of Hertfordshire in the United Kingdom devised a study to get people to break their usual habits.[1] Each day, the subjects picked a different option from poles of contrasting behaviors—lively/quiet, introvert/extrovert, reactive/proactive—and behaved according to this assignment. So, an introverted person, for example, would act as an extrovert for an entire day. Additionally, twice weekly, they had to stretch to behave in a way outside their usual life pattern—eating or reading something they would never have done.

The remarkable finding was that after four months, the subjects had lost an average of 11 pounds. Six months later, almost all had kept the weight off. The weight-loss impact of a nondiet was the result of this study focusing on change and its impact.

The rationale: Requiring people to change routine behavior makes them actually think about decisions rather than habitually choosing a default mode without consideration. This is story busting in an indirect way. In having to process decisions actively, they exercised their choice- and decision-making abilities, extending to other choices, such as what and what not to eat. Once you become aware that you are actively making choices, you can decide what's in your best interest and what furthers your story and what doesn't.

To create the money story you want, you first have to have a plan, then know specifically how to live the plan.

Many of the recommended methods for facilitating change are contrary to how the mind and brain work. Some of the exercise and work pages of these steps incorporate research in psychology, neuroscience, and strategic coaching to address change more effectively. At times, in order to deal with our innate resistance to change, we have to outsmart our brains.

The Mental Research Institute of Palo Alto on Cybernetics and Communications developed a model to focus on obstacles that interfered with people's forward movement in life rather than on the origins or dynamics of those obstacles.[2] One approach was to look at an exception: an instance where there was no existing problem. The exception—that is, the solution—became the focus rather than the problem. People derive significant benefit from directly focusing on solutions rather than on problems; by doing so, problems dissolve as some move ahead.

Neural Conditioning: Three Steps to Rewire Your Brain

Austrian psychiatrist Viktor Frankl, a Jew, was in a Nazi concentration camp during World War II. While death was certain, he observed that about one out of 25 of his fellow prisoners somehow managed to survive. He set about studying the characteristics of those who survived.

As he wrote later in *Man's Search for Meaning*, he found that it was what the survivors *associated to* that made the difference in their survival. While 24 out of every 25 focused on their pain and inevitable death, those who survived created meaning—a purpose—for their suffering rather than accepting their fate and wondering why God was allowing them to die. For example, they constructed a reason to survive so that they could tell their story to their children—to make certain that this kind of atrocity would never happen again. It changed the meaning of their suffering to something that would make a difference—a purpose that provided a will to live.

What you link inside your head—the meaning that you give—determines your behavior. You can change your behavior when you change the meaning. You can reprogram your associations and rewire your brain.

How do you condition yourself to make changes that last?

When you change the meaning of an association (neural conditioning), you change your behavior. There are three key principles of neural conditioning to make lasting change.

1. *Recognize what to change.* You must get to the point where you feel you *must* change something and change it *now* and that you *can* change it. Believe that change will ultimately bring pleasure. Recognize that not changing would be ultimately more painful than the immediate pain of the change process:

   - If you don't change your pattern, what will be the consequences?

   - What is the pain associated to the current choice?

   - What will be the pleasure with changing?

2. *Identify the cues/triggers for the behavior. The meaning you attach to a trigger determines your behavior.* Observe the cues (usually emotional) that trigger an automatic behavior pattern. For example, if you want to accumulate wealth yet do not, you immediately associate money to some pain or negative meaning. This shadow story may be "I'll have to work too hard and won't have time for my family." Or "Money will keep me from being spiritual." Or "I'd feel guilty about having a lot of money when so many others don't."

   - What are the cues or triggers for the automatic behavior pattern?

   - How can you interrupt your own pattern once you have identified it?

3. *Create a new association that empowers you.* Condition a new, empowering association to the same cue. For example, if you have limited yourself or feel stuck in that you're not making more money, link making money with strength, power, and possibility:

   - What is the new association to the familiar cue?

   - What is the change you want to bring about?

   - What, specifically, will you gain and enjoy with the change?

The science of success is the neuroscience of neural conditioning—of reprogramming your mind to attach meanings to generate success.

Self-Reflections on Change: Twelve Principles

1. *Each person's life story is created.* You create whatever you think, feel, and experience at each moment. Every day is a blank page until you begin writing on it—even though it seems to "just be the way things are." The first step is taking ownership of your story, including the assumptions that generate default behavior.

2. *Understanding begins with examination of which storylines work and which do not.* The next step is changing the ones that do not work while keeping or even enhancing those that do work.

3. *Knowing what not to do is at least as important as knowing what to do.* You may not always know what the next right thing is, but you can almost always know what it isn't.

4. *Questions are more powerful than advice.* Questions can direct, clarify, illuminate, and even story bust. Advice invites acquiescence or resistance; questions move the process from compliance to collaboration.

5. *When people create their own answers, they have signed on to invest in the outcome.* This investment elicits a sense of effectiveness and mastery.

6. *Identify four things: what to change, accept, let go, and enhance.* Doing this allows you to put your energy into what works and allows you to accept and let go of what you can't change. Making this simple distinction both liberates and enhances effectiveness.

7. *We don't see things as they are; we see things as we are.* Learn to recognize your own assumptions and beliefs and how they color what you perceive. Assumptions manifest as feelings and behaviors. By making assumptions explicit, you become able to perceive those that facilitate your process and those that interfere.

8. *Change is constant and inevitable; resistance to change is what generates most problems.* We are most successful when we learn from yesterday, anticipate tomorrow, and integrate the impact of new experience.

9. *Small changes lead to big changes.* Issues that seem overwhelmingly large and insurmountable can be approached by looking at the simplicity of the issue, then specifying a small step to take for progress. For example, someone who feels overwhelmed at work by the number of tasks expected of him or her can identify one issue to deal with effectively within the next day. This focus on a specific action exercises effectiveness and initiates a model of mastery.

10. *Solutions, causes, and problems are not always related or even interconnected.* Resolving a problem, even emotionally coming to the end of the past, does not create a blueprint for success. Strategic planning for specific goals is necessary. For the person with an eating disorder, there are no prepackaged answers awaiting discovery. He or she is moving into new developmental territory without a map.

11. *A collaboration keeps both individuals on the same side, looking at the same scene together.* Empathic listening keeps the professional aligned with the client's point of view and builds common ground for work.

12. *The benefit of doing more of what is working and less of what isn't working will become evident and self-perpetuating.*

Navigating Transitions

We can foster change by conscious practices and effective tools. An infinite sea of new patterns and possibilities can be created to further new goals. Here's the caveat: You have to take action to diminish preprogrammed responses and to write new script for new experiences; a new story has to replace the old one. There are no shortcuts since long-term change requires consistent practice—repetition—to groove new neural pathways and establish new neuronal networks. There are, however, effective and efficient methods to accelerate optimum change and ensure transformation.

Any new venture or stretch of current capacity naturally generates uncertainty and anxiety. For anyone, any really significant accomplishment always begins with unfamiliarity and risk. "Comfortable" is not where you begin but rather where you arrive with mastery of new experiences. Even a good and planned change is at first a discontinuity, like a gap in the experience of self. And although the change may be anticipated, it still requires adjustment.

You can't learn to swim on paper, so you have to jump in the pool for the first time as part of the process of mastery. The only way to learn to swim is to proceed despite anxiety: to let go and jump in the pool the first time. In order to ride a bicycle, the only way to *learn* balance is to *lose* it. If you perceive tasks such as these as terrifying, you'll avoid them. If the perception of danger and the feeling of fear trump everything else, stopping will seem logical.

If, on the other hand, you change your perception to *possibility* and *benefit*, you shift your perspective. Then you have to *experience* something new in order to make your commitment come true and change your reality. Choice becomes a conscious selection rather than a default behavior.

Recognition of oneself as the author, the creator, of the story challenges an assumed model and leads to deeper questions: "How do I create something else instead?" "What will the 'something else' be?"

To simply stop doing something is not complete change; a new story means incorporating new behavior and beliefs. A person has to embody— actually live—this new story. Abstaining from an old story—stuckness or compromising repetitions, such as abstaining from excessive drinking or eating—is a beginning. But someone has to engage a new story before an old story can be given up.

Strategic Goal Pursuit

SMART Goals

Goals are exciting and energizing. They make it easier to focus and make distractions clearer when they occur. SMART goals cocreate moving ahead and specifically honing strategies. SMART goals include these components:

- Specific: Be very specific about a goal—for example, "getting fit" is not a goal but an outcome.

- Measurable: There must be a way to track efforts and sustain energy and motivation.

- Achievable: The goal must be attainable.

- Realistic: Make sure you are willing to pay the price of your goal.

- Time bound: There needs to be a beginning and an end—time framed.

Initiatives

For each goal, establish three key initiatives that move toward the goal.

Next Best Action

For each initiative, decide on the next best action.

Application

People with repetitive behavior have spent time understanding an old story or focused on old behaviors and patterns. But understanding and further analysis aren't enough to bring about change. These individuals need a new story to be in before they can give up an old one.

I begin each mentor coaching session after a progress note to update; I ask what my client wants to focus on for this session. Then we decide on a desirable end point or takeaway for the end of the session.

Setting specific goals enhances motivation. Establishing strategies enhances focus.

This is also a model for the outside world: setting a next-step goal and having a strategy to reach it. Setting long-term goals, such as saving for retirement and emergencies, can replace the default pattern of spending everything earned.

Your Money Mission Statement

To have a successful relationship with money, you must have a plan. In business, a mission statement is a statement of an organization's primary purpose, the strategies to achieve that purpose, and its fundamental values. A personal mission statement can clarify and provide meaning to your daily activities; it adds focus and commitment to what you are doing.

A mission statement contains four elements: ideals, purpose, strategies, and goals.

Ideals: The core values that motivate and guide you, such as helping people, mastery, being your own boss, putting family first, and making a difference. They come first because they define what's important to you.

Purpose: What you wish to accomplish—to be successful, to make money, to be happy, or to retire early. Purpose must be consistent with your ideals.

Strategy: The art and science of a plan of action. Strategies include how you intend to serve a purpose—such as develop skills, meditate, minimize expenses, and implement a plan to do what you do uniquely well.

Goals: Not the end point of the journey but rather signposts along the way. If your purpose is to retire early, you'll need to achieve some interim goals, such as funding a retirement plan or increasing your savings or earnings.

We are always reaching our goals, consciously or not. Make your goals explicit and tangible to ensure that you reach the ones you intend.

Ideals: List your three most important ideals, in order of priority, that will guide your financial decision making.

Purpose: Why do you want X amount of money in your life? How will it serve you?

Strategy: How will you realize that purpose? What steps will you take?

Goals: What are your SMART goals (Specific, Measurable, Attainable, Relevant, Time limited)?

For each goal, identify the next two or three steps you will take to move yourself toward that goal and set a time line for each.

Your Money Mission Statement: One Sentence

In one sentence, what is your mission statement regarding your money?

Nine Steps to Advance the Plot of Your New Money Story®

1. *Construct an outline for your money story.* An outline orients your money story: to determine where you are, to measure how far you've come, and to see how far you have to go to reach certain goals. It's your map to identify what fits into the plot, what is distraction or detour, and to determine the best route.

2. *Keep your money mission statement visible and in focus.* Your money mission statement defines the essence of your financial goals and the philosophies underlying them. It proclaims the meaning, use, and value of money to you, including short- and long-term plans. Regular review and refinement of this statement orients decisions with your purpose and philosophy.

3. *Design a successful money story plot.*
   Establish three SMART goals (time frame: 90 days).
   Determine the three most important initiatives for each goal (time frame: the next week).
   Determine the next best action for each initiative (time frame: the next day).

4. *Create positive terms for success.*
   Rather than stating what you don't want or want to avoid, state your plan and criteria in positive terms: what you want and what you will do.

5. *Be specific, simple, and concrete.*
   Concrete and specific goals include time, amount, ultimate goal, precise measurements, and when and how you will bring this about. Distinguish goals (such as travel, retire early, pay off mortgage) from values (such as freedom, security, happiness).
   Vague, abstract, and theoretical criteria are not useful because you cannot live inside a theory. Wanting to change, to be happy, or to be content with money constitutes imprecise and abstract goals.

6. *Engage what you can determine.*
Recognize what you can and what you can't determine. Place all your energy only on what you can determine—the ways you can be effective.

7. *Make success finite and quantifiable with specific results and measurable progress.*
Knowing what is "good enough" determines when you have achieved a goal that is realistic, timely, and measurable.
A thesis and plot form the basis of organized and successful money and investment stories.

8. *Have your money story consistent with your needs and values.*
Living up to your ideal generates a sense of worth and esteem. Know the purpose of money in your life.

9. *Stick to the plan.*
"It is never too late to be what you might have been." —George Eliot
I would add, *or too soon to become who you want to be.*

Success Insurance for Completing Goals

Goal setting and, especially, using the proper tools to structure progress strategically is crucial for long-term achievement. The usual problem is not setting goals but rather completing them. Goals and strategy require management and dedication.

Two essential components include understanding why people give up on goals and how effective goal setting can help ensure long-term achievement.[3]

Six of the most important reasons that people give up on goals follow:

- *Ownership.* People must "buy in" to their goals and take ownership. This shifts the ownership and initiative to an internal point of reference. Then effectiveness and mastery can come about.

- *Time.* Goal setters tend to underestimate the time it will take to complete the task (an "optimism bias"), a habit that can lead to giving up.

- *Difficulty.* Along with the factor of time, the optimism bias applies equally to difficulty.

- *Distractions.* People tend to underestimate potential distractions and competing goals.

- *Rewards.* Disappointment sets in when achievement of a goal doesn't translate into other goals or to the desired happiness.

- *Maintenance.* Maintaining changed behavior is difficult, and there is always the pull of the old and the fear of the new.

Eleven Steps to Ignite Change

- Have needs and values in sharp focus.

- Know what you do uniquely well.

- Assess specific strengths, passions, and weaknesses.

- Establish SMART goals: Specific, Measurable, Achievable, Relevant, Time bound (time frame: 30 to 90 days).

- Determine three key initiatives to take for each goal (time frame: one week).

- Decide on the next best action for each initiative (time frame: one day).

- Structure a strategy to reach and stretch each goal.

- Increase tolerance of planned risk with associated fear.

- Focus on specific results, action, and momentum regarding goals.

- Continue assessment of disciplined activity with refinement of goals.

- Endorse your progress.

The AAA Principles of Change to Author a New Money Story: Awareness, Acceptance, Action

1. You're writing your own story. *Is it working?* For each component, what are the results? Honestly assess each of these story lines with the question, "Is it working?" And make that a "Yes" or a "No."

- Your personal wellness story: mind, body, spirit

- Your business/career story

- Your relationship story

- Your money story

When I ask people what they most look forward to and what they are most afraid of for the next chapters of their lives, they often respond with vague dreams yet specific fears. The top of the lists of long-term concerns are health and money.

A not-so-secret of success is that you have to pay in full for it. So you might as well find out what the price is, pay it in full, pay it as soon as possible, and then enjoy the benefits of success. The price is always some form of energy, whether that energy is money, time, work, or experience. If you get something for which you haven't provided value or benefit, you will still have to pay in some way. If you purchase something before you've earned the money, you simply end up paying more for it.

Another nonsecret: people who truly enjoy getting what they want are those who enjoy paying the price. This makes paying easy. The price is whatever you need to give in order to generate exactly what you want.

2. You're writing your own story. *It takes just as much energy to create any belief in your story.* Positive or negative, based on past/present/future, adaptive or maladaptive—*the same energy.* The belief of scarcity takes just as much energy as abundance. You generate the energy and give power to your story. Simple math says that when you use your attention to focus on what

you don't have, you deplete your energy to engage what you do have. Here's the subtle but crucial distinction: You give specific power to your story, and it assumes a momentum and power of its own. Remember that you're not the subject of that process—you're the creator of it.

Here's a short list of some results when you focus on what you don't want: fear, anxiety, anger, confusion, annoyance, helplessness, and guilt.

3. You're writing your own story. *Decide what you want.* The primary reason people don't get what they want is that they're not sure what they want.

A neuroscience/law-of-attraction question: How does the brain work like a travel agent? The first two questions a travel agent asks, "*Where* do you want to go?" "*When* do you want to get there?" A goal is like MapQuest: You program in where you want to go, make a map, and determine the time.

What you resist you draw toward you. Resistance is an engagement, just as anger is as passionate an attachment as love. If you find yourself resisting change, it has already occurred.

Most suffering is the result of resisting what already is. People resist going to the doctor but not because they're afraid of doctors. They're afraid their denial may be confronted.

4. You're writing your own story. *Do you have specific, measurable goals?* In a Harvard study begun in the mid-1950s, 10 to 15 percent of Harvard Business School graduates fashioned a vision and specific goals for their life in business. Five decades later, that 10 to 15 percent had 90 percent of the assets of the entire group.

Motivation increases as soon as you're clear about the goal and the payoff. A specific plan and strategy enhances your focus.

It is estimated that less than 10 percent of people have measurable goals, yet 100 percent of people have good ideas—at least some. The difference between a good idea and a goal? Measurement and time. Where? When? (again, travel agent questions).

Good idea: I'd like to lose weight.
Goal: I will reach 185 pounds by 5:00 p.m. on December 31.

Good idea: I want to save more money for retirement.

Goal: I will pay myself first by setting up an automatic transfer of $300 to my retirement fund the first day of each month.

Then: Write a breakthrough goal—something that would stretch you, bring incredible opportunities, and move you to a higher level. A quantum leap. Getting a book on the *New York Times* best-seller list. Spending every March skiing in Steamboat Springs or every August writing on the coast of Maine. (You'll have to substitute your own goals here.)

Then: Reread your goals—regular and breakthrough—twice a day: when you wake up and when you go to bed.

5. You're writing your own story. *Small changes lead to big changes.* During my specialty training in psychiatry, one of my first-year supervisors had a puzzling picture on his wall. It was a photograph in which everything seemed curiously out of focus. As I met with him each week, I glanced at the photograph until finally, toward the end of the year, I asked him about it.

"Look carefully," he said. "What do you see?"

I walked over to the photograph to get a closer view. Closer didn't help. It still seemed out of focus. I saw no particular aesthetic value. My experience and considerable interest in photography didn't help.

"Steven, the only thing I notice, is that there's only one branch of one tree in focus in the entire picture."

He nodded. "That's why I have it hanging there. It's my reminder that while things may seem confusing and blurry, there is always at least one thing that you can have in focus and see clearly." (Explains why he was a great supervisor for first-year residents.)

Issues that seem overwhelmingly large and insurmountable can be approached by looking at the simplicity of the issue to single out a step to take for progress. For example, if you feel overwhelmed at work with the amount of tasks, identify one specific thing that you can do in the next 24 hours that will give you some traction. This focus on a simple, specific action creates a sense of effectiveness and initiates a model of mastery.

Terry Fox started the Marathon of Hope—a cross-Canada run of 3,339 miles. Because he has an artificial leg, his running style was a shuffle and hop. He managed about 24 miles a day and completed the run in 143 days. Asked how he kept himself going when he was exhausted and knew he had thousands of miles ahead, he said, "I just kept running to the next telephone pole."

Divide up your work. Focus on and complete one thing at a time. There's always something you can focus on.

6. You're writing your own story. *Be consistent in the pursuit of your goals.* It takes 25 to 30 days to etch a new pathway in your brain to make it permanent. Remember the NASA astronauts.

Write your new story consistently for it to become the default mode.

The difference between a genius idea and a true story of success, Malcolm Gladwell tells us in *Outliers,*[4] is about 10,000 hours of dedicated work to develop mastery.

7. You're writing your own story. *The benefit of doing more of what is working and less of what isn't working will become evident and self-perpetuating.* This is all so simple—good parents have known this for centuries. Sometimes it just takes human science and cognitive research to remind us of the obvious.

We can foster change by conscious practices and effective tools. An infinite sea of new patterns and possibilities can be created to further new goals. There's one caveat: You have to take action to diminish preprogrammed responses and to write new script for new experiences; a new story has to replace the old one. There are no shortcuts since long-term change requires consistent practice—repetition—to groove new neuronal pathways and establish new neural networks. But there are effective and efficient methods to accelerate optimum change and ensure transformation.

8. You're writing your own story. *Ask for feedback.* Ask your spouse or partner, "On a scale of 1 to 10, how would you rate the quality of our relationship?" If you do this, you can get direct feedback—and learn what you can address.

Ask your employees and colleagues, "On a scale of 1 to 10, how am I doing?" Then ask, "How can I get to 10?"

A tribe in southern Africa called the Babemba has an interesting practice. When they hear of a person doing something wrong, something that destroys the social net of their tight community, all work in the village halts. The people gather around the offender and, one by one, recite all that that person has done right in his life: good deeds, responsible behavior, and thoughtful acts. This honest feedback on misbehavior has a time-honored consequence to allow the person to reclaim the better part of himself. He remembers who he is and why he is important to the life of the village.

This may have been an original 360-degree feedback.

Even without this kind of social network and feedback, we can *relax and remember* our way back into alignment with our true selves. We can get centered and reconnect with our true essence.

Find people who already successfully do what you want and get what you want. Research what they do in order to do your own version of it. Ask. Learn. Question. Do your homework. Build connections. Make a reasonable request, something easy and mutually beneficial. But make it *your story*.

An interesting statistic: After giving a complete presentation about the benefits of their service or product, more than 60 percent of the time, seasoned salespeople never ask for the order.

How to ask is a crucial factor. Ask clearly, confidently, and sincerely.

Virginia Satir, the well-known family therapist, was hired by the Michigan State Department of Social Services to submit a proposal on how to restructure the Department of Social Services to better serve the client population.[5]

Sixty days later, she provided the department with a 150-page report. Those who read it said two things: "This is the most amazing report!" and "How did you come up with all these brilliant ideas?"

She said, "I just asked all the social workers in your department what it would take for the system to work better."

You may have noticed that each of these AAA principles of change to author a new money story begins the same way: "You're writing your own story." That's the first four steps of the ROADMAP—Recognize, Observe, Assess, Decide—compressed into the shorthand of Awareness and Acceptance. What's the third A? It's mapping change and authoring new experiences in 12 action steps.

9. You're writing your own story. *Get success insurance.* Instead of waiting for good luck. Luck is defined as probability taken personally—which is to say narcissism meets chance.

   A review of research on goal setting helps us understand two essential components: why people give up on goals and how effective goal setting can help ensure long-term achievement.

10. You're writing your own story. *Take a chance.* You didn't have a *New York Times* best seller before you sent your manuscript to an agent. If you get it rejected, you still don't have one. So what have you got to lose? There's the problem—you've spent your whole life *not* having a *New York Times* best seller.

    A young chiropractor just out of professional school wanted to open a practice in Carmel, California. He was told he'd never make it—there was already one chiropractor for every *eight* people in Carmel.

    He went to 12,500 homes and talked to 6,500 people. He asked three questions:

    - In which location should I open my office—the north or west side of town?

    - Should I have extra office hours from 7:00 to 9:00 a.m. or 5:00 to 7:00 p.m.?

    - Which newspaper should I advertise in?

    He added, "When I have an open-house party, would you like an invitation?" He took in $72,500 the first month and netted more than $1 million his first year.

11. You're writing your own story. *It's never too late to start.* Don't let conventional wisdom or limiting assumptions ghostwrite your story.

Cliff Bion was a 61-year-old Australian sheepherder. He heard about a cross-country race from Sidney to Melbourne and decided to enter. When he showed up in Oshkosh B'Gosh overalls and work boots, the officials looked at him like he was crazy. "This is a race of more than over 800 kilos," they told him. "The most seasoned runners in the world compete. Do you have any running experience and equipment?" He said, "Yeah, I run after my sheep every day. And I got these boots and this baseball cap."

When the race began, the world-class runners took off as they were trained to begin. Cliff started shuffling along in his boots. In this particular race, you're supposed to run 18 hours and sleep 6, but no one told Cliff, so when the other runners were sleeping, he kept shuffling along. They were all asleep and couldn't tell him he wasn't supposed to keep running. He just shuffled along for over three days.

He cut five and a half hours off the world record.

Each of us has beliefs that limit us. Find the story that will improve you, then start believing it.

If there were no barriers, what would your ideal life be?

12. You're writing your own story. *Everything is okay in the end. If it's not okay, it's not the end.* Ed Lorenz conceptualized chaos theory in the 1960s in this way: The initial state of events may seem unrelated and random, but eventually a pattern emerges, and in the end, all the pieces fit together.[6] It's the study of phenomena that appear random but that in fact have an element of regularity that can be described eventually using a different organizing perspective. In the end, all the pieces fit together.

Virginia Woolf put it very simply: "Arrange whatever pieces come your way."

STEP 7
Program New Identity:
Rewire for Wealth

All changes, even the most longed for, have their melancholy. For what
we leave behind us is a part of ourselves. We must die to one life before
we enter another. —Anatole France

The most fundamental quality of the human psyche is that we resist
any change that is not part of our identity—our internal model of
self. And if we do change a behavior, we will ultimately return to
who and what we conceive ourselves to be unless a new model of identity
is programmed into the brain.

To sustain a change, a corresponding internal shift must occur.

A new money story must incorporate the changes to evolve your identity. Internalizing the change creates a new model of your money story
and, in part, of who you are. Let's consider some guidelines for sustained
change and continued growth that will impact identity.

Twelve Basic Principles for Change and Transformation

1. *Awareness of your plot and story lines.* The beginning of change is recognition that you are the author of your story. In the face of a personally
created problem, barrier, or obstacle, the task is not getting over it, push-
ing through it, or adapting to it; rather, it is recognizing that the obstacle
is not there until you create it. Consider the possibility of not creating it
and creating something else instead.

2. *Assess the story lines that work and those that do not work.* In order to change, you first need to know what you want to change and what you want to create instead in each aspect of your life: career, ideals, personal life, functioning at full capacity, happiness, relationships, and finances. The bottom line, no matter how entrenched the process or strong the hope, is "Does it work?"

3. Recognize passive versus active positions. *Active:* You are the author, the casting agent, and the director of your story. *Passive:* Fate, luck, destiny, or assuming that you are the victim of the feeling you create, as in "I got butterflies in my stomach" or "My fear took over."

4. *Listen to your language—it speaks your assumptions.* Words reveal an internal model. *Pressure words* reveal an external point of reference and authority rather than an internal one: "should," "have to," "ought to," "need to." *Passive language* indicates perceiving yourself as the subject rather than the initiator of action: "The thought occurred to me. My anger got the best of me. It just happened." *Limitation words* reveal the assumption of constraint and limitation: "impossible," "can't," "shouldn't."

5. *Address resistance to change and repetition of the old story.* Repetition ensures predictability. We repeat behavior that doesn't work because it offers familiarity. Doing the same thing leads to a known outcome. We sometimes mistake predictability for effectiveness. There is no future in repetition. Any departure from the familiar, even a positive one, creates anxiety and uncertainty. You need a new story to be in before you can give up the old story.

6. *Take ownership of your story to become your own authority.* Reinvention begins with taking ownership of what you do and what you do about what happens next—rather than living out what just seems to happen or feeling victimized by forces beyond your control.

7. *Decide what you want to change.* Your life is the manifestation of your beliefs. Old beliefs do not generate new ideas. Changing your mind changes your life, as beliefs, goals, and visions drive action. Choose carefully what you engage.

8. *Excitement and fear are the same feeling, just viewed and experienced differently.* Excitement counters anxiety when your mission is stronger than your fear.

9. *Construct a map to determine where you are.* Without a map to determine where you are, proceeding with an organized and successful story

(life, career, relationship, investment, and so on) will be difficult or impossible. With a map, you can see where you are, how far you've come, and how far you have to go to reach your goals.

10. *Decide where you want to go.* Having a map allows you to filter distractions, determine the route, and discern what is tangential or a detour. Distinguishing what you want to achieve, preserve, and avoid is an ongoing process.

11. *Figure out how to get there.* Create a game plan of realistic, attainable goals with measurable results.

12. *Stick to the plan.*

Your Personal Life and Money Balance Sheet

- Establish a clear boundary between your work life and your private life: each day, each weekend, and for designated vacation periods. Setting and respecting this boundary allows you to be fully present for both work and private life.

- Assess the amount of time you spend talking about your work with family and friends as well as the amount of time you spend associating with people related to your work. The ability to set these boundaries balances a potential overinclusive identity or time with your work.

- Determine specific, measurable money goals: income, expenses, investment, and retirement.

- If you feel guilty or vaguely uncomfortable with taking time off or relaxing, consider reframing the time, even the play, as a necessary component of your work. In order to be maximally effective when you are at work, making time for a private life and for play is crucial.

- Schedule time for introspection and self-growth.

- Establish daily goals of performance rather than hours spent working. This shift from work ethic to performance ethic values results.

- Distinguish between feedback, criticism, and setbacks on work projects as they relate to the work itself—the task you've performed—rather than taking it personally.

- Develop your emotional, interpersonal expertise as well as your technical expertise. Both can be finely tuned. Consider, for example, when different listening positions may be most effective. At times, a colleague or employer may need your empathic ear; at other times, an objective, even confrontational, position may be needed.

- Know the difference between thinking, feeling, and imagining as opposed to acting. Physical action is not the only form of doing something. Thinking and contemplating are active forms of doing something. This distinction may seem obvious, but it is not clear in the minds of many people.

- Surround yourself with like-minded people who are resourceful, creative, and confident.

- Maintain a high level of optimism with sustaining short-term goals toward an ultimate vision. Convert challenges into motivators and ultimately to advantages.

- Engage the aspects of your vision you are passionate about and do uniquely well. Delegate the rest.

- Be responsible for your own happiness.

- Know what motivates you in order to synchronize your values and needs.

- Take ownership and control of your life and career.

The Old Art and New Science of Visualization

The Old Art

A vision crystallizes possibility into a fundamental, articulated idea. A vision gives hope possibility—a shape and form—for programming your future, at the same time rehearsing it. You program a message for success in your mind by creating the experience of having achieved it.

Proven guidelines include the following elements:

- You must construct your *own* vision.

- Clearly define your criteria to measure success.

- Be specific, simple, and concrete. Wanting to change, to be wealthy, or to be happy are all imprecise and abstract goals.

- Create positive terms for success: what you want and what you will do.

Picture yourself as you have just succeeded at your goal at a specific time in the future. Create this success experience specific to time, place, how you would experience yourself, and your body through all five senses. Hold the energy of the precise outcome you've just achieved with the goals met and the feelings it brings. Imagine the details of the scene of your success inside and outside, engaging all senses, thoughts, feelings, and bodily experience along with details of the scene. For example, for a successful transaction, include the values and needs fulfilled, the money you have made from it, and the details of what you are doing, such as shaking hands and ushering someone out of your office.

Carve out a few moments at the beginning and the end of each day to replay your vision. This vision *begins the experience and outline of a goal that you can realize strategically.*

The New Science

Recent positron-emission tomography (PET) scans of the brain have confirmed several things about visualization:

- Mental visualization of a complex movement can actually improve performance.

- Visualization brings about actual physical changes in the brain.

- The brain assimilates a mental picture, whether the stimulus is actual from the optic nerve or imagined. The brain cannot distinguish between a mental image and an actual image.

- When you repeat a vision of successfully attaining a goal, the act programs neural networks and neuronal pathways to etch the experience more strongly.

- This new vision must be consciously incorporated into an ongoing story to be ultimately metabolized as part of the self. Unless you envision it, you will "lose" this vision.

- The more detailed your visual image, the more specifically etched your brain will be about achieving the goal.

- Write it down. Research on memory tells us that a new idea or fact lasts an average of 40 seconds in short-term memory before it's gone, unless you write it down to review. Read each one at the beginning and the end of each day.

- Visualization *crystallizes possibility* into an *articulated idea*—the experience changes the brain. A vision serves as a guide and inspiration to design ways to realize it—to live into it.

When you program your system with a visualized goal, you create structural tension in your brain—cognitive dissonance—the difference between where you are and where you visualize and affirm yourself. Your brain then strives to end this tension by actualizing the goal. Structural tension (dissonance) in your brain will do the following things:

- Give you creative ideas

- Help you see things in your environment not seen before—a perceptual shift

- Provide motivation to take action

Affirmations to Support Visualizations

Affirmations make visualization a complete story. To achieve a goal, reprogram your automatic pilot by affirmations. Affirmations are positive statements that state the goal as if it has already been achieved. For affirmations to be optimally effective, the following characteristics need to be incorporated:

- Present tense

  Begin with, "I am . . ." State the goal as if you have already achieved it.

- Positive

  Your brain will strive to achieve the image you focus on. A positive image is more powerful than ideas.

- Personal

  Make your affirmations about your own experience and accomplishment, not aimed at changing other people's behavior.

- Visual

  Use all five senses and different lenses: include wide angle and close-up and make a complete picture of experiencing the success of your goal.

- Emotional

  Include a feeling word (*happily* interacting, *peacefully* experiencing). A primary reason we do things is how we imagine we'll feel when we do it

- Brief

  Brevity is the soul of wit—and affirmations.

- Specific

  Clearly focused, specific detail makes it real. No abstractions.

- Action words

  "I am driving . . . acting . . . living . . ."
  If you say, "I am going to . . ." you will always be on the way.

- Consistent

  As soon as you let up on the disciplined, focused pursuit of a goal, your automatic pilot will revert back to the familiar.
  How long do you do this? Until you reach the goal.
  How many goals should you generate affirmation for? A reasonable number—at least three—that you're working on daily.
  In this way, you etch the vision and specifics of success in your brain. Then you strategically inhabit the experience.

Money and Success: Eighteen Caveats to Live a New Money Story®

1. *When both your head and your gut (what you think and feel) agree and you act accordingly, you optimize positive results.* Disregarding or deleting one or the other results in compromise. Emotional goals and internal values must be consistent with external plan and vision. Align your internal ideals with your financial goals. Your ideals—the internal model of who and what you are—generate the unspoken assumptions on which you operate.

2. *Having a definition of success and an internal ideal of "good enough" are essential for satisfaction.* The most outstanding characteristic of the happy superachievers I have known is that all of them love their work and their play. Succeeding is not an event or an act but rather a process.

3. *Rich is knowing you have enough.* An internal definition of success may not be easily mapped. And it may be defined differently by men, by women, and individual by individual. Internal success is measured by ideals, relatedness with important others, and comfort with one's self. Self-esteem results from having internal ideals and living up to them.

4. *Long-term goals are necessary to keep perspective, while short-term goals are necessary to sustain enthusiasm and tolerate frustration.* Short-term setbacks are an essential part of achieving success within the orientation and organization provided by long-term goals. In learning to walk, the toddler's fall is not a failure but rather part of the process of learning to walk. When you have the end point of your purpose clearly in mind, you can more easily keep setbacks in perspective. Anything important requires a commitment to go forward despite discomfort.

5. *Respect the boundaries between business and personal life.* In order to be fully immersed in your work and in your private life, a clear boundary must exist between the two. Although you may enjoy and feel rewarded by your work, play is equally important. You may even find it useful to set aside a brief time at the end of the day to allow closure of work activities, to have an official transition time that puts a period at the end of the sentence of each day so that private time is distinct.

6. *Develop your emotional and interpersonal expertise as well as your technical expertise.* Part of establishing a goal is identifying whom you need to work with. Then you can identify the skills, knowledge, and abilities you need to develop in order to reach the goal.

7. *Thinking, feeling, and imagining are all active forms of doing something.* Yet thinking, feeling, and imagining are different from physical action.

8. *Judgment resides in the potential space between urge and action.* Impulsivity collapses this space. This space requires creation: at a time when you may be caught up in details or in the grips of excess emotion, a necessary question is, "What is in my best interest?" This question can always be in the background. At times of stressful or stimulating distractions, it needs to move to the foreground. Creating a contemplative space is necessary at times when you feel the urge to act impulsively or prematurely or sense the pressure from others to act. There are few true emergencies in life.

9. *You'll never do anything important that will feel comfortable in the beginning.* The only familiar territory is behind you. Mastery requires you to proceed despite your anxiety. Uncertainty in doing anything new is to be expected. Comfortable is not a place you begin.

10. *Assess what reaching a goal will do.* It is important to know what achieving a goal will do in order to distinguish clearly what it will not do. For example, reaching a career goal will not undo the past or make other troubles go away. Having more money won't make a marriage relationship better. Monetary wealth will provide pleasure, luxury, and financial security, but it may not make your marriage better. A common mechanism for keeping hope alive is stopping short of a goal, keeping you stuck in the illusion that reaching the goal will provide all the hoped-for solutions. Getting what you've always wanted in the past may not feel as good as you expected because it's no longer the past.

11. *Just having a choice can make choosing the same thing feel very different.* Insight and understanding are internal change; external change is another step in and of itself. Every step of growth and change involves its own mourning. You have to relinquish a past position in order to move ahead. Mourning the fantasy of what might have been is more difficult than saying good-bye to what actually was. What you decide to accept undergoes a change.

12. *Growth and change are hard. The only thing harder is not growing or changing.* If you are uncertain or concerned about change, it is already occurring.

13. *Recognize your limits in order to achieve success.* It may be difficult to recognize those limits and to seek the advice of others. Consulting an expert is not a weakness or an acknowledgment of limitation. Failing to

recognize the limits of your knowledge in any area or being unable to admit mistakes can profoundly hamper your judgment.

14. *Admit mistakes in order to cut losses.* The prospect of selling a plunging stock at a loss may make the loss so real that you will have difficulty selling. As long as the stock isn't sold, you can retain the hope that it will rise again and avoid the "reality" of the loss.

15. *Continue to seek suggestions, critiques, and advice—and don't take it personally.* Consulting only with those who mirror and agree with your opinion is far easier than listening objectively to critical or contradictory information. The decision to seek consultation from individuals knowledgeable in specific areas may be as logically sound as it is emotionally difficult.

16. *Distinguish lack of information and organization from unconscious conflict.* Further information, strategy, and redoubled efforts will persist in not working if emotional conflict creates a barrier. A new plan is not the remedy for an unexecuted existing plan. Only when a plan is fully executed can you make an informed decision about its effectiveness.

17. *Planning and strategy are essential components of a game plan.* Establishing a goal will enhance motivation. Developing a strategy will focus concentration on efforts.

18. *Examine the process that gets you to a good result. Examine the process that gets you to a bad result.* You can learn immensely from both.

Thirty-two Guidelines to Further A New Money Story

1. *Distinguish need from want.* You can get sick if you don't have enough of what you need, and you can get sick if you have too much of what you want.

2. *You always have the right to say "No" or "Yes."* Don't hesitate to say "No" or "Yes" when you are clear about what you want and need. Also, as a wise mentor once told me, never speak more clearly than you think. The other person also has a right to say "No" or "Yes." So don't hesitate to ask.

3. *You have to be free to say "No" before you can be free to say "Yes."* Unless you are free to say "No," "Yes" has no meaning.

4. *Coming to the end of your past, especially resolving emotional issues, isn't enough: you have to have a purpose, a dream, in order to give hope a blueprint.*

5. *Have a "big picture" and bring it into focus whenever necessary.* The big picture comprises your own ideals, principles, and objective organization of your life and decisions according to what you believe to be in your best interest.

6. *Establish priorities.* Every day, you will redefine and refine priorities and make decisions about what is really important in each area of your life: family, work, health, friendships, leisure, self-care, and finances, to name a few. Neglect in one area creates imbalance.

7. *Have specific, attainable goals on a short-term, daily basis as well as in the big picture.* Setting specific goals allows self-affirmation once you attain them.

8. *Disengage from "what might have been."* You may lose today looking back for yesterday. "If only" fantasies idealize the past and erode today.

9. *Engage what you can be effective in doing and disengage what you have no determination over.* Discerning the difference between these two tenets and adhering to them can create a powerful impact on your life.

10. *Seek out suggestions, critiques, and advice.* Consult with people knowledgeable in specific areas. At times, this may be difficult emotionally when it would seem easier to consult (collude) with someone who would mirror and agree with your own opinions rather than listening objectively to critical or contradictory information. Don't limit yourself with your imagination because your imagination has to evolve from your present model. Other points of view may be a catalyst.

11. *Sleep on it. Recognize that there are few true emergencies in life.* Weighing different factors, gathering data, and perhaps consulting experts are the best approaches to making most decisions. Rarely does any legitimate crisis demand that these steps be skipped. A classic example is the promoter who tries to push you into an overnight decision, to make money decisions in a fraction of the time it took to earn the money. Decisions based on impulse, frustration, or anger may need to be postponed until objectivity is regained. Calling a time-out is a useful maneuver for emotionally charged matters.

12. *Select goals consistent with your self-image.* This is necessary to have all of you going in the same direction. We live our lives based on our beliefs and assumptions; to change your life, you must first change your belief.

13. *What you decide to accept undergoes a change.* To forgive someone is to free yourself.

14. *Getting what you always wanted in the past may not feel as good as you expected because it is no longer the past.* Just having a choice can make choosing the same thing feel very different.

15. *For an end point, ask yourself, "What is good enough?"* Driven pursuit of perfection arises from not having a standard of good enough—of not having established an end point.

16. *The question "What is in my best interest?" should always be in the background and, at times, in the foreground as well.* Asking this question is just another way to assess the big picture at a time when you may be focusing on details or in the grips of excess emotion.

17. *The past may not be the best or the most relevant context in which to understand the present.* The model of understanding must fit the situation, your style, and your personality; it should be consistent.

18. *Create a contemplation space to ponder decisions, especially emotionally freighted ones.* Between an urge and an action lies a potential space in which judgment resides.

19. *Growth involves enduring uncertainty.*

20. *Not only can we change, but we can also choose how we will change.*

21. *Insight and understanding may initiate internal change, but both internal and external change need to be addressed.* The more you think about how much you missed out on, the more you miss now. When you stand up, your lap is a memory—it can be re-created, and if you continually have to return to it, it interferes with proceeding. A client commented, "I wish there were some magical words you could fill me with so I didn't feel bad." My gentle but firm response was, "There are: Stop searching for magic."

22. *Growth and change involve their own mourning.* You have to relinquish a past position in order to move ahead.

23. *The only familiar territory is behind you.*

24. *Growth and change are hard. The only thing harder is not growing or changing.*

25. *Our experiences are always consistent with our theories.* Most often, we attempt change by changing our experiences, which often only produce new editions of the old experience.

26. *Clarify your external goals.* Be certain there is a fit between your internal and external goals, that what you want to accomplish is consistent with your ideals. This consistency can provide an organizing structure and direction to your ambition.

27. *Anything important requires a commitment to go forward despite discomfort.* A commitment is a decision you have to make only once—then you can direct your energy to fulfilling the commitment.

28. *Know what reaching a goal will do.* Then you can distinguish clearly what it will not do. For example, reaching a goal will not undo the past or make other troubles go away. Monetary wealth may bring many things, but it may not make your marriage better.

29. *You'll never do anything important that will feel comfortable in the beginning.* Anxiety about the new and unfamiliar do not equate to the old anxiety coupled with danger, warning about the need to head to safety. This new anxiety can be a signal, an affirmation, that you are moving ahead to do things new and unknown.

30. *Trying to change your past is not change; it will always be the way it was.*

31. *Decisions always limit choices while activating others.*

32. *We suffer most from our anticipations and limit ourselves most by our assumptions.*

Twelve Maxims to Sustain Growth

1. Get all of yourself going in the same direction: ideals and needs aligned with passion, goals, and strategy.

2. If you want to change your life, change your mind.

3. Have inside and outside match to move yourself, your life, and your career to new realms of capacity and function.

4. Believe in yourself; doing so will determine how much others believe in you.

5. Stick with yourself no matter what.

6. When you change your mind, you change your life and your vision of potential, goals, and results.

7. To leave an old story, you have to have a new story to be in.

8. People may hear what you say, but they will always remember how you made them feel.

9. What you believe will show.

10. As with any new experience, some fear and uncertainty are natural in the beginning.

11. You are always creating outside to match inside; your experiences are always consistent with your assumptions.

12. What you believe will become true because you will live it.

An Overview of the Seven Steps: The ROADMAP

We've examined money as reality and metaphor and the power we give it as well as its own inherent power.

This journey has illuminated seven steps to change and enhance your money story:

Recognize authorship of your money story.
Own your present money story.
Assess your money story plot and story lines.
Decide what to change in your money story.
Map changes: Inscribe new code.
Author new experiences: Write new software.
Program new identity: Rewire for wealth.

These seven steps articulate some of the secret language of money—how some money issues are really about money, how a bunch of other things hitchhike on money, and how our money stories are a large part of our life stories.

These basic steps deconstruct how you write your money story and live it; they are building blocks to revise a money story or to write a new one.

A Final Story

For tens of thousands of years before there were books or computers, we transmitted our essence and principles by story. Story linked to the past, organized the present, and illuminated the future. Story allowed us to connect with each other's humanity in the paths crossed on the long journeys out of Africa to populate the rest of the world. Later, the anatomy and physiology of our brains grew by putting thoughts and feelings into stories. Stories informed, instructed, inspired, governed, and organized. Story is the most powerful way humans communicate. Stories give birth to possibility.

Stories are a way that we resonate with our earlier selves, connect with others, and create a road map to proceed.

Your story is yourself, your life, and what will survive you. At some point in the distant future, all that will be left of you, all that will survive you, is your story.

Be sure to get it right.

Part 3

BELIEF SYSTEMS AND CHOICE ARCHITECTURE

THE ABCS OF MONEY MISTAKES AND FINANCIAL FALLACIES

- Do you make spending decisions based on how much you've already spent on a particular project?

- Do you sell winning investments and hold on to losing investments without sound underlying investment reasons?

- Do you spend more with credit cards than you would for the same purchase with cash?

- Would you spend the same amount regardless of the source of the money, including unexpected and windfall sources?

- Do you have trouble saving money?

- Do you pay yourself each month, such as an automatic savings plan?

- Are you aware of how sensitive you are to losing money and honest with yourself about losses, "real" or "paper"?

Some recurring psychologically based fallacies affect money behavior and financial choices. These patterns of mental dynamics can be identified to help you avoid mistakes and generate productive strategies.

The following 25 common fallacies, along with a prescription of cure (Rx) for each, offer a psychological nomenclature for an aspect of financial literacy.

The ABCS: Affect (Emotional) Biases

Nostalgia Bias

Nostalgia looks backward with rose-colored glasses. Nostalgia remembers things not as they were but as we wished them to be, as better than they were at the time—airbrushed memories backlit by idealization. Nostalgia recalls the ideal rather than the real.

By airbrushing memories, people overestimate their own ability; this can create a tendency toward bad decisions. This tendency inflates present expectation. People believe that they make better financial decisions than they actually do and that they are healthier than average.

People attribute negative results to external factors beyond their control: the market or the economy. This tendency to marginalize the negative and enhance the positive relates to nostalgia.

Rx

Review the negative and warning signs that you overlooked in previous compromised decisions. Be sure you understand any tendency to dismiss what you don't want to see, to minimize mistake patterns, and to disregard what you hope won't happen. There is a place for rose-colored glasses, but you have to take them off to make financial decisions (rose-colored glasses make red ink invisible).

Invincibility Bias

Invincibility bias involves self-deception by self-inflation. People naturally tend to estimate risk poorly and to exaggerate anticipated performance. Of the U.S. population, 19 percent believes they are in the upper 1 percent of income. And 90 percent believe they are better drivers than average. In the same way, 94 percent place themselves at the top half of their profession. Among both men and women, 75 percent believe they are healthier than average.

Rx

Set limits prior to an activity. For example, gamblers can set a predetermined daily amount of maximum money exposure.

Research variations of outcome. List them to focus on real possibilities.

Substitute alternative excitement for real danger. The brain does not distinguish between real and manufactured thrill, so thriller films and roller coasters can be an alternate excitement to financial risk. Actively trade a fantasy portfolio.

Optimism Bias

The optimism bias inflates expectations and minimizes potential negative outcome and warning signs going forward. Excess optimism idealizes the future just as nostalgia idealizes the past. In 1990, people pushed AOL to a price that an earnings model supported only if it had 18 billion subscribers, which would be triple the population of the Earth.

Optimism bias also minimizes fearful possibilities. People indulge in risky behavior despite being aware of the danger involved. Gamblers underestimate the risk and inflate their chances despite knowing the odds against them.

Rx

Examine those areas in which you are "probability blind." Notice patterns that you are likely to expect although they have no basis in reality. For example, if the roulette wheel stops on red four times in a row, you may expect it to do so a fifth time—knowing logically that the next spin has a 50/50 chance of landing on red or black. Or if a stock goes up 14 quarters in a row, rather than expecting it to follow its trend, objectively assess its current fundamentals and value.

Don't listen for what you want to hear. Look for the shadow side of every story.

Tilt

Poker experts indicate that the difference between winning and losing is often the ability to stay off "tilt." In poker terms, tilt—the emotional reaction to winning big or losing big—alters a state of mind that carries over to the next hand. When poker players are on tilt, they make decisions they normally would not make because they're upset, disappointed, irritated, or extremely happy and excited.

Increased tension produces emotional regression—a pattern characteristic of a much earlier age. Additionally, increased emotion narrows perspective and restricts focus on the most recent event (recency effect).

Rx

When you're in a state of upset, the first order of business is to regulate feelings. Break the state of mind; get centered and grounded. "I'll think about it" is a decision. "I'll sleep on it" is a choice. "I'll get back to you" is an option. There are few true emergencies in life; investing isn't one of them.

Emotional Valuation

Regardless of how logical you think you are, your first register of a new stimulus is emotional. Any new input goes directly to the amygdala (in the midbrain), then the hippocampus (still in the midbrain) attaches meaning, and then the forebrain consciously processes.

At times, this emotional coupling can overwrite brain valuation and blur logic. An emotionally significant equation can be one that became coupled in the past. For example, money can be equated with emotional signifiers, such as power, freedom, evil, and greed. Decision-making processes in the brain also involve shortcuts in analysis, such as brands, familiarity, and trust.

Rx

Recognize and understand emotional links that can derail logic. Question your ideas. Probe your reasoning. Monitor your choices. Determine how much each choice costs.

Loss Aversion

The average person experiences negative feelings from losses more acutely than pleasurable experiences from gains. Studies show that there is about twice the pain from a $100 loss than there is pleasure from a $100 gain.[1] Even the expectation of loss can create a sensitivity to overreact, such as selling stocks too quickly when hearing negative news.

Loss aversion can create inertia to retain losing investments too long, to hope for a rebound, rather than sell and "lock in" a definitive loss. A paper loss is nonreality as long as selling does not concretize it. Additionally, loss aversion can prompt abandonment of an investment too quickly.

Rx

Predetermine criteria to balance emotional reactivity. Move the choice architecture from an emotional position to a logical, objective assessment of present value.

Assess the equally compromising position of inertia—staying in a comfort zone—that can blind you from making an objective assessment and decision.

Probability Blindness

The tendency to inaccurately judge risks based on wish or habit can result in probability blindness. If someone sees a roulette wheel stop on red six times in a row, a false belief exists that the chances are higher than 50/50 that it will stop on black the next spin. When as few as two things happen in a row, the brain expects a third to occur. Unlike your brain, the roulette wheel has no memory and sticks with the possibility of 50/50 red/black on each spin.

The human brain, capable of complex mathematical calculations, succumbs to probability blindness to purchase a lottery ticket with a 1 in 15 million chance of hitting. A triad of illusion includes underestimation of risk, overestimation of performance, and bad math.

Rx

Specifically consider alternatives. Alternatives may force you to look at biases, emotional valuation, and probability blindness.

Seek dissenting opinions. Although emotionally and intellectually challenging, seeking opposing views and exposing alternatives is a useful strategy.

Track prior decisions. Once we make a decision or an event has passed, we tend to believe we did better and knew more about the outcome beforehand than we actually did. This hindsight bias can distort accurate assessment.

Avoid decision making at emotional or stressful times.

Understand alternatives and incentives. Both financial and nonfinancial incentives can distort decisions, such as brand or nostalgic coupling.

Set limits prior to an activity. Savvy gamblers set a predetermined daily amount of maximum money exposure.

The ABCS: Behavior Biases

Transference Fallacy

In psychoanalysis, transference is carrying over perceptions and response patterns from a past context to a current one. In a transference fallacy, investors tend to draw analogies and see identical situations that distort a current situation. Another company, sector, or market environment becomes colored with the same brush even though there may be only a remote resemblance between the two situations.

The transference direction can also go forward to project the present onto the future. Whenever a stock doubles in value, the tendency is to expect it to continue to grow. This self-reinforcing story can create a bubble in a stock, sector, or market.

Rx

Ground your decisions in the present time. Transference is the result of existing mind and brain software—the organizing effort based on how we see, perceive, and process. Independently assess the assumptions of similarity and dissimilarity based on past experience to evaluate whether the software is outdated. Recognize what will require a new or revised model.

Spending Justification

Justification occupies a place of dubious distinction: It gives a legitimate support and just cause (by definition) to an endeavor but uses the same reasoning to deceive its author. The relentless and even addictive pursuit of money, for example, sustains the pursuit of the extreme, justified by the American work ethic and ideal of capitalism.

Rx

If you have to justify a decision, it needs to be examined, under bright lights, and with at least one witness.

Examine each financial decision in terms of the entire system and the principle involved rather than segmenting the decision as stand-alone.

Spending Rationalization

How many times have you spent "found money" or gambling money, rationalizing it as extra money that was not there otherwise? Perhaps spent it many times over? A variation of rationalization can be the concept of amortization over time. Any purchase can be rationalized if extrapolated over a period of time.

Rationalization applied to credit card purchases makes spending and getting in debt a theory.

Rx

Like justification, if you have to rationalize a decision, it needs to be examined under bright lights, with at least one witness, and scrutinized in terms of your overall plan.

Sunk Cost Fallacy

We sometimes make continued spending decisions based on how much money we've already spent on a project. It's hard to let go of a loser or not complete an expensive project though the cost far exceeds reason.

Rx

Research worst-, likely-, and best-case scenarios on the front end as part of a business decision.

Have internal and external (contractual) agreements in place from the beginning. Make sure you don't register only what you want to hear—such as logging in the lower figure of a range of cost possibility.

Each decision you make is a present choice regardless of your previous decisions.

Pattern Bias

The brain naturally seeks patterns. Studies have demonstrated that people see patterns too quickly in data that are actually random.[2] The brain links patterns to rewards. The limbic system tells us that if we see a stock go up several days in a row or as few as two quarters in a row, it will continue to go up, and we had better buy. The limbic system does not know that the stock has no memory and that past performance is no guarantee of future results.

Rx

Recognize what psychological tendencies have worked and which have sabotaged investment returns. Understand those patterns to create principles for times of stress, such as panic in a sharp market downturn or greed in a sharp market upturn.

Predict and mentally rehearse everything that could go wrong with a plan, the worst- and best-case scenarios. Understand your reactions to emotional news and vulnerability to external influences.

Review core holdings and basic decisions periodically. Base this review on calendar time, such as once a year, rather than as precipitated by an emotional event.

Status Quo Bias

The status quo bias is another name for inertia—the resistance to leave a comfort zone. The power of inertia accounts for why we do things the way we've always done them rather than looking at decisions in a present context with fresh eyes and objective evidence.

People stick with default choices even when the choices are costly or compromised. Marketers know that when they set up a continuity program, such as a free three-month trial with automatic continuation unless canceled, the inclination is to stay with the familiar and not cancel. This keeps 75 to 80 percent of initially free subscribers on for the long haul of paid subscription.

Rx

For any situation, look at the data and also the hypothesis—the default assumption that appears as a "given."

Examine what works and what doesn't work.

Challenge your thinking and assumptions. Interact with diverse people and keep an open "beginner's mind" rather than a quick foreclosure to a new idea.

Decide what you want to keep, avoid, let go, and enhance.

Convert good decisions into a commitment device and a status quo model, such as regular automatic deposit into a retirement account, regular dental and medical checkups, or automatically recurring beneficial acts.

Ask, "If I had not always done it this way, knowing what I know now, what would I do?"

The ABCS: Cognitive Biases

Diagnosis Bias

Once we label a person or situation, we're prone to then seek data to confirm that notion more vigorously, coupled with blindness to evidence that contradicts. We then use the "diagnosis" as a paradigm or mental map for subsequent categorical decisions.

Rx

Remain flexible and examine a situation from different angles. Take your time and consider options available before deciding. Impose a waiting period before reaching a judgment. Consider objectively: "Is this an emotional issue or a business decision?" Seek alternate—especially dissenting—opinions.

Confirmation Bias

We cherry-pick data to fit our beliefs. We decide about everything from the likability of a person to the value of an idea, then consciously and unconsciously seek validation. Confirmation bias is a distortion based on the search for information to validate beliefs and impressions. More insidiously, this bias precludes someone from questioning and examining the premise. First impressions have powerful impact because of the ensuing process to seek supportive data.

Rx

Monitor your choices. Be aware of the tendency to find the story you want to hear.

Question your ideas. Objectify your assumptions as much as possible.

Probe your reasoning. Beware of a tendency to see only what you already believe.

Ask clearly and honestly, "Does it work?" Ask for feedback whenever possible and be open to what you hear.

Money Equations

Money can make any statement. A few of the most common include worth, autonomy, security, freedom, love, opportunity, and power.

Money equations are established by early couplings and developed by emotionally powerful desires. Money is the legal tender of desires. Money becomes the inkblot of the Rorschach test: When our eyes look straight at it, there is only a design on paper, but when offered the chance to imbue the design with meaning, our interpretations will be as wishful and varied as our fantasies.

Rx

See the section "Your Money Equations" in chapter 7.

Anchoring

Anchoring sets an arbitrary figure as a starting point of reference to place value in ambiguous situations. Adjustments move from that point. If someone takes a recent trading range as the anchor value of a stock, this precludes an analysis of the intrinsic value of the stock itself.

The person who buys a stock at $100 is much less likely to sell when it goes to either $90 or $110 than the person who brought it at $40 because the anchor is the purchase price of $100. Meanwhile, what is the underlying value of the stock itself?

People can also "anchor" their predictions in the present and resist believing that the future will be much different.

Rx

Rather than accepting the current price of an equity or the marked price of an item as the anchor, research the true value. Be objective in your comparison and due diligence.

An example of setting your own anchor price is to preview an auction item and establish the maximum price you will pay before you get caught up in the excitement of bids.

Framing Decisions

A dollar, the same unit of money, is treated differently—as if it has a dissimilar value—depending on its context. Framed as a gambling win, a tax savings, or a salary, it is regarded differently. "Found money" (as in found on the street or in a forgotten coat pocket), an unexpected bonus, or a tax return is spent more freely than if it came from salary and especially more so than if it came from savings.

How we frame an issue determines how we think about it. The metaphors we use can help us respond more effectively to what we encounter.

"This is found money. I have to blow it on a horse," George Costanza said memorably in an episode of *Seinfeld.*

Rx

Consider each decision objectively as an independent choice regardless of the source of the money. Would I make this purchase if I had to take it from my salary? From my savings? Is this a choice I will be proud of tomorrow? And will have no regrets about one year from now?

Extrapolation Errors

When we predict the future based on the past, we forget that anything can happen. We do not and cannot know the future.

Two simple concepts are valuable in investing:

- No one knows the future.

- The brain automatically imposes patterns and predictions on repeated events, making it difficult to override both emotion and brain patterns in order to make wise and balanced decisions. The emotional components of investing account for the perception that the public has not gotten smarter; it's why people repeat financial mistakes.

Rx

Do not assume that the future will be a replica of the past. To balance extrapolation mistakes, consider whether you can take a risk based on the probability that you are right and also on the consequences if you happen to be wrong.

Consult with an expert financial planner and include a range of good to bad scenarios going forward; include saving for a rainy day. Consider a personal or business board of advisers or mastermind group to brainstorm financial plans.

Internal Bargaining

Internal bargaining involves the self-deception of equating plan with action. The internal bargaining of "I'll make this purchase now and start my savings plan next month" creates the illusion of commitment. The idea of a future plan, even a promise to oneself, has never led its author to add a single dollar to a savings account.

An investor makes carefully planned decisions to minimize risk and maximize reward. He makes money consistently. As his gains accrue, he relaxes his criteria and departs from his principles, making unplanned trades. Losses follow.

Rx

A commitment is a decision you have to make only once. The truly challenging, courageous part of change is not the initial decision. Nor is it the initiation of a new order of things. It's the willingness to stay the course. Success is never final. Don't get complacent. Testing is as important as postulating.

The ABCS: Social Biases

Affinity Bias

We underestimate the risk of things we like, such as alcohol, tobacco, or favorite stocks. We overestimate the risk of the things that we do not like, such as foreign enemies or an out-of-favor investment. We overestimate the value of what we most like, such as prized possessions or a favorite stock. We underestimate the influence of what we don't like, such as an opposing team or political party.

Rx

Be aware of explicit affinity biases, such as bets on your alma mater's football game. Reflect on hidden influences that elevate regard of the familiar and favorite while marginalizing both risk and value of the unfamiliar and disliked.

Value Attribution

We tend to imbue a person or thing with certain qualities based on our initial perceived value. Value attribution is our own shortcut to determine how we judge what we see, even what is worthy of our attention. Then the assigned value shapes subsequent perception.

Value attribution incorporates the endowment effect, a related bias in which someone assigns a greater value to what they own than to what they don't own, whether or not that value is warranted.

Rx

Be mindful to observe objectively rather than what you wish or how things appear. Recognize that you make judgments based on your assumptions or personal value. Accept that your initial perceptions can be wrong. Ask yourself, "If I were just now exposed to this situation for the first time, what would my decision be?"

Availability Bias

When we try to figure out how likely something is to happen, we scan through our memory of similar events, pulling up data for comparison.

What we may not realize is that our access to similar events is highly skewed toward recent experiences. More recent events, especially more salient and emotionally charged ones, are always more memorable. So if you recently had a car accident, you will have "kindling" and be more skittish about driving. Or if you had a close friend who was robbed, you are more likely to conclude that your neighborhood is dangerous.

Rx

My favorite athletic coach consistently said, "Keep your eye on the ball and your head in the game."

Keep your eye on the ball: Focus on the immediate, the present moment, without distraction.

And keep your head in the game: See the big picture, the purpose and game plan, so that everything you do moves you forward.

Recognize the distinction between avoidance and contemplation. "I'll get back to you" is a response. "I'll think about it" is a decision.

Recency Effect

Whatever has happened most recently basically determines what seems most likely to happen next. Our human tendency estimates possibilities more on the basis of recent events than long-term experience or longitudinal analysis. Recency trumps both reason and history. We tend to over-weight recent events because of more vivid recall as well as greater emotional impact.

The brain contributes to the recency effect by predicting a third re-iteration when two events occur in a row. Marketing devices take advantage of this fact, such as slot machines with two matches while the player waits expectantly for the third match or scratch-off lottery cards with two matching symbols leading to the excited expectation of a third.

Rx

Create a long-term plan that reflects your values and priorities. Have a money map. See the section "Your Money Mission Statement" in chapter 12.

Collective Tilt (Herd Mentality)

Although we say we buy companies, we really buy stories. Although we say we judge logically, we really decide emotionally. And we are vulnerable to social contagion.

Bandwagon jumping on hot funds, sectors, or stocks causes artificial inflation. Or, if the herd mentality goes the other direction, it causes premature sell-offs. Wall Street analysts are not immune to this phenomenon. Research consistently indicates that consensus analyst forecasts range too high or too low by an average of 40 percent. When the stock market rises, we reach for our calculators to plan early retirement. Yet when the market declines, we worry if we'll ever be able to retire. Individual psychology, as well as group reaction, exaggerates this reaction to short-term trends. Herd mentality overreacts to trends as well as to events.

Rx

Have a plan and stick to it.

Take in new information but distinguish emotional information from fundamental business data.

If it seems that you're making an urgent or emergency decision, sleep on it. Consult a trusted adviser.

Remain active in your investment plan as chief executive officer of your finances. Even a financial planner is still your employee.

Seek excitement in other areas of your life rather than using finances, investments, or trading as a source of excitement.

Use different wallets, such as having a core investment holding, a higher risk/higher reward investment portion, and a secure, no-risk portion.

BELIEF MANAGEMENT

Believing: The Neuroscience of Reverse Truths

In traditional science, truth is arrived at by proffering a hypothesis, then accumulating data to prove or disprove it; the data force the conclusion. Reverse truths work the opposite—the hypothesis or belief *creates* the data.

Our assumptions select what we perceive in the world and determine what meanings we attach. Not only is believing necessary in order to see; we also bring about what we expect to happen. A story creates a reality. For example, a placebo is an inert pill plus a story. The patient is prescribed expectations that, in the majority of cases, manifest. By anticipating an experience, we can create it. The story generates a truth so powerful that it can *reverse* the pharmacological effects of the real medicine. The placebo's story is a white lie, a fiction that becomes a truth.

While my children's adolescence cured me of most of my theories, a few fundamental ones survived and are even more boldly illuminated against the backdrop of passing years. One of these survivors is the principle of reverse truths.

A vital reverse truth is our belief in our children. They look to us as a mirror of who they are, and they become what they see. If we trust and respect them, they become trustworthy and respect themselves.

Some parents have this reverse truth backward, thinking that they will trust a child only after he or she has proven to be trustworthy. There are forward truths, but this isn't one of them. Our belief in our children is taken in by them and metabolized into their own belief in themselves. We convey to them in an unspoken message, "I'll believe in you until both of us can." When that affirmation isn't there, they may spend their lives looking for that elusive approval.

Carlyle was right. "Tell a man he is brave and you help him to become so." As a parent, the trick is that you have to believe what you say, for feigned praise and inauthentic interest are forgeries immediately discernible to a child's expert eye. I see this reverse truth professionally as well. When I work with practicing professionals (health care, financial, and legal)—and performance professionals (actors and athletes), I have to believe in them so they can believe in themselves. Since people can imagine only from their own systems, they may not be able to authentically and completely imagine immense personal and professional success—which is why I work only with clients in whom I really believe.

A corollary of believing in my children was to believe their words, their truthfulness. When both my children were very young, I told them that I would never lie to them and would always believe everything they told me as well. I knew then the responsibility that that placed on them to always tell the truth.

On a Father's Day many years ago, my son's last before leaving home and starting college, I found a letter from him at my bathroom sink. A passage offered a progress note on this reverse truth: "You never lied to me and I have never lied to you. Sounded stupid at first, but as time passed, it became more important, and I realized that I never would. This is a relationship few others have ever had."

Keep Your Eye on the Ball (and Your Head in the Game)

This regular admonition by my favorite athletic coach was an often-repeated encouragement that served as inspiration and template for success as he mentored me daily for four years. His frame for this mantra was a principle he taught me that became the foundation for why I would devote a first career to psychiatry and a second to mentor coaching: Your mind is the most powerful thing in the world. These two phrases were catalysts to win championships and later served as a guide for professional choices.

Keep Your Eye on the Ball

When you enter a bank to buy money (also known as applying for a loan), your concern may focus on being good enough, about how you will be viewed, if you and your income and credit are adequate.

The simple process of an application for a loan can even resonate with the dynamics of shame: "I have to prove my worth." This process is one we all wish was more unconscious than it really is.

When an acceptance does come—and relief with it—the exact terms, conditions, and cost of your purchase of money may remain unquestioned. This temporary abandonment of focus is as common as it is illogical.

In contrast, consider an unemotional purchase. When you go to an appliance store to buy a refrigerator, you've probably already done research, cost comparisons, and perhaps an assessment of the store. You pay particular attention to the cost, features, warranty, and even the efficiency. Still, it is a simple transaction involving just the facts. The purchase of the refrigerator is unemotional and does not overshadow the business transaction.

Keep your eye on the ball: Focus on the immediate, the specific, and its importance.

And Your Head in the Game

The chemicals of emotion alter mind and body. Personal experience determines what software program (state of mind) we use to process and respond to a particular situation. An emotional response with its bio-chemical consequences in the brain can trigger an emotional state of mind geared more for survival than for logic.

Money sometimes speaks to us just below the level of our conscious awareness: as confidante, seducer, adversary, protector, or drug. It can serve as a tangible container for hope, freedom, ambition, love, or disappointment. It can become a currency of caring, a symbol of success, a promissory note for happiness, or a filler for a sagging sense of self. Money is the one true metaphor that can stand for anything else.

We make money mistakes because we use money to accomplish non-financial goals. We give money meaning. We breathe life into it, give it emotional value, build relationship with it, and make it bigger than it is.

Keep your head in the game—and never forget the cost of money.

Two Questions That Can Change Your Life

What's My Sentence?

Dan Pink and I were discussing our recent books and the application for the professional coaches I train. From his already best-selling *Drive*,[1] Dan highlighted a brief section about two questions that seemed most beneficial to life and business coaches.

The first comes from Clare Booth Luce, one of the first women to serve in the U.S. Congress. In 1962, concerned that President John F. Kennedy's attention was divided among many priorities and worried that he was trying to do too many things, she told him of her concern that he would be less than effective with his attention scattered.

She told him, "A great man is one sentence." Abraham Lincoln's sentence was that he preserved the Union and freed the slaves. Franklin Roosevelt's sentence was that he lifted us out of the Great Depression and helped us win a world war. It was up to Kennedy, she implied, to formulate his own sentence, to focus his efforts.

Perhaps your sentence is "I raised two children who became happy and productive adults" or "I helped many people grow to become more of who they really are."

As you reflect on your purpose, begin with the question, "What's my sentence?"

Am I Better Now Than I Was Yesterday?

Small questions can be like single steps in creating a new life story. At the beginning of each day, you may ask what you will do that day so that you're better than yesterday. What will you learn or do to be better? Look for the small things, such as writing two pages, eating five servings of vegetables, learning a new word, or working out.

As you go to bed each night, ask the small question, "Am I better now than I was yesterday?"

To Change or Not to Change

More than a century ago, William James wrote that the greatest discovery of his generation was that human beings could alter their lives by altering their attitudes of mind. Neuroscience validated his assertion and added that creating new experiences changes neuronal pathways in the brain (neurotransmitters) and even alters gene expression.

Many years ago, a wise, elderly colleague of mine would simply tell his patients, "Sometimes you just gotta change the way you act before you can change the way you think and feel."

How surprised we are to learn that our fears are not in the dim shadows of the past's unknown but in the hopeful light of this moment's change.

Precommitment and Commitment

Precommitment: Ulysses Contracts

Ulysses, king of Ithaca and hero of the Trojan War, embarked on a protracted sea voyage after the war to go back to his home island of Ithaca. He had a rare opportunity ahead in that his ship would pass the island where the beautiful sirens sang melodies so enchanting that no one had been able to avoid their magnetic pull. Every time they lured the sailors and their ships toward them, the ships were dashed on the rocks, drowning all aboard.

Ulysses—knowing that when he heard the music, he too would be unable to resist—created a present plan to deal with his future self. In his present rational state, he ordered his men to lash him to the mast of the ship and not untie him no matter how much he begged or pleaded. He then had them fill their own ears with beeswax so the voices of the sirens couldn't seduce them. He made it clear to his crew that they must not release him until the ship was well past the sirens, nor were they to take out the beeswax until then.

Every one of us is free to make a Ulysses contract, to create a plan for a future self, a precommitment. Someone determined to break an alcohol addiction must ensure that they avoid exposure to alcohol. Someone determined to save for the future has an automatic transfer on the first day of the month from his or her checking account to a retirement fund—a good one-time decision. People in the old-fashioned Christmas clubs regularly deposited a fixed amount each month for their December selves.

Another example of a Ulysses contract, a way to proactively commit to a future self, is to put down a deposit of $100 with a promise that you will lose 10 pounds by a certain time. If you lose the 10 pounds by the date you set, you get all the money back. If you don't lose the weight by that time, you lose the money. Perhaps a charity gains or, worse, your good friend keeps it. As people get closer to the date that they can win back their money, their present emotional selves will care more and more about the past self that made a future commitment.

Ulysses contracts are made in medicine when someone signs an advanced medical directive to pull the plug in the event of a coma.

Commitment Devices

One of the roles of a mentor coach is being an accountability partner. There have been studies on how people self-impose as well as cocreate commitments for behaviors that they know are in their best interest. We help our children do this. A piggy bank is a commitment device to counter impulsive purchases.

People can counter their own vulnerability and bolster commitment to a better response in a variety of ways:

- In one study, college students were given the option to create their own earlier deadlines for three papers due by the end of the semester. Out of the total group, 75 percent of them jumped at the chance. Of course, this is always an option of personal choice.

- People find ways of saving themselves from immediate cravings. A study at the Harvard Business School looked at the ways people dealt with purchasing "want" products and "should" products.[2] They would devise ways to either put off purchasing or put off having the "want" products delivered to ensure that they would do what they should do first.

- Freezing a credit card in ice to mandate a contemplative pause before a purchase.

- Automatic retirement deposits to make commitment a one-time decision.

Consider how to prioritize your *shoulds* and reward doing them with your *wants*. This reframes *wants* as part of a performance ethic. It removes guilt, and it links performance with what you know you're going to do anyhow. And planning is a different scenario from impulsivity.

Belief Management Narratives

Thoughts, assumptions, and beliefs about money that can limit a money story. The story in your mental theater can contain any of a number of limiting beliefs:

- I have to work hard for money.
- I have to sacrifice for money.
- Money's just not for me.
- You have to get lucky.
- It will hurt someone else.
- People won't like me as much if I'm rich.
- It will change who I am.
- Making money is stressful.
- I'll have to give to the government anyway.
- It's hard in this economy.
- Money's running out.
- There's not enough.

In the same way, the story can include abundance beliefs:

- Abundance is a mind-set I can create each day.
- There's plenty for everyone.
- Abundance is good for me, my friends, and my family.
- The more I have, the more I can offer to the world.
- Money creates opportunities for my loved ones. And for me and my life.

- Creating money feels good.

- Creating money brings joy to me and to those around me.

- Money loves me.

- It wants me to be there for me.

- It wants to be there for me and my friends and my family.

You'll be using your energy either spending money or creating it. It's a choice.

Money Psychology and Information Avoidance

> Fate has a way of putting in front of us that which we most try to leave behind. —Mozzie in the TV series *White Collar*

We want more money, but we resist examining our money stories. We hit a money glass ceiling, but we avoid information about ourselves.

In a recent panel on money stories that I conducted for financial coaches, one woman spoke of money being a source of anxiety throughout her adulthood ever since she had to flee her home country as a child. With a forced exodus from her homeland, her family lost its fortune. Her experience was that money had wings and could be taken away. She indicated that she refuses to eat out of paper plates because it resonates with that traumatic time. She now owns 10 sets of dishes.

Research has shown that credit card users underestimate significantly how much they owe on credit cards. Cardholders admit to only $4 of every $10 they owe. Intelligent people willfully disavow 60 percent of their debt.

Most people are secretly dissatisfied with their money stories. This dissatisfaction often stems from feeling either unfulfilled or ashamed of certain aspects of that story. Each of us has beliefs about money that we don't speak about out loud to ourselves. This avoidance can create a bias; it can preclude taking in essential, important new information. Earlier downloads of certain expectations and experiences about money remain intact and unchallenged despite the passage of years, even decades. What are some of the main reasons people use to avoid new information about themselves?

- It may require a change in beliefs. People seek information that confirms their beliefs and blind themselves to reasons that disprove those beliefs.

- It may cause unpleasant emotions. If we expect bad news, we tend to avoid this information.

- It may require us to take undesired actions. At times, it may seem better not to know, such as ignoring a symptom that requires us to gather new information. People aren't scared of doctors; rather, they're scared that their denial may be confronted.

- It may feel like lack of control. If people anticipate a loss of control over the consequences of information, they will stay with what they know and avoid the unknown.

- It activates the brain's error-detection mechanism. New information will trigger that mechanism, generating a reading that something isn't right and should be avoided.

- The information may be difficult to understand. If the information is difficult to interpret, overwhelmingly complicated, or not clear and simple, we may tend to avoid the work of interpreting it.

Here's the important principle to keep in mind when considering new information about ourselves: *The key element in writing a new story is to design the story from what is possible, rather than what existed in the past.*

Create New Beliefs

How we tell our stories of the past will shape our future. Some stories get told so much or so often that they achieve the status of becoming a personal myth:

- If I were just loved enough.

- If I just have enough money.

When you are ready to write a new belief, focus on it frequently and return to it often and in every way that you can. The new belief has to replace the old belief. Create a vision of yourself getting the results from the new belief.

Nathan Handwerker put in a new food stand in 1916 in Coney Island. Handwerker's hot dogs were pure beef, made from his wife's recipe, and every bit as delicious as those of his competitors. But he priced his at 5 cents, and the other hot dogs were priced at 10 cents. He attracted no customers. People wondered if his hot dogs were inferior; they attributed poor-quality ingredients to his products. Nor did his sales increase when he offered free root beer and free pickles—that just furthered the perception that the value must be substandard.

Then Handwerker came up with a new ploy. He asked doctors from a nearby hospital to stand nearby eating his hot dogs while they were wearing their white coats and stethoscopes. And he raised his price. The franks began selling well. People assumed that if physicians were eating his food, it had to be good. His hot dogs became a national phenomenon: "Nathan's Famous Hot Dogs."

The value we attribute—the belief—can fundamentally change how we perceive something.

Creating a new belief is not an instantaneous thing. It's a process. It can take some period of time. It can occur quickly, or it can take years to complete. The process of changing a belief is just that: the process, not an event. It can be planned, though, step-by-step, with incremental progress.

It takes however long it takes. It's your process, not anyone else's. Don't compare your inside to someone else's outside. Don't compare your journey, your timetable, and your progress with anyone else's. It is uniquely yours. Your story. However long it takes, you can make it worth it.

In changing your belief and the result of the change in your action, you are also changing your mind as well as your brain.

The choices generate the moment-by-moment life you create. The programming of your internal map of reality—your software—determines how easy it will be.

At any moment in time, neural networks are influenced by three factors: *genes*, *experiences*, and *focused attention*. Regardless of someone's unique brain architecture and individual complexity, these three factors intersect at any moment, at any nanosecond.

Our DNA downloads information from the expression of its code. We now know it can also go in the other direction. Our experiences—our beliefs—can turn genes on and off to determine the major extent of the expression of DNA-based information. Dr. Bruce Lipton summarized this finding, emphasizing that although genes can't turn themselves on or off, they can adapt to our beliefs and experiences.

CHOICE ARCHITECTURE

Frame

Alocal car wash ran a promotion featuring loyalty cards. Each time customers bought a car wash, their cards were stamped, and when they filled up their cards with eight stamps, they got a free wash. Another set of customers, at the same car wash, got a loyalty card with which they needed to collect ten stamps for a free car wash rather than eight. They were also given a head start in that when they received their cards, two stamps had already been added.

The goal was the same for both sets of customers, requiring the purchase of eight car washes to get a reward.

But the psychology and therefore the motivation were different. Those who had the two-stamp head start were already 20 percent of the way toward a goal rather than starting from scratch.

Several months later, the results were in:[1]

- Of the eight-stamp customers, 19 percent earned a free wash.

- Of the head start group, 34 percent earned a free wash. And this group earned their free wash faster, meaning they were ready to start over and spend more money sooner. Almost a fourfold difference was based solely on how the offer was framed.

People are motivated by feeling they are partly finished with a longer task or journey rather than just beginning an even shorter one. Therefore, a way to motivate action would be to frame the task in such a way that people feel that they are closer to the finish line.

How you frame something can change the meaning. The meaning can change your mind, and your mind can change your brain. Meaning derives from the frame we place around an event or situation. The structure of meaning is an inside job: a bridge between an external event and an internal state. Each meaning and each frame is yours to construct. It is not there until you create it.

In an original experiment done by Daniel Kahneman and Amos Tversky, subjects spun a wheel that would supposedly stop at random numbers between 1 and 100.[2] Then they were asked what percentage of African countries belonged to the United Nations:

- For one group of subjects, the wheel was preset to stop on 10.

- For the second group, it stopped on 65.

The first group guessed that 25 percent belonged to the United Nations. The second group guessed 45 percent.

Even when informed, the subjects insisted that the number the wheel stopped on had no relation to the correct answer to the question, yet the number the wheel stopped on had a profound influence on their responses. Irrelevant information can influence judgments, which can then influence decisions.

The way you frame the question makes a great deal of difference. When companies automatically enroll their employees in retirement savings plans, the employee has to *opt out* to not participate—to actually make a choice that says *I will not save for my future*. When it's automatic, it's 100 percent initially (by definition). Then it levels to between 86 and 94 percent. At companies where it isn't automatic and someone has to *choose to opt in*, 20 percent participate—over a fourfold difference.[3]

Another example of how people are sensitive to things that shouldn't matter:

- One group of countries in Europe expects people to donate their organs *unless* they check a box saying they don't want to (opt out). The rate of organ donation: 95 percent.

- In another group of countries, people can be organ donors only if they check the box *to donate* (opt in). The rate of donation: 18 percent.

To discern meaning, you need a context to surround it. The frame can even determine your state of mind. Our decisions are astonishingly reliant on the context of our experiences. Priming is what psychologists define as "the incidental activation of knowledge structures by the current situational context"—in other words, the booting up of a particular mind-set.

The practical effect of priming is that our perception influences how we make decisions even if the two are irrelevant and the connection is illogical. A test was done in which French and German wines were offered in a supermarket.[4] The wines were matched for price and quality. After the customer made a choice, a researcher approached the customer and asked why he or she picked that particular wine. The customer typically mentioned things such as price, quality, or anticipation of the match with a meal. The researcher then asked whether the customer noticed what kind of music was being played and if it had any bearing on his or her decision. Most customers acknowledged hearing the music, but almost all felt it had nothing to do with their selection.

Actually, when French music was played, French wines were selected 77 percent of the time. When German music played, German wines were selected 73 percent of the time.

When told of the study and the findings of the music influence, 86 percent of all participants said that the tunes had no influence on their choices.

Focus

The reticular activating system (RAS) at the base of the brain decides what, out of all the information streaming into the brain, is allowed into consciousness. You pay attention to whatever fits your story—the framework you use. For example, part of your story is your self-image. If someone says something really nice about you and you don't believe it, it won't register. It will be disavowed with an internal comment, perhaps, "What are they trying to sell me?"

How do you reframe and reprogram your RAS to let in what you want to achieve? You change your natural filters:

- Beliefs

- Self-image

- Goals

This three-step combination can help you reframe your comfort zone:

1. Visualization: You can create powerful and stimulating internal images. Visualization reprograms the RAS by programming awareness.

2. Affirmations: The positive validation of doing and being what you want—the story that frames the visualization.

3. Change your behavior.

New behavior and new experiences create new pathways in the brain. With each repetition, those pathways become more deeply etched. When well grooved, the new behavior becomes a habit, automatic, the default mode. Your future self lives in your present mind. If you can visualize it clearly, it is then up to you to actualize the vision.

Where you have direct impact, what you can determine, and where you can be effective is your *circle of influence.*

When someone cuts you off on the freeway, will getting angry inoculate you against the next occurrence? Will your getting upset in a traffic jam speed up traffic? Circumstances like these are your *circle of concern*— things such as overpopulation and housing prices that arouse concern but over which you're not immediately effective.

Engaging a negative or fear-based belief in order to counter it will create what you are most trying to avoid. The more you keep running away from something, the more you engage it. Positive affirmations need to be based on positive beliefs that are believable.

Every day, several times a day, we say "Yes" or "No" to things in our lives.

The results you get in your life are the result of your focus. If you automatically and unconsciously focus on what you don't want, you have polarized yourself to become a magnet for it and direct yourself toward it.

Without being consciously aware, you can focus on something you don't want and bring it about. If you believe that certain relationships can be painful and that you have to watch out for and avoid certain people, you have focused your mind on precisely that: dead relationships and people who can hurt you. This focuses specifically on what you do not want and attracts it to you. When those people appear in your life, you are unconsciously drawn to them but consciously repelled by them. This ultimate paradox is why people keep having the same relationship with different people.

This paradox occurs in every aspect of life: What you do not want, you ironically make happen. Focusing on not making mistakes creates mistakes. Focusing on not being late creates lateness. Focusing on not wanting to be financially insolvent creates scarcity. Focusing on not smoking makes you want to smoke.

Your mind is an energy field and responds to focus. Whether the focus is negative or positive, the response is to the focus. Your mind precisely and effectively creates what you focus on.

Brain research shows that focusing on problems or negative behavior reinforces those problems and behaviors. Additionally, the harder you push people to change, the harder they will push back. The best mentoring strategies focus on the present and future—on possibilities and solutions rather than problems. This requires the development of new neuropathways in the brain and learning new thinking patterns.

The most important principle is to focus on what you do want rather than on what you don't want.

In addition, become consciously aware so that you can direct this power of focus to the specific outcomes that you want. Here's one exercise to help you do it:

- Discover all the things that you focus on that you do not want. Make a list of all the things that you do *not* want as you notice yourself focusing on them or thinking about them.

- Be very specific about what you *do* want. Make a list. Be certain that what you do want is not just what you do not want in disguise. An example: "I want a relationship in which I am treated well and regarded positively." This statement focuses on the expectation of not being treated well and having to reverse it. You may say, "I want a reliable car" because of a focus on the possibility that a car will break down and need repairs. The desire to avoid something is usually the result of negative emotional experiences with what you want to avoid. Trying to avoid those things paradoxically creates them.

- Work on these two lists over time because much of your awareness is not conscious. These two lists will crystallize many beliefs and assumptions that you may not have been consciously aware of.

- Each time you think about an outcome that you do not want, stop and consciously change your thinking to focus on precisely what you do want.

- Keep being aware and working on both lists. Practice changing your focus. Persist in positive focus. Write down the lists and the revisions.

- These changes are a hard-work miracle. Practice in persistence is paramount.

- The questions you ask determine your focus. Ask yourself questions that help you focus on positive outcomes. Rather than "Why can't I do this?," ask yourself questions that are positive and lead to furthering a positive focus, such as "How will I do this?" and "How can I grow from this?"

Decision Clarification

West Virginia University researchers Steve Booth-Butterfield and Bill Reger devised a study that ran ads indicating that one glass of whole milk has the same amount of saturated fat as five strips of bacon.[5] At a press conference, they showed reporters a tube full of fat—the equivalent of the amount in a half gallon of whole milk. By making these healthy choices specific and tangible, the market share of low-fat milk moved from 18 to

41 percent. They moved "eating healthily" from an admirable goal to a specific choice and behavior.

When you want to effect change, you need to script these specific behaviors. When you want to catalyze change in others, you need to help them circumscribe and specify clear options. Change always has to begin at the level of individual decisions and specific behaviors.

Understanding these leading reasons that people resist change can help inform decisions:

- Ambiguity aversion: The risk of change is seen as greater than the risk of standing still. "Better the devil you know than the one you don't." People prefer a known risk to an unknown risk even if the known risk is high. To make a change requires a leap of faith—it is a move in the direction of the unknown and unexperienced. You have no proof.

- People feel connected to other people identified with the present situation. Change threatens losing those identified with the old way. This resonates with emotional bonds of loyalty as well as individual status quo and group inertia.

- There may be no new role models for the new activity or at least no mentors who have been there before. Moving beyond those who have been both mentors and colleagues is challenging.

- You can't know that you have the competence for a new situation that you've never been in before. This may be a subtle but pervasive fear, with people concerned they won't be able to make the transition well.

- The proposed change threatens both people's notions of themselves and how others perceive them. They don't know whether others will respond with support or with competitive jealousy.

- Too many choices. Remember the jam-tasting study. Decide what "good enough" is and narrow choices to fit a goal.

A caveat: Always consider whether the proposed change is a good idea or a bad idea. Sometimes, idealizing change or focusing on the dynamics of change and the transition process occludes clear judgment about whether it is really a good idea worthy of your full engagement. Those who automatically see change as a challenge that calls for engagement may not carefully consider this notion.

Shrink the Change

The experience of reaching attainable short-term goals creates the experience of effectiveness, the most basic of human motivations. This experience of mastery builds on itself. The strategic application of the series of next-best actions to pursue an initiative toward a SMART goal is a fundamental mission of mentoring strategy. Facilitating steps of effectiveness and the resulting experience of mastery fosters hope.

From Bill Parcells, quoted in *Harvard Business Review* on winning two Super Bowls: "When you set small, visible goals, and people achieve them, they start to get into their heads that they can succeed."

And from John Wooden, the greatest college basketball coach of all time: "When you improve a little each day, eventually big things occur. Don't look for the quick, big improvement. Seek the small improvements one day at a time. That's the only way it happens—and when it happens—it lasts."

Two fundamental applications of shrinking the change:

- By investing $1.50 per day beginning at age 20—based on the stock market average growth since 1926—by age 65 you'll have $1 million. Wait until age 21 instead of 20, and the difference is $109,000.

- By investing $2,000 per year in an individual retirement account beginning at age 18, then stopping all investment by age 30, by age 65 you'll have $1 million.

Why Don't We Do the Next-Best Thing?

At a recent World Economic Forum, eight Nobel Prize winners were asked, "What do you see as the world's biggest challenges?"[6]

While the laureates ranged in discussion from overpopulation to un-employment to the environment to inequality, all spoke of one common denominator: problems we create ourselves. The most basic theme: We don't make a connection between our current behavior and the future consequences. As two-time Nobel Prize winner astrophysicist Saul Perl-mutter stated, "We're limited by being human. We want results fast, and we discount the future."

Our brains are wired to be in the present and to respond in the here and now. Our medulla is alert to immediate threat and pleasure, we are pulled to immediate gratification, and we have trouble visualizing our fu-ture selves. The most common mistake we have in investing, according to Daniel Kahneman, is to choose a little now rather than a lot later.

Three Harvard researchers presenting at a recent Davos session found that the savings from wellness programs in organizations averages $3.27 for every dollar spent.[7] But the quality and depth of such programs is very limited. We decide visually and organizationally based on the more primitive parts of our brain and become myopically short term in our perspectives.

And yet we can learn to be far more intentional and more aware in our behavior and less short term in our perspective. Doing so requires plan and practice. To transform others, organizations, and the world, we have to begin with ourselves. Consensus studies find that we have to systemati-cally train the regulation of negative motion and increase our practice of calm reflection in the face of stress.

Specific rituals—behaviors and practices that eventually become auto-matic—create sustainable effectiveness and overall well-being.

Most Frequent Mistakes in Writing a New Money Story

1. *We avoid the truth about ourselves.* We are reluctant to leave the secu-rity and familiarity of our own stories. New information may demand a change in beliefs, while we tend to seek information to confirm our beliefs rather than disprove them. New behaviors are uncomfortable, and the outcome is uncertain.

To know to ask is half the answer.

2. *Stopping at the first right answer.* When we are solving problems or writing a new story, we may stop at the first reasonable action. While this may be a correct strategy, it stops us from considering other right answers—other correct strategies that could be more effective.

Ask yourself, "And then what? What else?"

3. *Procrastination.* Five frogs sat on a log. They all considered their options. Four, however, planned their strategy and then decided they would jump off. How many were left?

Five were left because they only planned and decided and didn't commit to act.

Consider some of the broad themes of procrastination, the big patterns: putting off an exercise program, not paying yourself first, not saving for emergencies, not saving for retirement, or taking care of others but not yourself.

Most of us live our lives as though we have an unlimited amount of time ahead of us. We have little sense of urgency, contributing to a lack of focus.

When the two-minute warning sounds in a football game, a team sometimes achieves more in the final two minutes than they did in the previous twenty-eight. This imminent deadline—a limited, finite amount of time to accomplish goals—focuses concentration and increases effort. In our lives, only rarely do we have a two-minute warning. We play as if the notion of finite time is only an abstraction, something we acknowledge but seem not to internalize. Life is finite; it's just that the game clock is invisible.

4. *Inefficient energy management.* Managing energy is a key to success. It starts with knowing your strengths and limitations, your biological cycles, and when you perform best:

- Know how to enter and exit various states of mind—and which works best for a particular task. For example, writing and editing are two different states of mind—to be done at two different times.

- Cluster activities that require the same state of mind.

- Identify what enhances your energy: anticipation, creativity, pleasure, meditation, or prayer.

- Identify what depletes your energy: toxic people or situations, a negative mind-set, or a lack of focus.

5. *Ambiguity.* If you are unclear about what options are available and don't know what it would be like to pursue them—since you haven't done it before—this uncertainty adds to decision paralysis. What looks like resistance can be simply a lack of clarity.

People are more likely to change when new behavior is crystal clear, not vague or absent. "Eat a healthier diet" or "Save for the future" are both vague and abstract.

When you want to effect your change, specifically script behaviors. When you want to enhance active decision making, limit and specify clear options. Change begins at the level of individual decision and specific behavior.

6. *Too many choices.* Studies show that a human relations department or individual investment adviser can provide too many choices and the extra options backfire, leading to decision paralysis. Many investment options of different kinds of stock-and-bond funds, real estate investment trusts, and various international and domestic market funds, including money market accounts, are usually offered as options, and each category may have several subchoices. For every 10 options offered, the employee's rate of participation goes down by 2 percent.

At some point, choice debilitates rather than liberates so that the person being asked to choose retreats to the default mode of not choosing.

A classic study in decision paralysis was done at a gourmet grocery store.[8] The research project offered a display of six jams for tasting. On an alternate weekend, there were 24 jams available for tasting. For both weekends, customers were given a coupon for $1 off if they purchased any jam. While the larger display of jams attracted more potential customers, in both cases people tasted an equal number of jams. When 24 varieties were available for tasting, 3 percent purchased. When only six varieties were available for tasting, 30 percent purchased. With too many choices, actual purchases declined *10-fold*.

With too many choices, we feel overwhelmed and resort to our comfort zone: to do nothing.

7. *Lack of persistence.* The truly challenging, courageous part of change is not the initial decision, nor is it the initiation of a new order of things. Rather, it's the willingness to stay the course.

A clearly defined goal can capture imagination and inspire passion. It can cut through the fog like a beacon in the night. *One extra degree* of effort in business and in life separates the good from the great:

- Fifty-one publishers turned down Richard Bach's *Jonathan Livingston Seagull*. He took it to number 52.

- One hundred and forty-one publishers turned down a guy who then decided to publish his book himself and sell it out of the back of his car. It had an unlikely title for a book: *Chicken Soup for the Soul.*

- To get what you've never had, you'll probably have to do what you've never done. *Perseverance is not a long race; it is many short races, one after another.* —Lord Eliot

8. *Not following success trails.* Have you said some version of the following?

- I want to play a bigger game, but I'm not quite sure what it is.

- I want to create wealth, but I don't have a plan.

Decide how you want to expand, then pick success trails to follow.

When my good buddy Art heard that I was transitioning from psychoanalytic practice and had completed my professional coach training and certification, he flew to Houston to take me to dinner. A few years earlier, he had left a senior executive position at IBM to start his own consulting corporation. He told me how he chose five very successful people who had done something similar to what he was planning and asked them to lunch or dinner to pick their brains about what he was about to do. He advised me to do the same. Now some businesspeople with instant global recognition pick his brain for substantial picking fees. It has worked for both of us.

Create a support team. Construct an advisory board or networking group, engage a mentor coach, or join a mastermind group.

9. *Not having enough mental models.* The brain functions like a Google map: it creates multiple independent maps while finding its way in the

world. When a new situation arises, another map boots up. If we have too few mental models—paradigms—we tend to overuse the ones we have. To someone with a hammer, every problem looks like a nail.

10. *Not visualizing your future self.* A study by Princeton psychologist Emily Pronin found that making financial decisions, especially how much money we put away toward retirement, depends on how closely we identify with our future selves.[9] Brain imaging reveals that the greater activity in an area of the brain called the anterior cingulate cortex is activated when imaging yourself in the future, the greater your alignment with that future self, including the greater amount of savings for the future since it is aligned with identity.

When people showed a lesser activity in thinking about their current and future self, they tended to save less money. People who see their current and future self as more alike will create more financial assets.

The conclusion of this study was that encouraging people to imagine themselves in the future may help them save more.

11. *Losing a neural tug of war.* Contemplating future rational plans stimulates more activity in the prefrontal cortex. Focusing on immediate rewards activates the brain areas associated with emotion—the dopamine system and nucleus accumbens. Good decisions require both sides of the brain; this may require delaying a decision in order to restore brain balance.

And sometimes, not getting what we want is exactly what we need.

Engineering Effectiveness

Some essentials of engineering an effective New Money Story®:

1. Make changes *tangible and concrete*. Construct a yardstick or a map to determine where you are and where you are going, to be able to measure progress along the way, and to tell what is detour and distraction.

2. Make progress *measurable*. Demystify the journey. Create a specific destination with a tangible focus on the next step.

3. Make progress *visible*. Small, specific, attainable milestones make progress visible—celebrate each small victory.

4. *Specify* the next step. Not abstract or too global: "some" is not a number; "soon" is not a time; "act healthier" is not a strategy.

All you ever have to do is the next right thing. This shrinks the change to immediate steps of effectiveness and the experience of momentum.

Principles of Facilitating Successful Change

A review of some principles to facilitate successful change:

1. *Each person's life story is created.* In adulthood, you create whatever you think, feel, and experience each moment. Every day is a blank page until you begin writing on it—even though it seems to the individual as "just be the way things are."

2. *Knowing what* not *to do is at least as important as knowing what to do.* You may not always know what the next right thing is, but you can almost always know what it *isn't.*

3. *When people create their own answers, they have signed on to invest in the outcome.* Doing so establishes the beginning of a sense of effectiveness and mastery. The antithesis is having someone tell you what to do. We'll talk later about how the brain lights up with an "Aha!" or insight experience, something it does not do when receiving advice or directives.

4. *We don't see things as they are; we see things as we are.* Assumptions manifest as feelings and behaviors. When you make assumptions explicit, you can more clearly see which ones facilitate and which interfere.

5. *Change is constant and inevitable; it is resistance to change that generates most problems.* We are most successful when we learn from yesterday, anticipate tomorrow, and integrate the impact of new experience.

6. *Small changes lead to big changes.* Looking at the simplicity of the issue in order to specify progress can approach issues that seem overwhelmingly large and insurmountable. For example, when you feel overwhelmed with the amount of tasks, first clarify one issue that, if done today, would be progress. This focus on a specific action exercises effectiveness and initiates a model of mastery.

7. *Problems, causes, and solutions are not always related or even interconnected.* To resolve a problem, even emotionally, to come to the end of the past does not create a blueprint for success. That's why there are a lot of

frustrated therapy refugees. Strategic plans for specific goals are necessary. In a totally new experience, you may need a guide, even for something like a healthier diet or exercise.

8. *The benefit of doing more of what is working and less of what is not will become evident and self-perpetuating.*

9. *You need to know where you're going—goals and strategies.* Setting a goal will enhance motivation. Establishing strategies will facilitate focus. If you don't know where you're going, any map will do. The end should be in mind from the beginning. Lewis Carroll said it well:

Alice came to a fork in the road. "Which road do I take?" she asked.

"Where do you want to go?" responded the Cheshire cat.

"I don't know," Alice answered.

"Then," said the cat, "it doesn't matter."

10. *You need the correct paradigm.* A paradigm is an internal map—the way you see, interpret, and understand something. It needs to be correct. If you're in Dallas and need to navigate the city, a map of Houston is useless no matter how hard you try. And it needs to be current, not a paradigm from an old story.

11. *Decide what you want. Believe it's possible.* A belief is a filter between reality and our perception—just like the filter on a camera alters the image that the camera records.

We now know that beliefs can actually turn genes on or off. You can change your life by changing your beliefs.

Our possibilities are limited only to the ones we allow ourselves to see. A destitute young housewife has almost no money. She can't afford a babysitter or a computer, but she has a story to tell, and she is determined to do it. She decides to write. As soon as she starts writing, her mother dies at age 45 from multiple sclerosis. Her marriage to an abusive husband ends in divorce. She has a miscarriage. She gets fired from her job and lives on government welfare.

She takes her baby to a coffee shop in the middle of the afternoon and writes on a legal pad while her baby takes a nap. She does it every day for four years.

And then, after much work, she finally finds a publisher—for *Harry Potter*.

How to Be Brilliant (Hint: Reach Beyond and Fail Frequently)

Significant new research suggests that we do not come close to tapping into—or actualizing—our true potential.

David Shenk, in *The Genius in All of Us*, believes that we have a "latent talent abundance" that scientists call our "unactualized potential."[10] Since intelligence is made up of the skills that we develop, we can train ourselves to be successful. Deliberate practice changes the brain.

Epigenetics—the study of how our environment and experience determines the way genes are expressed—shows that there are no fixed genetic limits.

Superior talent, rather than being a rare gift of a few, is a result of the art and science of highly concentrated effort. Malcolm Gladwell gave us the 10,000-hour rule of success in *Outliers*: It is not innate genius or talent that creates great achievers but rather seized opportunities to put in an extraordinary period of time—a minimum of 10,000 hours—to develop their talent.

Another fellow who made something of a name for himself concurred with that theory before it was a theory: "It is not that I'm so smart, but that I stick with problems longer." (That was Einstein.)

Talent is not a thing but a process. It is not something we have but something we can do by creating the discipline to practice and cocreating a supportive environment.

The repeated attempts to reach beyond our present level can produce changes in the brain and create new heights of achievement. Because this deliberate practice can lead to frequent failures, make it an organic process to reach beyond and fail frequently.

And remember to learn from the failures while you keep practicing.

Fourteen Ways to Outsmart Your Brain to Spend Less

1. *Don't use credit cards*: In numerous studies, individuals spend significantly more—on average 23 percent—when using credit cards versus paying cash. Credit cards make money an abstraction as well as relegating payment to a future time. The immediacy of real money makes it a real consideration.

2. *Estimate expenses in detail; pay in cash*: Studies at the Robert H. Smith School of Business at the University of Maryland found that people spend less when they have to estimate expenses in detail as well as when paying cash than when using credit.[11]

3. *Pause between the pick and the purchase*: Wants are the language of the initial intoxicating exposure to dopamine. Anticipation causes a dopamine release, making action feel compelling. Neuroscientists at Emory University found that this delay disrupted dopamine release. Dopamine is the same chemical that, once a purchase is made, diminishes, with "buyer's remorse" the result. Create a contemplative pause—a space of time between choosing something and paying for it at checkout. Time cures wants.

4. *Simplify your symbolism*: Designer brands are marketed to symbolically represent quality, desirability, and the experience of having arrived. The symbolism of specialness costs more. The qualities that we attribute to brands create a relationship with the brand that produces both desire and the commitment to pay more.

5. *Leave emotions at home*: Emotions hijack the logical brain and, with it, reasonable decisions. Under stress, we may relieve that stress by buying, by hoarding, or by purchasing out of other emotional needs, such as insecurity or a desire to win approval.

6. *Don't be special*: Special offers or other indications that you are in a select group—an inner circle of consideration—will make you buy more than you need. Special, exclusive, unique offers induce a desire to respond with gratitude and with purchase. Be suspicious of special offers.

7. *Shop alone*: The social contagion of shopping with friends induces a relaxation of usual constraints as well as the desire to impress friends with purchase.

8. *Know what "good enough" is*: Rather than an impossible quest for perfection or for the unattainable endpoint of "more," define specifically what good enough is. Having an end point lets you know when you arrive, when you can feel satisfaction.

9. *Keep your eye on the ball*: Focus on the immediate, the specific, and its importance.

10. *And keep your head in the game*: Be aware of the big picture—the scope of importance. In the United States, about 1 percent of the people own 96 percent of the wealth. Keep the big picture in mind. "Good enough" is the antithesis of "more."

11. *Consider the opportunity cost of your purchase*: Calculate what the money would be worth in 5 years and in 10 years.

12. *Consider the absolute value rather than the anchor price*: Evaluate an item you purchase on the basis of the item itself rather than the stated initial price. Our brains are wired to log in an initial anchor price, then to judge everything subsequently in reference to that anchor price.

13. *Consider the actual product and what you will do with it if purchased*: Disregard the brand, the esteem of ownership, and how you will be perceived as its owner. Marketing produces desires we didn't know we had.

14. *Use "free" as a cue to spend more slowly*: Evaluate carefully. "Free" is designed to induce action and minimize consideration.

Eighteen Caveats to Live a New Money Story

Once you have an understanding of your relationship with money, you can then systematically change your money story. Here are some considerations in that process:

1. You'll never do anything important that will feel comfortable in the beginning.

2. Having a definition of success and an internal ideal of "good enough" are essential for satisfaction.

3. Rich is knowing you have enough.

4. Long-term goals are necessary to keep perspective, while short-term goals are necessary to sustain enthusiasm and tolerate frustration.

5. Respect the boundaries between business and personal life.

6. Develop your emotional and interpersonal expertise as well as your technical expertise.

7. Thinking, feeling, and imagining are all active forms of doing something. (Yet they are not physical action.)

8. Judgment resides in the potential space between urge and action.

9. When your head and your gut agree and you act accordingly, you won't go wrong.

10. Assess what reaching a goal will do.

11. Just having a choice can make choosing the same thing feel very different.

12. Growth and change are hard. The only thing harder is not growing or changing. (If you are uncertain or concerned about change, it is already occurring.)

13. Recognize your limits in order to achieve success.

14. Admit mistakes in order to cut losses.

15. Put your ego in a blind trust and seek suggestions, critiques, and advice.

16. Distinguish lack of information and organization from unconscious conflict.

17. Planning and strategy are essential components of a game plan: establishing a goal will enhance motivation; developing a strategy will focus concentration on efforts.

18. Examine the process that gets you to a good result. Examine the process that gets you to a bad result. You can learn immensely from both.

Thirty-two Guidelines to Further a New Money Story

1. Distinguish need from want.

2. You always have the right to say "No" or "Yes."

3. You have to be free to say "No" before you can be free to say "Yes" (or else "Yes" has no meaning).

4. Coming to the end of your past, especially resolving emotional issues, isn't enough. You have to have a purpose, a dream, in order to give hope a blueprint.

5. Have a "big picture" and bring it into focus whenever necessary.

6. Establish priorities: what is really important in each area of your life.

7. Have specific, attainable goals on a short-term daily basis as well as in the big picture.

8. Disengage from "what might have been."

9. Engage what you can be effective in doing and disengage what you have no determination over.

10. Seek out suggestions, critiques, and advice.

11. Sleep on it. Recognize that there are few true emergencies in life.

12. Select goals consistent with your self-image.

13. What you decide to accept undergoes a change.

14. To get what you always wanted in the past may not feel as good as you expected because it is no longer the past.

15. For an end point, ask yourself, "What is good enough?"

16. The question "What is in my best interest?" should always be in the background and, at times, the foreground as well.

17. The past may not be the best or the most relevant context in which to understand the present.

18. Create a contemplation space to ponder decisions, especially emotionally charged ones.

19. Growth involves enduring uncertainty.

20. Not only *can* we change, but we can also choose *how* we will change.

21. Insight and understanding may initiate internal change, but both internal and external change needs to be addressed.

22. Growth and change involve their own mourning.

23. The only familiar territory is behind you.

24. Growth and change are hard. The only thing harder is not growing or changing.

25. Our experiences are always consistent with our theories.

26. Clarify your external goals.

27. Anything important requires a commitment to go forward despite discomfort.

28. Know what reaching a goal will do.

29. You'll never do anything important that will feel comfortable in the beginning.

30. Trying to change your past is not change; it will always be the way it was.

31. Decisions always limit choices while activating others.

32. We suffer most from our anticipations and limit ourselves most by our assumptions.

CHAPTER SIXTEEN

A New Operating System for Wealth

Computers have operating systems. Within the hardware and constituting the programs is a complex system of software that contains instructions, protocols, and couplings that enable the system to function smoothly. Usually, we think about the operating systems only when there are problems or failings.

Our society also has operating systems of laws, customs, and social and economic arrangements that make up protocols and assumptions about how we conduct ourselves.

Your money story has a similar operating system with a set of beliefs and assumptions about your behaviors. Among the various theories and disciplines, each has unique perspectives on this system of human behavior that ultimately download as your own story that you tweak to make it uniquely yours. Consider those downloads that operate smoothly within a system but don't work—that is, the operating system doesn't fail, but the downloads are faulty. These faulty downloads can become glitches in creating wealth:

- Thinking that if you're not born with money, you will never have money.

- Equating education with an entitlement to wealth.

- Assuming that book-smart will make you street-smart.

- Focusing on rich and forgetting about wealth.

- Focusing on making and spending money rather than on making your money work for you.

- Not seeing yourself capable of making a lot of money, with the result that you don't make a lot of money.

- Waiting for motivation in order to generate the energy and personal business plan to succeed.

- Expecting things to happen quickly.

Your money story is a paradigm to understand your relationship to your life story. Your fundamental beliefs, assumptions, convictions, and personal truths about money are the same ones as about life. If you get behind in your paperwork in your life, you will likely be behind on your financial paperwork. If you put off doing necessary things that will reap a larger benefit later, you will probably be doing the same thing with long-term savings and retirement.

To find out what you believe about your life, what your fundamental convictions are, and the ultimate truths you hold, look to your money story.

Remember the subtle, persuasive influence of the status quo. The status quo can masquerade as the blessing of being Sisyphus. As long as you struggle to push the boulder up the mountain, almost but never actually arriving, you are always certain of both your focus and your work. You always have something specifically to do. This also translates to always knowing who you are—someone trying hard at something that can never quite be done, someone with a weight problem who always works hard to be thin but never gets there, someone who is always about to do well and become debt free and make really big money—almost. You're never lost or helpless because there is always that elusive goal.

You can write your new programs in your mind—reverse your mind software. Then they can be repeated until they become automatic.

Be clear about exactly what you are doing and the programs that you are writing. There are two equal myths:

- Money buys happiness.

- Wealth does not matter.

We sometimes fail to distinguish between *correlation* and *causality*—or we equate the two. We assume that when we or researchers observe a correlation between two variables, one must have *caused* the other.

An example is the Super Bowl indicator. The stock market goes up when a National Football Conference team wins and goes down when an American Football Conference team wins. The Super Bowl winner has correctly correlated to the stock market direction 80 percent of the time between 1967 and 2008.

David Leinweber's analysis showed a 75 percent correlation between butter production in Bangladesh and the level of the Standard & Poor's 500 stock index. He was pleased to find that "a simple dairy product explained so much."

To consider the correlation-versus-causality conundrum, we have to consider whether the theory behind a decision accounts for the circumstances.

Consider this: If you had an endless supply of money, how would you live your life differently?

As you write down your answers, focus on the process of your life—the skills and qualities you want to achieve. Rather than focusing on the things you would buy with that money, consider how you would actually live your life differently:

- What mind-set would you have?

- When you wake up in the morning, how would you feel?

- What beliefs and assumption would change for you?

- How would you think differently?

- How would you approach each day differently?

- What would it mean to you to come from a place of abundance, your scarcity mind-set no longer relevant?

- How many of your beliefs and assumptions about money—the story lines of your money story—would become irrelevant?

Twenty-five Guidelines to Fulfill Your New Money Story

In the end, your actions are the language in which your money story speaks. Whether you choose to buy or not, to save, to invest, or to decide not to decide, your money behaviors will be the final expression of your beliefs and will determine your financial success.

Consider these guidelines to live your New Money Story:

1. *Keep your money mission statement always visible and in focus.* Your money mission statement defines the essence of your financial goals and the principles and ideals underlying them. It proclaims the meaning, use, and value of money to you, including short- and long-term plans. Keep this statement where you can see it often—on your desk, on your wall, on your computer—and review it periodically, refining it as needed, to make sure that it accurately orients your decisions with your purpose and philosophy.

2. *Have a plan.* Create a strategy and a fully informed, well-structured financial plan, with provisions for saving and investment in alignment with your money mission statement, based on facts rather than on emotions. Periodically review your plan to make sure it reflects your purpose, your values, and your most up-to-date information and advisements from counsel you seek and trust.

3. *Stick to your plan.* In times of trauma, crisis, or circumstances beyond your control, stick to your plan.

In times of elation, unexpected growth, and great success, stick to your plan.

When you are most prone to overreact, stick to your plan.

When you recognize procrastination or failure to act or react, stick to your plan.

When your plan isn't working well, review whether you are fully executing the plan; if you are, then review the current validity of your plan. Once you are satisfied that your current plan is solid, stick to your plan.

4. *Seek out suggestions, critique, advice, and expertise.* Consult with people knowledgeable in specific areas. At times, this may be difficult emotionally when it would seem easier to consult (read: collude) with someone who will mirror your views and agree with your opinions. The search for validation aims to maintain your comfort zone and avoid change. Consulting a mirror for advice is what the wicked queen does in "Snow White." Leave the mirror for touching up makeup; for your plan, consult objective experts.

Seek those expert in areas other than your own, including those with different points of view. Listen from another's perspective without abandoning your own. Use that new information from a flexible and informed position.

In addition to a financial adviser and other experts in specific fields, consider using the services of a coach, mentor, or mastermind group; they can provide invaluable perspective on how (and whether) your actions, decisions, and ideals are in effective alignment, and if they are not, they can help you reassess and realign.

5. *Estimate expenses in detail.* Don't ballpark what your life and the things in it will cost. This is not a ball game; it's your life. Get down to hard numbers.

6. *Establish priorities.* Prioritize plans and pursuits based on core ideals and needs. Money and finances must be balanced with family, work,

health, friendships, leisure, making a difference in your community, and taking care of yourself. Neglect or imbalance in one area may generate overcompensation in other areas.

Priorities are not static; they are not something you can figure out on a weekend and then set aside for the rest of the year. You will likely reconfront, refine, and even redefine priorities every day and make decisions based on your fresh answers to the fundamental question "What is really important?"

7. *Align your internal ideals with your financial goals.* Your ideals, the internal model of who and what you are, generate the unspoken assumptions on which you operate. Clarify your external goals to be certain that they are consistent with your ideals.

The clarity and consistency of your principles and goals can be called on in times of emergency or confusion to help bring the big picture into focus. Be certain there is a fit between your internal and external goals, that what you want to accomplish is consistent with your ideals. This consistency can give your ambition an organizing structure and direction.

8. *Distinguish needs from wants.* A need is an essential requirement, a necessity for mind, body, or spirit. You can get sick if you don't have enough of what you need: nutrition, touch, rest, or security. A need can be satisfied.

You can also get sick if you have too much of what you want (e.g., Mexican food, alcohol, sexual freedom, or solitude).

Wants (wishes and desires) are replaceable with other wants, but a need cannot substitute for another need. And you can never get enough of that which you don't need.

9. *Determine what is good enough.* The pursuit of perfection comes from not having a standard of what is good enough. "More" is not a goal. More money, like perfection, is a quest never satisfied. For perfectionists, failure may even be a relief, ending the relentless and impossible pursuit of perfection. The undefined pursuit of "more" is a guaranteed plan for failure.

As playwright Neil Simon said, "Money brings some happiness. But after a certain point, all it brings is more money."

Having an end point lets you know when you arrive, when you can feel satisfaction, when you can experience effectiveness and mastery at reaching a goal.

10. *Know what reaching a goal will do. And what it will not do.* Monetary wealth can provide pleasure, luxury, and financial security, but it may not make your marriage better. It is important to know what achieving a goal will do so that you have the clarity to distinguish what it will not do.

A common mechanism for keeping hope alive is stopping short of a goal so that there is no need to confront the illusion that reaching the goal will provide all the hoped-for solutions. Reaching a goal will not undo the past or make other troubles go away.

11. *Don't invest with your heart.* Never fall in love or hate with a stock—it won't love you back. It doesn't even know that you own it. Invest in the stock or bond of a company that you genuinely want to own, not in a "hot trend" or "good story." Remember that if someone tells you it's "a sure thing," it isn't.

12. *Don't use credit cards.* Numerous studies have shown that people spend significantly more (on average, 23 percent more) when using credit cards than when paying with cash or check. Credit cards make money an abstraction as well as relegating payment to a future time. Pay in cash.

13. *Consider the opportunity cost of your purchase.* Before you spend significant money on an item, calculate what it would be worth in five or ten years if you were instead to invest that same money.

14. *Consider the absolute value rather than the anchor price.* A 75 percent discount on a jacket overpriced by 300 percent is not a deal. A "sale price" is meaningless if it is anchored in an inflated initial price.

15. *Consider the actual product and what you will do with it if purchased.* Will you really use it? For how long? One year from now, what choices will you be glad you've made?

16. *Be suspicious of being "special."* Special offers or other indications that you are in a select group—an inner circle of unique consideration—will make you buy more than you need. Special, exclusive, unique offers induce a desire to respond with gratitude—and with purchase. Be suspicious of special offers.

17. *Simplify your symbolism.* Designer brands are marketed to symbolically represent quality, desirability, and the experience of having arrived. The symbolism of specialness adds cost. The qualities that we attribute to brands create a relationship with the brand that results in both desire and the commitment to pay more. Ask yourself whether you'd pay the same amount for a product if the logo were changed and nothing else.

18. *Leave emotions at home.* Emotions hijack the logical brain and, with it, reasonable decisions. Stress may seek relief through buying, hoarding, or purchasing out of other emotional needs, such as insecurity or a desire to win approval.

Make financial decisions independently of emotional decisions and distinguish between the two. Worry about the right things.

19. *Shop alone.* The social contagion of shopping with friends induces a relaxation of usual constraints as well as the desire to impress friends with purchase.

20. *Remember that you have the right to say "No."* Don't hesitate to say "No." And don't hesitate to say "Yes" either when you are clear about what you want and need. The other person in your interaction also has a right to say "No" or "Yes." Don't hesitate, for example, to make a simple request for a fee for service equal to its value.

21. *You have to be free to say "No" before you can be free to say "Yes."* Unless you are free to say "No," "Yes" has no meaning.

22. *Disengage from "what might have been."* Getting what you always wanted in the past may not feel as good as you expected because it's no longer the past. If you attempt to reenter an old story and acquire what you missed in the past, it won't work. "If only" fantasies erode the power of today.

To keep a goal just out of reach maintains the "someday" fantasies associated with it. "I'll lose the 10 pounds, and then I'll be happy." The weight-loss goal must remain elusive, or the hope of happiness contained in the loss of the last 10 pounds would be exposed as illusion. The unattainable becomes addictive.

It's difficult to sell a stock that has declined significantly. The sale makes a reality of money loss rather than a theory of paper loss. The sale also banishes the hope of future gains.

You have to relinquish a past position in order to move ahead. When you let go of the past, you reclaim your aliveness (and effectiveness) in the present.

23. *Keep the big picture in mind.* A study by the Joseph Rowntree Foundation found that wealthy Londoners do not feel rich because they never mix with people less affluent than themselves.[12] When you take a good look at the global neighborhood and realize that half of humanity lives on less than $3 a day, it puts things in perspective.

The big picture consists of your own ideals and principles, of objectively organizing your life and decisions according to what you believe to be in your best interest. Whenever you might be caught up in details or in the grip of emotion, stop and ask, "What is in my best interest?"

The next right step may not always be clear, but you can almost always be clear about what the next right step isn't.

24. *Strike while the iron is cold.* A study from the University of California, Los Angeles, found that when purchases were interrupted by a conscious break in the buying process, purchasers became more objective and discerning about the need to buy. Neuroscientists at Emory University found that this delay disrupted dopamine release.[13] A drop in dopamine after you buy is called "buyer's remorse." That same drop before you buy is called "coming to your senses."

There are few true emergencies in life. Most decisions involving money really do allow time for consideration. Weighing different factors, gathering data, and perhaps consulting experts works best to make most decisions. Rarely does any legitimate crisis demand that these steps be skipped.

In between urge and action lies a gap: Impulsivity erases that gap, while emotional intelligence seeks it out. Create a contemplative pause—a space of time between choosing something and paying for it. Postpone all decisions based on impulse, frustration, or anger until you have regained objectivity.

25. *You'll never do anything important or fulfilling that will feel comfortable at first.* Growth and progress always feel uncertain in the beginning. At the point of jumping into the pool for the first time to learn to swim, you can either proceed despite your discomfort or abandon your task and immediately stop the anxiety. Anxiety signals that you are moving ahead into a new experience—it is not an indication of danger or inability. In order to master the task, you have to proceed despite anxiety.

If worrying about the future fills the present, both are diminished. A plan is only a guideline, not a certainty. The capacity to endure uncertainty is the essence of growth.

Growth and change are hard. In fact, the only thing harder is not growing or changing.

EPILOGUE
Money Lessons from Others

The Neuroeconomics of Thinking
More Like a Woman

Both men and women share a desire for autonomy and effectiveness as well as for connection and emotional caring. Yet the unconscious whispers of "you have evidence of worth by doing these things" differ considerably for each:

- For men, the early models and reinforcements probably had more to do with being strong, unemotional, doing more, and making more money.

- For women, the model more likely leaned toward being perfect, pretty, thin, quiet, loving, and giving to others.

These gender-specific expressions of attempts to live into an ideal—and thereby counter shame—can hitchhike on money as an emblem of care, worth, power, or any assigned meaning; money is a Rorschach ink blot of our own individual strivings.

Three considerations of gender-specific money psychology and investing lessons from women:

1. For elite investors, self-awareness is an important characteristic. Self-awareness fosters both objectivity and balance in decision making. Women tend to be more empathic with others

and thereby more empathic with themselves. Women tend to share emotions, regard of friendships, discussion of relationships, and collaboration of feelings more than men.

2. Unlike men, women are less likely to let their narcissism and pride get in the way of decision-making processes. Unlike women, men are significantly less likely to ask for directions, viewing it as a weakness. (Not me—I asked once back in February 1993.)

3. When men have disagreements, they tend to act on their feelings. Typically, they revert to physical activity or some form of action. Women are more likely to create a contemplative pause to reflect, plan, and engage more mentally. This means that men get on "tilt" more often. Poker players use this term for the emotion following a significant loss or significant success, causing them to respond emotionally to subsequent hands.

But money has no gender. It can convey any message and represent any message—the one true metaphor that can represent anything. It's a stand-in for what we idealize and desire yet fear and lack, for what we covet, crave, spurn, chase, or follow.

Money is a simple unit of value. It can't speak, promise, regret, or forecast. Money doesn't even know who owns it any more than the war bonds knew about the war. So it can't possibly create fiction. Yet the owner can, and the money stories that we consciously and unconsciously write become powerful influences in our lives.

What Can We Learn from Bernie Madoff?

And how was he able to con so many smart people?

We make money mistakes and financial fallacies because of the ways that our minds and our brains work. The Madoff tragedy illuminates some of the more prominent errors:

- *Exclusivity*: The desire to be special, even "chosen," catapults someone beyond common sense to an emotional choice. Madoff appealed to his target's desire for status by including

them in an exclusive club, even turning down potential investors. One investor said, "You had to go to him—he didn't
come to you. The first two or three times he said, 'Not yet.'
Until finally when he said 'Yes' you gave him every penny."

- *Transference fallacy*: Madoff was believable as an authority
  figure, especially confirmed by the fact that he was chairman
  of the NASDAQ and a philanthropist and had a huge following of admirers. We tend to idealize figures who portray
  confidence and manifest wealth in the hope of participating in
  some of their glory.

- *Social contagion*: People are persuaded by group momentum in
  order to participate, especially not to be left out. By reacting to
  trends, herd mentality creates trends.

- *Confirmation bias*: Once you make a choice, the tendency to re-
  inforce the belief that this is the best choice obscures evidence
  to the contrary. We tend to cherry-pick data to confirm that
  we've made the right decision. People continued to invest with
  Madoff and invited their friends to do the same.

- *Proving your worth*: Often, the victims of a scam want to prove
  their worth. Madoff's scam could have been his self-statement:
  Insiders said he wished he had gone to Wharton or Stanford,
  but instead he went to Hofstra University, so he always felt he
  needed to prove something.

- *Specialness*: Someone who offers an evocative promise that
  crystallizes vague, hazy dreams to make them seem vividly
  within reach can generate a cult-like following. The scam artist
  paints a picture to allow people to see what they want to see,
  then the victims project their own desires onto a promising
  story that crystallizes a fantasy of magical wealth. The scam
  artist is half of the cocreated scam.

- *Greed*: Emotion and immediacy will trump logic and thinking.
  The excitement of an opportunity creates a collaboration of
  neurocircuitry with a promise—a good story. When someone makes money, the region of the brain called the nucleus

accumbens lights up. This is the same pleasure center that responds to other highs, even those of cocaine. The drive to obtain a reward can resemble the addictive response of cocaine: Both are processed by the pleasure center. When financial incentives present a strong allure, reason as well as motivation can be hijacked by the pleasure center.

What can we learn from the Madoff debacle?

- Do not make significant financial decisions when you are vulnerable. Greater vulnerability occurs at times of crisis, such as divorce, job loss, death in the family, or economic downturn.

- Be wary of hearing what you want to hear. Once you make a decision, continue to examine the decision objectively and look for evidence that it is right and that it is possibly the wrong decision. Notice when you cherry-pick data to confirm your decision. If it seems too good to be true, it's probably too good to be true.

- No matter how chosen, special, or select a group you're in, no matter how exclusive the club you belong to, continue to ask questions. Madoff's creation of exclusivity obviated questioning by the time a client was accepted. Jerry Oppenheimer, in his book *Madoff with the Money* (the best title for a book since adolescent psychologist Dr. Anthony Wolf's *Get Out of My Life, but First Could You Drop Me and Sheryl Off at the Mall*), noted that Madoff surrounded himself by associates and staff who would not question him.[1]

- Be willing to sleep on it. There are few true emergencies in life and investing is not one of them.

- Following the lead of famous people into an investment is meaningless unless they became famous by investment success.

- Three basic tenets of good writing apply to good investing: clarity, brevity, and simplicity. Madoff had a complex investing scheme that even other money managers admitted they didn't understand.

- You are the chief executive officer of your own finances. It's an ongoing job.

- Our brains are wired for instant gratification from the pleasure center, the nucleus accumbens. The logic of financial decisions resides at a different neural address—the prefrontal cortex—which can be hijacked and held hostage by the pleasure center *unless there's a plan and you stick to it.*

- When someone's stock portfolio does well, he or she may attribute this to talent and smartness. And it could be. Or not. My wife and I play heads-up poker, and she finally confessed that one of my "tells" is that, when I happen to draw a lucky hand, I have a slightly smug look, like I think I'm brilliant.

Portrait of a Money Story: How Annie Leibovitz Lost Her Focus

Annie Leibovitz, perhaps the most famous living photographer, had a contract with *Vanity Fair* alone worth tens of millions of dollars. Unfortunately, that's also the estimated amount of debt she had. One chunk of that, $24 million, came due on September 8, 2009, to Art Capital Group, and unless she paid up, she would lose the rights to her famous photographs (including well-known shots, such as the naked John Lennon and Yoko Ono and a pregnant Demi Moore).

Rather than looking more closely at Leibovitz's dynamics, let's examine what we can learn about *our own* dynamics from this tragedy and take a look at how our minds and brains operate to sometimes persuade us into money mistakes and financial fallacies.

1. *Why are we intrigued by a sad story of a famous woman's misfortune?* When we hear of something bad happening to someone we envy, the result is that we may feel good. Neuroscientists at the University of Cambridge found that news of the downfall of the rich and famous activates the dorsal interior cingulate cortex of the brain. Their humiliation activates this region of the brain that responds to conflict and social rejection. In fact, the study showed that the more we envy someone, the greater the pleasure in his or her downfall. This accounts for our pleasure in seeing a high-powered chief executive officer who earned several million dollars

in bonus get humiliated in front of a congressional committee exposing indiscretion or doing the "perp walk." (When Madoff got shoved on the sidewalk—be honest—how many times did you rewind?)

2. *Making or spending money activates the same pleasure center in the brain as cocaine.* This makes the act of spending money potentially addictive. A lifestyle of increasing accomplishment, fame, wealth, and power can all be state changing and cumulatively challenging.

3. *Good decision making is a balance in which the right (emotional) brain and left (logical) brain operate together.* Stress, whether good or bad, can shift decision making to the right brain, overriding reason. We are reminded to delay significant financial decisions when vulnerable, such as at times of death in the family, divorce, or job loss. In recent times, Leibovitz lost her mother, her father, and her longtime companion Susan Sontag and added two children to the family.

4. *Our minds are drawn to the stories of the extreme to compare ourselves and feel better.*

- To reflect: "At least my debt isn't as bad as hers."

- To anchor an envy of fame or wealth: "I'm glad I'm not her."

- To watch dysfunctional people on reality and talk shows: "My problems are *nothing* compared to *that.*"

5. *Any* thing *(like money)* or any process *(like spending) can become its own story and eclipse its author.* Success has made failures of many men, Cindy Adams reminds us.

6. *Understanding insatiable appetite does not inoculate against its effects.* Leibovitz's fame as a photographer in the 1970s and 1980s provided gratification to people's limitless hunger for stargazing.

7. *Expertise in one area does not equate with expertise in another.* From successful physician to famous artist, people may not translate their accomplishments to money or investment savvy. Different parts of the brain are involved. Even Warren Buffett recognized this about himself: "I don't think being able to allocate capital means you're good at anything else."

8. *Money can solve many problems—or at least make them easier.* But then we overreach and make money solve more than it should. It gets

pressed into service because it's a commonly accepted social and personal resource—it makes people feel self-sufficient.

9. *We compare our inside to someone else's outside and may think money can bridge the differences.* Stories such as Leibovitz's confront this illusion. Her creative work has exposed more than just the surface for decades.

10. *Money is the legal tender of desires.* It becomes the ink blot of the Rorschach test. Emotional valuation can overwrite brain valuation. Money can be equated with emotional and social signifiers, such as power, freedom, and limitless opportunity.

11. *Credit cards and loans decouple buying and paying.* The pleasure of the purchase is segmented from the pain of future payment. Our optimism bias then makes rainy days and repayment an abstraction.

12. *Like perfection, "more" is not a goal.* It's unreachable—no end point. Leibovitz was supplied with an almost limitless budget to shoot her increasingly exotic and expensive photographs. Jane Sarkin, a *Vanity Fair* features editor, said, "Her demands became bigger . . . whatever she wanted she got."

Tiger and Mastery: With Sidebars on Bernie, Kinky, and Us

Tiger Woods, called the greatest golfer of all time, stated from the beginning of his career as an amateur and repeated regularly throughout his professional career that he could—that he must—become better. He said it after his finest seasons and biggest championships. He's still saying it now about his personal and professional life. He understands mastery. He assures himself, with us listening in, that he still pursues it despite his self-induced setbacks.

Daniel Pink tells us in *Drive* that mastery is an asymptote—a straight line that a curve approaches but never quite reaches.[2] Mastery—the urge to get better at something that matters—is a mind-set. The motivation of effectiveness, demonstrated in the first months of life, evolves in various expressions throughout life. With a mind-set of mastery, improvement continues. Our minds are drawn to the stories of the extreme, at times to compare ourselves and feel better. Our *minds* respond in reaction formation to the envy of their wealth and fame; our *brains* fire in reaction to their humiliation and shame:

- "At least my debt isn't as bad as hers."

- "I'm glad I'm not him."

- "My problems are *nothing* compared to *that*." (Reality shows regularly take this one to the bank.)

And remember the words of my fellow Texan Kinky Friedman, smart enough both to run for president and to withdraw before any possibility materialized: "If you look deep enough inside yourself, you will see everyone else."

What about the rest of the story? For Tiger, Kinky, and us, a perpetual series of occasions is available for the pursuit of effectiveness and mastery, to get better both personally and professionally at what really matters.

Inside the Brain of a Super Bowl Champion

With 64 seconds remaining in the Giants–Patriots 2012 Super Bowl, the Giants were trailing the Patriots 17–15 and were within striking distance to score. With an immediate Giants score, the Patriots would get the ball back and have time to attempt a scoring drive. So the Giants wanted to score, but first they wanted to use up most of the time remaining on the clock. The Patriots needed the Giants to score immediately so they would have enough time for a drive to keep hope alive that they could win the game.

The Giants' Ahmad Bradshaw was handed the ball, having been instructed to ground himself a yard away from the goal rather than scoring the touchdown. The Patriots cleared the path for an immediate touchdown.

Bradshaw tried to stop himself at the one-yard line. It was not only counterintuitive, but it also opposed well-grooved superhighways in his brain traveled for many years. His trained instincts and brain wiring told him to take the ball and run across the goal line. The Giants' season-long mantra, "Finish," provided further context. His brain wouldn't let him do it. Instinctively, he kept going even though he clearly heard quarterback Eli Manning say, "Don't score." Bradshaw later told reporters, "I tried, but I couldn't do it."

If this accomplished professional athlete could not outsmart his brain with a world championship on the line, how can we hope to make rational decisions while browsing at Macy's or making an online stock purchase?

Many high-stakes decisions are made at stressful times. Mentor coaching with pro athletes and executives has repeatedly shown me how decision makers are often under emotional stress, skewing their potential to evaluate options, leading to a greater reliance on emotional decisions and default options. At times of stress, we do two things:

1. Our minds reduce decisions to rely on heuristics—rules of thumb. Heuristics work well on a daily basis for simple decisions. They are generally right, and the cost of errors is small. Yet in high-stakes decisions, simple rules of thumb (heuristics) tend to be a poor method of forecasting and decision making.

2. Our brains rely on default programming that has been conditioned by numerous repetitions of stimulus–response. This neural conditioning is simple: The meaning we attach to a stimulus determines our behavior.

The neuroscience of high-stakes decisions becomes prominent at crucial times. The paradox is that with the pressure of time, the state of mind shifts so that deep thought, reflection on principles, and contemplative pause all become elusive. Bradshaw simply couldn't suddenly override years of training and tens of thousands of practice behaviors that etched default pathways in his brain.

A state of mind is vulnerable to emotional contagion, greed, and peer pressure, all of which can trump logic. When you see friends making significant profits trading stocks or flipping real estate, the natural inclination is to want in on the action. As more join the movement, prices rise for a while, and it's a self-fulfilling prophecy. But then some event reverses the momentum, bursts the bubble, and turns optimism into panic. Herd mentality then pushes people to join the momentum to buy or to flee the market. A hot stock tip, a business deal gone sour, or a family tragedy may create an alarm response with an emotional state of mind geared for survival rather than the use of logic.

Habits are difficult to change because of the way the brain functions. Many patterns of thinking and behaving are ingrained in circuits deep within the brain. Information is processed in the amygdala (the center of strong emotion) and the hippocampus (where meanings are attached), both in the midbrain, and these algorithms are automatic and not initially processed consciously.

An instant way of grounding and centering yourself to restore a balanced state of mind to access logic and reason may be to use a mantra.

GLOSSARY

Behavioral economics Studies of the social, cognitive, and emotional factors underlying economic decisions of individuals and groups. Behavioral economics studies how people really think and behave as opposed to how they think they think and behave. The assumption of conventional economics is that we are rational beings, that we compute the value of the options we face and follow the best path of action. Yet in reality, many factors skew fundamental rationality and reasoning abilities: expectations, emotions, social norms, and other illogical forces.

What are our minds made for? It looks as if we have the wrong user's manual. —Nassim Nicholas Taleb, *The Black Swan*

Change To modify or convert from past to present or back again—such as the "system restore" of a midlife crisis when someone who has previously altered a value system in order to succeed in a competitive corporate environment shifts back to what is more authentic. Change uses the past as a point of reference to alter recognizable patterns; reinvention focuses on now and the future to create a new story. A new story can move problem to possibility, obstacle to desire. The key element in writing a new story is to design the story from what is possible rather than what has existed in the past.

No human quality is beyond change. —Daniel Goleman

Choice architecture The determination of informed choice and the recognition that each moment's choice is actively determined. Choice architecture involves the recognition that you write your own story, own it, can assess it, and decide the choice generated each moment. Mentor coaching collaborates with clients to help them make the most informed choice possible moment by moment. Choice architecture helps someone understand how the mind and brain work in order to create optimum maps and paradigms in order to make informed, strategic choices.

It's taken me most of my life to know which notes not to play. —Dizzy Gillespie, master jazz trumpeter

Concessions Something an individual puts up with that takes time, energy, peacefulness, or money in a recurring, unsatisfying way. We have four major arenas of concessions: physical, emotional, relationship, and financial. Concessions at home include such things as physical repair needs, cleaning needs, messiness, or noise boundary violations. Concessions in work life can be inadequate space, wrong field of work, poor communication, lack of mission, improper technology, or dysfunctional hierarchies. Concessions regarding family, friends, and colleagues include imbalance of support or friendship, blurred boundaries, misunderstandings, or the need to change fundamental agreements. Concessions usually arise through procrastination, conflict avoidance, or creating a certain appearance.

Nothing prevents our being natural so much as the desire to appear so. —François de La Rochefoucauld

Emotional Economics® The study of the interactions of mind and brain impacting money behavior and financial decisions. Emotional Economics integrates and applies developmental psychology, neuroscience, and quantum physics with strategic coaching principles to understand and remedy money mistakes and financial fallacies. The study of Emotional Economics incorporates the principles of understanding how the mind and brain work in order to revise mind software and rewire brain hardware regarding money behavior and financial decisions.

Our core beliefs and emotions require a portal of expression, a path to the tangible.

Empathy A listening perspective positioned inside the experience and subjective reality of another. This attunement with another's internal experience permits appreciation of that person's own framework of thinking,

feeling, and meaning. Empathy is resonance, not sympathy, commisera-
tion, or condolence. Empathy positions one foot in the shoe of another's
experience without losing any of oneself. Empathy is neutral—equidistant
between two sides of a conflict—not knowing what that person's answer
will be and not needing it to go one way or another. An empathic failure
causes another's hurt that's often quickly repaired by anger—a reaction to
the helplessness of not being understood.

> Could a greater miracle take place than for us to look through each
> other's eyes for an instant? —Henry David Thoreau

Explicit and implicit learning Acquiring conscious, specific, and focused
content is referred to as explicit learning. Explicit learning focuses on data
and factual information. Implicit learning takes place outside awareness.
Implicit learning includes a body memory, such as riding a bicycle, or a
procedural memory, such as complex behavioral patterns, for example, a
parent who repeats with children the same behavior or attachment pattern
the parent experienced as a child. Implicit learning and memory operate in
the flow of a process, so you ultimately don't have to think about it each
time. A "choke" or "slump" can be associated with a switch from implicit
to explicit processes.

> What is remembered is what becomes reality. —Patricia Hampl

Ideal An internal standard of excellence. Ideals serve as a personal model
of value—an internal guide of purpose and principles. Examples of ideals
include being able to relate, to create, to teach, or to contribute. Living
up to a personal, attainable ideal generates self-esteem. When ideals are
respected and protected, the result is integrity. When ideals are not attained or when there is no tangible evidence of what "good enough" is,
the result is shame.

> Ken Townsend's mother, after reading that Townsend won an Eng-
> lish prize said, "There must be some mistake." Townsend "took her
> remark as proof that whatever I did, it would not be good enough."
> —*Raritan* magazine

Internal point of reference Ownership of one's life story: the self as the
source of initiative, esteem, and regulation. Autonomy to become one's own
authority allows the person to fully realize passion and potential. Examples
of an external point of reference—of not being one's own authority—include

passive language: "Anger seized me," "I came to an impasse," or "My mind played tricks on me." Other examples are external pressure words: "Have to," "Ought to," or "Should." Or the direct abdication of one's own initiative: "You made me feel that way." Dependence on others, as well as perpetual defiance of authority, indicates ongoing struggles with autonomy.

> Both conformity and opposition occupy the same prison. —David Krueger, *Destiny*

Intuition A knowing not formulated from data or intellectual processes. An impression, gut feeling, hunch, flashing image, or fantasy may occur before someone knows what to think. Intuition is imaginative, sometimes surprising.

> Intuition is the source of all scientific knowledge. —Aristotle

> But what would happen if we took our instincts seriously? We would end up with a different and better world. —Malcolm Gladwell

Mental models A representation of external reality inside your head. A mental model attempts to understand knowledge and principles about the world. Each of us has several mental models—or mind-sets—inside our heads. A mental model is a way to identify core principles and organizing concepts to make a story out of isolated facts. A mental model needs to come from multiple disciplines, as one discipline cannot encompass all the necessary wisdom. If a physician or a philosopher sticks to his own model, his understanding of the real world would be limited. Mental models are simply stories—stories composed of metaphors that explain both the tangible and the intangible. If we have too few mental models, we tend to overuse the ones we have. To a man with a hammer, every problem looks like a nail. Mental models are stored in the hippocampus, the brain's memory focal point.

> Alice came to a fork in the road. "Which road do I take?" she asked.
> "Where do you want to go?" responded the Cheshire cat.
> "I don't know," Alice answered.
> "Then," said the cat, "it doesn't matter." —Lewis Carroll

Mirror neurons Mirror neurons are a function of actual networks in different parts of the brain that reflect the behavior or feelings of others. We unconsciously imitate what we witness, ranging from movement to behavior patterns to yawning. Mirror neurons help us directly and indirectly imitate actions and create experiences. Stick out your tongue at a newborn baby, and the baby will immediately return the gesture. A baby smiles, and her mother smiles back. Mirror neurons are instrumental in our acquisition of empathy, language, and social behavior. This mirroring activity explains how children download beliefs and behaviors beginning in the first years of life. We experience and take in how our parents approached money—the behaviors, messages, attitudes, biases, meanings, and regard of money. Mirror neurons help us understand emotional and social contagion.

> A loving person lives in a loving world.
> A hostile person lives in a hostile world.
> Everyone you meet is your mirror. —Ken Keyes Jr.

> Tell me what you pay attention to and I will tell you who you are. —José Ortega y Gasset

Money story People breathe life into money and give it personal meaning to make it a story. Every important relationship, including money, has its own history, develops its own story, and evolves its own language. What money means to you, what it says to you, and what you say with it constitute your money story. Everyone has a money story—a money autobiography with a plot, story lines, conflicts, and strivings. A money story reveals your relationship with yourself as well as to money. Otherwise, money is only a fact—a piece of paper or set of digits. People create internal and external conversations about money. Some of the money issues are really about money, but many are about other matters, private or even secret, hitchhiking on money.

> I don't know how to tell my money story to myself in order to see what elements need to be changed. —Jeremy Tarcher, personal communication

Narrative The basic components—the running commentary—of a life story that comes alive in various ways. Narratives include the themes of verbal expression, the body language that expresses feelings in psychosomatic lexicons, and recurring behavior patterns. A life story unfolds through its narration. Personal narratives, unlike other narration, may not be announced directly. Some of the narrative may be left out, invisible to the speaker; the narrator may not be fully aware of the story he or she is telling.

> Myths are the stories we tell ourselves to explain the world around us and within us. —Pamela Jaye Smith

Needs An essential requirement for mind, body, or spirit. Early in life, our needs include physical nurturance, empathic attunement, attachment, effectiveness, exploration, assertion, feeling regulation, and sensory requirements. The adult version includes providing for physical requirements, comfort, identity, affirmation, love, communication, safety, mastery, freedom, and sexual/sensual needs. When a need is met, a sense of effectiveness and optimum functioning results.

> Needs and values form core themes of personal story plot. An unmet need results in someone getting sick. —Henry Miller

Neuroeconomics The neurobiological foundations—the brain basis—of economic decision making. Neuroeconomics combines psychology, economics, and neuroscience to study how people make financial decisions. Neuroeconomic studies demonstrate how people buy with their emotions first and their reason second. Logic comes in afterward as the brain justifies the decision that has already been made. Neuroeconomics extends behavioral economics to direct observation of brain functioning—how the brain interacts with the environment to produce economic behavior. This study extends to how the brains of groups of people interact to produce economic behavior. By studying the neuromechanisms underlying decisions about rewarding and losing outcomes, we can create situations that avoid suboptimal decisions, as well as harm, while maximizing optimum decisions.

> Sometimes the hardest thing in life is to know which bridge to cross and which to burn. —*The International*

Neurogenesis The creation of new brain cells. With new experiences, new neuronal cells as well as pathways are generated throughout our lives. Neurons are both flexible and regenerative. The new brain cells connect with existing circuitry and developing networks to enhance function, such as memory. Two things above all other create neurogenesis: an enriched environment (intellectual and emotional stimulation) and exercise. As a corollary, chronic stress impairs neurogenesis.

> Life isn't about finding yourself. It's about creating yourself. —George Bernard Shaw

Neuroplasticity The capacity of the brain for creating new neural connections and pathways in response to experience. Neuroplasticity can occur throughout the life span. Neuroscience has demonstrated that the emotional and mental changes we craft by the process of "mind sight" transform the physical brain. By focusing on our experience, we can sculpt neural pathways and stimulate the growth of aspects of the brain crucial to well-being. Neuroscience shows us that we can grow these new connections throughout our lives. One of the most exciting and revolutionary discoveries in the past few decades is that how we specifically focus attention shapes the actual structure of the brain. The brain never stops growing in response to new experiences.

You become what you give your attention to. —Epictetus (AD 55–135)

Perception The process of how we select, register, and attach meaning to experiences. Someone registers information and experience that fits an existing belief pattern and ignores or disbelieves what doesn't fit that pattern. Two people with different cognitive styles can stand shoulder to shoulder viewing the same scene, then later describe it in ways that sound like two different events. Our inner beliefs determine our experience of what surrounds us; our interpretation becomes our story, which becomes our reality.

The percentage of Americans who believe they are in the richest 1 percent of the population: 19 percent. —Peter Strupp

One day our descendants will think it incredible that we paid so much attention to things like the amount of melanin in our skin or the shape of our eyes or our gender instead of the unique identities of each of us as complex human beings. —Franklin Thomas

Plot The skeleton of a life story that gives it structure, purpose, and pattern. A unique set of individual beliefs, consequences, and relationships that determine how one creates experiences. The plot is the arc drawn across the themes and story lines of an entire life narrative. Plot dictates what one looks for, how one perceives, and how one assigns meaning to an experience. All subsequent information is absorbed through that narrative plot. Basic beliefs and core assumptions generate experiences, behaviors, and meanings. All components of a life, business, or career story can evolve to a cohesive narrative and an organized coherent plot of action goals, strategic development, and results. Often, an individual's plot goes unquestioned because it is taken for granted—the person is unaware of its existence as an organizing model.

Every man's work, whether it be literature or music or pictures or architecture or anything else, is always a portrait of himself. —Samuel Butler (1835–1902)

Premise An organizing proposition on which a story is based. The preliminary statement of story purpose keeps the reader from straying from the story line while fully and richly developing the plot. Certain fundamental propositions on which life stories are based include parentage, social class, looks, and race. America lets one work out of some premises, such as social class. For example, the greatest reason people don't earn and keep a lot of money is the premise that they don't see themselves capable of it. Still other premises, such as one based on early childhood abandonment, powerfully affect subsequent relationship expectations.

The universe is made of stories, not atoms. —Muriel Rukeyser

Psychological symptom A somatic story authored by emotions. A symptom both reveals and conceals, making obvious to others what one hides from oneself, simultaneously attempting to engage and to flee. Symptoms give disguised voice to what their creator avoids knowing, a secret hiding in the open. A symptom is a component of a story that needs, indeed begs, to be told in its entirety, listened to rather than silenced artificially, respected rather than disregarded. It speaks literally: a pain in the neck, purging something, weeping skin, hypertension. As a story with its own history, dynamics, and meanings, a symptom answers a question not asked consciously; it will be repeated until translated.

It is easier to fall ill than learn the truth . . . so take care of your maladies . . . they always have something to tell you. —M. Pavic

Reinvention The creation or composition of different life or money story experiences. A process that begins with taking ownership of a life or money story rather than living out what just seems to happen or feeling victimized by forces beyond our control. The key element in writing a new story is to design the story from what is possible rather than from what has existed in the past.

History doesn't repeat itself, but it does rhyme. —Mark Twain

Resistance to change Both mind and brain become conditioned to respond in recurring patterns. The pull of the old and the fear of the new constantly vie with each other. Yet there is only a redundant future in repetition. Any departure from the familiar, even a positive one, creates uncertainty and trepidation. We repeat behavior that doesn't work because it offers security and familiarity. Doing the same thing produces a known outcome. We can mistake predictability for effectiveness, trade freedom for safety, or forgo aliveness for certainty. Overcoming resistance to change by creating new experiences literally changes the neuronal networks and neural nets within the brain.

> I am astonished I could let go of the drama of being a suffering artist. Nothing dies harder than a bad idea. —Julia Cameron

Secrets To hold onto something, to continuously engage by sequestering, reserves its place, frozen in time. The possibility of telling invites relinquishment of what the secret holds, threatens to unleash the feelings packaging it, and adumbrates dissolution of the illusion that is part of the secret. The threat of exposure risks stripping away everything pertaining to the secret, especially its companion: hope. Someone can engage something the first time by denying it. People can tell themselves secrets out loud by symptoms. Speaking secrets out loud in words distinguishes the present from the past. A secret is always about the past because it exists in a time capsule.

> The only secrets are the secrets that keep themselves. —Ralph Waldo Emerson

Self-empathy Being able to make yourself the focus of your attunement and resonance. Self-empathy is more difficult than focusing on another person, especially if you are unaccustomed to taking yourself as a point of reference and have been a caretaker of others to the partial exclusion of yourself. Being empathic with yourself is the same process as being attuned to others, only with yourself as the focus. Your feelings need to have a receiver (you), have an impact on and become known (by you), and be metabolized (by you).

> If you look deep enough inside yourself, you'll see everyone else. —Kinky Friedman

Self-statement A unique, personal communication of experience and point of view. What people say and do are inevitable, unavoidable self-statements of their beliefs and personal realities. Individuals actively construct their experiences. Narrative and plot reflect individual assumptions and self-concept. A life story manifests through self-statements ranging from broad themes, such as success, to simple statements, such as melancholy that sees and forecasts unhappiness. People believe according to their self-images; views are self-statements of our perception. All that you say is about yourself.

> People seem not to see that their opinion of the world is also a confession of character. —Ralph Waldo Emerson

State of mind A psychophysiological (mind–body) state, with an internally organized software program of expectations, attitudes, meanings, and emotions. Each state of mind has its own developmental history, its own expectations to filter and organize perception and attribute meaning. Each person has different states of mind, with more awareness of some than others. A normal range of mind states includes calm relaxation, focused alertness, or worried anticipation; some states have a dominant feeling, such as excitement, fear, anxiety, or euphoria. Each state of mind, like a software program, determines access and expression of memory, emotion, thinking, and behavior. Within a particular state of mind, people perceive, remember, feel, think, behave, and respond in a consistent mode.

> The mind seems to embrace a confederation of psychic entities. —William James

Story busting Although people are neurologically and psychologically conditioned to relate to the world in a preprogrammed repetitive way, change can occur. An internal working model can be transcended. New information may not fit into the existing framework and ultimately can't be ignored. For centuries, no one believed a human being could run the mile in less than four minutes. In 1954, when one man busted that story, the perception of reality and possibility changed. Within months of Roger Bannister's breaking the four-minute mile, several others did so as well, and today it is common. The obstacle of the impossible could no longer be constructed.

> And what happens when the stories we have relied on our whole lives stop making sense? —Monica Crowley, *What the Bleep Do We Know!?*

Story line The basic themes, or subplots, of a life or money story plot. Each story line has its own history, its own consistency over time, its own assumptions and motivations. The perceptions and suppositions within a story line become evident in behaviors. A story line is the manifestation of beliefs since one always finds or creates that which validates basic theories. Some of the major story lines of literature and life include entitlement and privilege, redemption through caring for others, hard work bringing prosperity and dignity, and penance absolving earlier mistakes. The victim always finds ways to suffer; someone who is hopeful will always create possibility and live into it.

> The unconscious speaks more than one dialect. —Sigmund Freud

Story metaphor The metaphor constructing a life or money story is based on the premise that whatever you think, feel, and experience is what you create each moment. You construct your entire story; every element of experience is created. Consider the different perspective in saying "I am sad" versus "I feel sad." "I am sad" is a self-definition that both defines and limits. "I feel sad" is the recognition of the act of creating a feeling and the inherent recognition of being able to create other feelings as well. The choice architecture of each moment actively constructs story narrative. Focusing on and recognizing story construction not only accepts that we create story but also presents us with possibilities for transformation.

> Money is the one true metaphor, the one commodity that can be translated into all else. —Dana Gioia

Success intoxication To become enmeshed in the escalating pursuit of success and lost in its stimulation and affirmation. Indications of success intoxication include a reliance on the extremes of accomplishment, accelerating success with heightened metrics, an evolving erosion of other important matters to the process leading to success, and blurred boundaries between work and personal life. The stimulation of extreme success, such as in business or athletic endeavors, can make it harder to regulate emotions and stay grounded in values and identity.

> Success has made failures of many men. —Cindy Adams

Success phobia Disturbance in a person's ability to comfortably handle achievement. Those who have the opportunity, intelligence, and imagination to succeed but do not live up to their potential or suffer when they do reveal an internal rather than external impediment to success. Success can be avoided in any area of life—academic, vocational, marital, sexual, and parental, to name a few. Fear of success manifests in so many ways that it often goes unrecognized. Three basic areas of phobic avoidance are avoidance of the final step to success ("I always stop just short of my goals," known as choking), erosion of successful accomplishment (a takeaway after success to spoil its enjoyment), and ambition without goal setting ("I can't set a specific goal.").

> We have met the enemy—and he is us. —Walt Kelly, creator of *Pogo*

Transference The active organizing process of the mind to understand a present experience but necessarily relying on existing software. What we expect in the present tells us instantly what has happened in the past. Relationships with original caretakers establish a story premise of expectations and patterns. When neuronal networks and neural pathways are activated, the basic story lines unfold. Transference is most obvious with a stereotypic or irrational response, such as currently reacting to a spouse in the same way as toward a parent in childhood. Unless shaped and changed by revision, repetition ensures a replay of the old story.

> You tricked me out of feeling solitary by being others for me. —Clive Wilbur

Visualization A scenario of the experience of arrival at a destination, such as the successful actualization of a goal. An author visualizes a scene and conveys it to the readers in such a way that they live into the process of being there. Constructing a vision gives hope possibility—a shape and form. Vision crystallizes an achievement into a full sensory experience and context in mind and brain. An individual inhabits the experience of a vision as guide to creating it. A vision serves as inspiration to design ways of realizing it. The most successful businesses have a vision that is also ubiquitous for each person in the organization. A vision leads you to it.

> But eyes are blind. You have to look with the heart. —Antoine de Saint-Exupéry, *The Little Prince*

Wants Wishes and desires. Wants are replaceable with other wishes, and fantasies are interchangeable, but one need cannot substitute for another need. Old unmet needs manifest as present wants, such as a childhood need for affirmation leading to a relentless adult pursuit of validation trophies and driven accomplishments. A need cannot be suppressed or segmented from awareness for very long. The frustration of a wish, such as the expectation of a gift, can lead to disappointment. While needs are universal, wants are tied to uniquely personal experiences and have their own particular history.

> I know what I am fleeing from, but not what I am in search of. —Michel Eyquem de Montaigne

Work addiction An unrestrained, unfulfillable internal demand for constant engagement in work and a corresponding inability to relax. A "workaholic" is incessantly driven, relentlessly active. Work is the one organizing and effective activity. Inactivity or activity other than work may give rise to guilt, anxiety, or emptiness. Some individuals view work as the only area in which they can establish and maintain their identities, feel effective, and enjoy feelings of importance, validation, and affirmation. Others may use work to counteract underlying feelings of inadequacy and ineffectiveness. Working passionately, long and hard, and deriving satisfaction does not make someone a work addict.

> *An addiction is something you can't do without, yet it is a promise never kept.*

NOTES

Chapter One: The Longest Relationship of Your Life

1. Loren Eiseley, *The Unexpected Universe* (New York: Mariner Books, 1972).

2. Hilke Plassmann, John O'Doherty, Baba Shiv, and Antonio Rangel, "Marketing Actions Can Modulate Neural Representations of Experienced Pleasantness," *Proceedings of the National Academy of Sciences* 105, no. 3 (January 22, 2008): 1050–54.

3. Hal E. Hershfield, Daniel G. Goldstein, William F. Sharpe, Jesse Fox, Leo Yeykelis, Laura L. Carstensen, and Jeremy N. Bailenson, "Increasing Saving Behavior through Age-Progressed Renderings of the Future Self," *Journal of Marketing Research* 48, no. SPL (November 2011): S23–37.

Chapter Two: Surface and Shadow Stories

1. Charles Dickens, *Dombey and Son* (London: Bradbury and Evans, 1848).

Chapter Three: Why Do We Resist Change?

1. Nassim Taleb, *The Black Swan: The Impact of the Highly Improbable* (New York: Random House, 2007).

2. Ronald Havens, *The Wisdom of Milton H. Erickson: Hypnosis and Hypnotherapy*, vol. 1 (New York: Paragon House, 1990).

3. Derren Brown, "How Not to Have Your Wallet Taken—Trick of the Mind," August 28, 2012, https://youtube/TpXNSg02zA4.

4. Kim Parker, "Yes, the Rich Are Different," Pew Research Center, August 27, 2012, http://www.pewsocialtrends.org/2012/08/27/yes-the-rich-are-different.

5. Twyla Tharp, *The Creative Habit: Learn It and Use It for Life* (New York: Simon & Schuster, 2003).

6. Howard E. Gardner, *Extraordinary Minds: Portraits of 4 Exceptional Individuals and an Examination of Our Own Extraordinariness* (New York: Basic Books, 1997).

7. Gudrun Heise and Fabian Schmidt, "How Brain Cells Control Orientation," *Tomorrow Today—The Science Magazine*, October 12, 2014, https://www.dw.com/en/how-brain-cells-control-orientation/a-17975917.

8. Kerri Anne Renzulli, "Poll: How Boomer and Millennial Couples Feel about Love and Money," *Time*, May 19, 2015, http://time.com/money/3882484/couples-money-survey-boomers-millennials.

Chapter Five: Master Money States of Mind

1. Max H. Bazerman and William F. Samuelson, "I Won the Auction but Don't Want the Prize," *Journal of Conflict Resolution* 27, no. 4 (December 1983): 618–34.

2. Jennifer Lerner, PhD, professor of public policy and management at the Harvard Kennedy School of Government and director of the Harvard Laboratory for Decision Science, http://www.decisionlab.harvard.edu/_oldsite/people/jennifer-lerner.

3. Andrew W. Lo, Charles E. and Susan P. Harris Professor at the MIT Sloan School of Management and director of the MIT Laboratory for Financial Engineering, http://alo.mit.edu.

4. Bessel van der Kolk, *The Body Keeps the Score: Brain, Mind, and Body in the Healing of Trauma* (New York: Viking, 2014).

Chapter Six: Nonsense Neuroscience and Bad Behavioral Economics

1. Emily Haisley, "The Appeal of Lotteries and Their Use in Incentive Design" (doctoral diss., Carnegie Mellon University, 2008).

2. Francesca Gino, Michael Norton, and Dan Airely, "The Counterfeit Self: The Deceptive Costs of Faking It," *Psychological Science* 21, no. 5 (May 2010): 712–20.

3. Daniel Kahneman, *Thinking, Fast and Slow* (New York: Farrar, Straus and Giroux, 2011).

4. Ibid.

5. Chris Crowley and Henry S. Lodge, *Younger Next Year: A Guide to Living Like 50 until You're 80 and Beyond* (New York: Workman, 2005).

6. Ray Kurdzweil, *The Singularity Is Near: When Humans Transcend Biology* (New York: Viking, 2005).

7. The Editors of *Time*, *The Science of Happiness: New Discoveries for a More Joyful Life* (New York: Time Inc. Books, 2016).

8. Daniel Gilbert, *Stumbling on Happiness* (New York: Vintage, 2007).

9. David G. Myers, *The American Paradox: Spiritual Hunger in an Age of Plenty* (New Haven, CT: Yale University Press, 2000).

10. Lawrence M. Ausubel, "Credit Card Defaults, Credit Card Profits, and Bankruptcy," *American Bankruptcy Law Journal* 71 (Spring 1997): 249–70.

11. Alfred Kahn, *The Economics of Regulation: Principles and Institutions* (Cambridge, MA: MIT Press, 1988).

Chapter Eleven: Step 5—Map Changes: Inscribe New Code

1. Steven D. Gjerstad and Vernon L. Smith, *Rethinking Housing Bubbles* (New York: Cambridge University Press, 2014).

Chapter Twelve: Step 6—Author New Experiences: Write New Software

1. Ben Fletcher, Karen Pine, and Danny Penman, *The No Diet Diet: Do Something Different* (London: Orion, 2005).

2. John H. Weakland and Wendel A. Ray, eds., *Propagations: Thirty Years of Influence from the Mental Research Institute* (New York: Haworth Press, 1995).

3. Marshall Goldsmith and Laurence S. Lyons, eds., *Coaching for Leadership: Writings on Leadership from the World's Greatest Coaches* (San Francisco: Wiley, 2005).

4. Malcolm Gladwell, *Outliers: The Story of Success* (Boston: Little, Brown, 2008).

5. Virginia Satir, *The New Peoplemaking* (New York: Science & Behavior Books, 1988).

6. Edward Norton Lorenz, "Deterministic Nonperiodic Flow," *Journal of the Atmospheric Sciences* 20 (March 1963): 130–41.

Chapter Fourteen: The ABCS of Money Mistakes and Financial Fallacies

1. Daniel Kahneman, *Thinking, Fast and Slow* (New York: Farrar, Straus and Giroux, 2011).
2. Ibid.

Chapter Fifteen: Belief Management

1. Daniel Pink, *Drive: The Surprising Truth about What Motivates Us* (New York: Riverhead Books, 2009).
2. Sarah Jane Gilbert, "Understanding the 'Want' vs. 'Should' Decision," Harvard Business School, July 16, 2007, http://hbswk.hbs.edu/item/5693.html.

Chapter Sixteen: Choice Architecture

1. Joseph Nunes and Xavier Dreze, "Your Loyalty Program Is Betraying You," *Harvard Business Review* 84, no. 4 (April 2006): 124–31, 150.
2. Daniel Kahneman, *Thinking, Fast and Slow* (New York: Farrar, Straus and Giroux, 2011).
3. Ibid.
4. Adrian North, David Hargreaves, and Jennifer McKendrick, "The Influence of In-Store Music on Wine Selections," *Journal of Applied Psychology* 84, no. 2 (April 1999): 271–76.
5. Steve Booth-Butterfield and Bill Reger, "The Message Changes Belief and the Rest Is Theory; The '1% or Less' Milk Campaign and Reasoned Action," *Preventive Medicine* 39, no. 3 (September 2004): 581–88.
6. Alvin Roth, Edmund S. Phelps, Robert J. Shiller, and A. Michael Spence, "Four Nobel Economists on the Biggest Challenges for 2016," World Economic Forum, January 17, 2016, https://www.weforum.org/agenda/2016/01/four-nobel-economists-on-biggest-challenges-2016.
7. Wellness Rebates, "What Is the ROI on Wellness?," December 7, 2012, http://www.wellnessrebates.com.
8. Sheena Iyengar, *The Art of Choosing* (New York: Twelve, 2011).
9. Emily Pronin, Christopher Y. Olivola, and Kathleen A. Kennedy, "Doing unto Future Selves as You Would Do unto Others: Psychological Distance and Decision Making," *Personality and Social Psychology Bulletin* 34, no. 2 (February 2008): 224–36.

10. David Shenk, *The Genius in All of Us: Why Everything You've Been Told about Genetics, Talent, and IQ Is Wrong* (New York: Doubleday, 2010).

11. Kristen Fanarakis, *The Real Color of Money*, University of Maryland Robert H. Smith School of Business, February 25, 2015, https://www.rhsmith.umd.edu/news/real-color-money.

12. "A London without Poverty," Joseph Rowntree Foundation, March 22, 2016, https://www.jrf.org.uk/report/london-without-poverty.

13. Anthony A. Grace, Stan B. Floresco, Yukiori Goto, and Daniel J. Lodge, "Regulation of Firing Dopaminergic Neurons and Control of Gold-Directed Behaviors," *Trends in Neurosciences* 30, no. 5 (May 2007): 220–27.

Epilogue: Money Lessons from Others

1. Jerry Oppenheimer, *Madoff with the Money* (New York: Wiley, 2009).

2. Daniel Pink, *Drive: The Surprising Truth about What Motivates Us* (New York: Riverhead Books, 2009).

SELECTED BIBLIOGRAPHY

Berger, Jonah. *Invisible Influence: The Hidden Forces That Shape Behavior*. New York: Simon & Schuster, 2016.

Chen, Kay-Yut, and Marina Krakovsky. *Secrets of the Moneylab: How Behavioral Economics Can Improve Your Business*. New York: Portfolio/Penguin, 2010.

Crowley, Chris, and Henry S. Lodge. *Younger Next Year: A Guide to Living Like 50 until You're 80 and Beyond*. New York: Workman, 2005.

Dickens, Charles. *Dombey and Son*. London: Bradbury and Evans, 1848.

Eagleman, David. *Incognito: The Secret Lives of the Brain*. New York: Pantheon Books, 2011.

Eiseley, Loren. *The Unexpected Universe*. New York: Mariner Books, 1972.

Fletcher, Ben, Karen Pine, and Danny Penman. *The No Diet Diet: Do Something Different*. London: Orion, 2005.

Gardner, Howard E. *Extraordinary Minds: Portraits of 4 Exceptional Individuals and an Examination of Our Own Extraordinariness*. New York: Basic Books, 1997.

Gilbert, Daniel. *Stumbling on Happiness*. New York: Vintage, 2007.

Gjerstad, Steven D., and Vernon L. Smith. *Rethinking Housing Bubbles*. New York: Cambridge University Press, 2014.

Gladwell, Malcolm. *Outliers: The Story of Success*. Boston: Little, Brown, 2008.

Goldsmith, Marshall, and Laurence S. Lyons, eds. *Coaching for Leadership: Writings on Leadership from the World's Greatest Coaches*. San Francisco: Wiley, 2005.

Havens, Ronald. *The Wisdom of Milton H. Erickson: Hypnosis and Hypnotherapy*. Vol. 1. New York: Paragon House, 1990.

Iyengar, Sheena. *The Art of Choosing*. New York: Twelve, 2011.

Kahn, Alfred. *The Economics of Regulation: Principles and Institutions.* Cambridge, MA: MIT Press, 1988.

Kahneman, Daniel. *Thinking, Fast and Slow.* New York: Farrar, Straus and Giroux, 2011.

Krueger, David. *The Secret Language of Money: How to Make Smarter Financial Decisions and Live a Richer Life.* New York: McGraw-Hill, 2009.

Kurdzweil, Ray. *The Singularity Is Near: When Humans Transcend Biology.* New York: Viking, 2005.

Myers, David G. *The American Paradox, Spiritual Hunger in an Age of Plenty.* New Haven, CT: Yale University Press, 2000.

Newberg, Andrew, and Mark Robert Waldman. *Words Can Change Your Brain: 12 Conversation Strategies to Build Trust, Resolve Conflict, and Increase Intimacy.* New York: Hudson Street Press, 2012.

Nisbett, Richard E. *Mindware: Tools for Smart Thinking.* New York: Farrar, Straus & Giroux, 2015.

Oppenheimer, Jerry. *Madoff with the Money.* New York: Wiley, 2009.

Pink, Daniel. *Drive: The Surprising Truth about What Motivates Us.* New York: Riverhead Books, 2009.

Pradeep, A. K. *The Buying Brain: Secrets for Selling to the Subconscious Mind.* Hoboken, NJ: Wiley, 2010.

Satir, Virginia. *The New Peoplemaking.* New York: Science & Behavior Books, 1988.

Shenk, David. *The Genius in All of Us: Why Everything You've Been Told about Genetics, Talent, and IQ Is Wrong.* New York: Doubleday, 2010.

Taleb, Nassim. *The Black Swan: The Impact of the Highly Improbable.* New York: Random House, 2007.

Tharp, Twyla. *The Creative Habit: Learn It and Use It for Life.* New York: Simon & Schuster, 2003.

The Editors of *Time*. *The Science of Happiness: New Discoveries for a More Joyful Life.* New York: Time Inc. Books, 2016.

Van der Kolk, Bessel. *The Body Keeps the Score: Brain, Mind, and Body in the Healing of Trauma.* New York: Viking, 2014.

Weakland, John H., and Wendel A. Ray, eds. *Propagations: Thirty Years of Influence from the Mental Research Institute.* New York: Haworth Press, 1995.

Yarrow, Kit. *Decoding the New Consumer Mind: How and Why We Shop and Buy.* San Francisco: Jossey-Bass, 2014.

INDEX

ABOUT THE AUTHOR

David Krueger, MD, is an executive mentor coach and CEO of Mentorpath, an executive coaching, training, publishing, and wellness firm. His work integrates psychology and neuroscience with strategic coaching to help executives and professionals write the next chapter of their life or business stories. Author of twenty trade and professional books on success, wellness, money, and self-development, and seventy-five scientific papers, his latest book, *The Secret Language of Money* is a Business Best Seller translated into ten languages. He is Mentor/Trainer Coach Faculty and Dean of Curriculum for Coach Training Alliance. Founder and director of his own licensed, specialty-certified New Life Story® Wellness Coaching and New Money Story® Mentor Training, he has trained professionals worldwide and develops internal mentor programs for corporations. You can learn more about his work at www.Mentorpath.com and www.NewMoneyStoryMentor.com.